# 마이갓 5 Step 모의고사 공부법

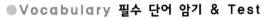

**1** ● **Vocabulary 필수 단어 암기 & Test**
① 단원별 필수 단어 암기 ② 영어 → 한글 Test ③ 한글 → 영어 Test

**2** ● **Text 지문과 해설**
① 전체 지문 해석 ② 페이지별 필기 공간 확보 ③ N회독을 통한 지문 습득

**3** ● **Practice 1 빈칸 시험 (w/ 문법 힌트)**
① 해석 없는 반복 빈칸 시험 ② 문법 힌트를 통한 어법 숙지
③ 주요 문법과 암기 내용 최종 확인

**4** ● **Practice 2 빈칸 시험 (w/ 해석)**
① 주요 내용/어법/어휘 빈칸 ② 한글을 통한 내용 숙지
③ 반복 시험을 통한 빈칸 암기

**5** ● **Quiz 객관식 예상문제를 콕콕!**
① 수능형 객관식 변형문제 ② 100% 자체 제작 변형문제 ③ 빈출 내신 문제 유형 연습

영어 내신의 끝
**마이갓 모의고사** 고1, 2

1 등급을 위한 5단계 노하우
2 모의고사 연도 및 시행월 별 완전정복
3 내신변형 완전정복

영어 내신의 끝
**마이갓 교과서** 고1, 2

1 등급을 위한 10단계 노하우
2 교과서 레슨별 완전정복
3 영어 영역 마스터를 위한 지름길

마이갓 교재
보듬책방 온라인 스토어 (https://smartstore.naver.com/bdbooks)

# 마이갓 10 Step 영어 내신 공부법

## Vocabulary

### 필수 단어 암기 & Test
① 단원별 필수 단어 암기
② 영어 → 한글 Test
③ 한글 → 영어 Test

## Grammar

### 단원별 중요 문법과 연습 문제
① 기초 문법 설명
② 교과서 적용 예시 소개
③ 기초/ Advanced Test

## Text

### 지문과 해설
① 전체 지문 해석
② 페이지별 필기 공간 확보
③ N회독을 통한 지문 습득

## Practice 3

### 빈칸 시험 (w/ 해석)
① 주요 내용/어법/어휘 빈칸
② 한글을 통한 내용 숙지
③ 반복 시험을 통한 빈칸 암기

## Practice 2

### 빈칸 시험 (w/ 해석)
① 주요 내용/어법/어휘 빈칸
② 한글을 통한 내용 숙지
③ 반복 시험을 통한 빈칸 암기

## Practice 1

### 어휘 & 어법 선택 시험
① 시험에 나오는 어법 어휘 공략
② 중요 어법/어휘 선택형 시험
③ 반복 시험을 통한 포인트 숙지

## Quiz

### 객관식 예상문제를 콕콕!
① 수능형 객관식 변형문제
② 100% 자체 제작 변형문제
③ 빈출 내신 문제 유형 연습

## Final Test

### 주관식 서술형 예상문제
① 어순/영작/어법 등
주관식 서술형 문제 대비!
② 100% 자체 제작 변형문제

## 전체 영작 연습

### 직접 영작 해보기
① 주어진 단어를 활용한
전체 서술형 영작 훈련
② 쓰기를 통한 내용 암기

## 학교 기출 문제

### 지문과 해설
① 단원별 실제 학교 기출
문제 모음
② 객관식부터 서술형까지
완벽 커버!

23년 고2
9월 모의고사

마이갓

연습과 실전 모두 잡는 내신대비 완벽
| workbook |

보듬영어

# 2023 고2

9
월
WORK BOOK

2023년 고2 9월 모의고사 내신대비용 WorkBook & 변형문제

(.hwp) (.pdf) → www.englishjmygod.com

# CONTENTS

2023 고2 9월 WORK BOOK

보듬영어

# Voca

| ❶ voca | ❷ text | ❸ [ / ] | ❹ ____ | ❺ quiz 1 | ❻ quiz 2 | ❼ quiz 3 | ❽ quiz 4 | ❾ quiz 5 |

| | | | | | |
|---|---|---|---|---|---|
| 18 | draw | 끌다, 그리다, 비기다; 끌기, 제비(뽑기) | | deal with | ~을 처리[해결]하다, 다루다 |
| | attention | 주의(력), 집중(력), 관심 | | in particular | 특히, 특별히 |
| | frequently | 자주, 흔히, 빈번히 | | exhibit | 전시하다, 보여 주다, 드러내다; 전시(품) |
| | be supposed to V | ~을 해야 하다, ~을 하기로 되어 있다 | | avoid | 피하다, 막다 |
| | unaware | 알아채지 못하는, 모르는, 부주의한 | | suggestion | 제안, 암시, 시사 |
| | grateful | 고마워하는, 감사하는 | | trait | 특성, 특색, 특징 |
| | remind ~ that ... | ~에게 ...을 상기시키다 | | suggest | 제안하다, 암시하다, 시사하다 |
| | look forward to | ~을 고대하다 | | acceptable | 받아들일 만한, 용인되는 |
| | improvement | 개선, 향상 | | perform | 수행하다, 행동하다, 공연[연주]하다 |
| | faithfully | 충실하게 | | focus on | ~에 집중하다, 초점을 맞추다 |
| 19 | desperate | 필사적인, 간절한, 절망적인 | | unreliability | 신뢰할 수 없음 |
| | border on | ~에 가깝다 | 21 | suspect | 의심하다, 수상히 여기다; 용의자 |
| | irritation | 짜증, 화, 따끔거림, 염증 | | fungi | 균, 곰팡이류, 세균 |
| | bother | 괴롭히다, 성가시게 하다, 신경 쓰다 | | forward | 전달하다, 전송하다; 앞으로 |
| | trivial | 사소한, 하찮은, 평범한 | | species | (분류상의) 종(種) |
| | glance | 흘긋 보다, 대강 훑어보다; 흘긋 봄 | | assume | 추정하다, (태도 등을) 취하다, 맡다 |
| | statue | 상(像), 조각상 | | emerge | 나오다, 나타나다, 드러나다 |
| | inscribe | (이름 등을) 새기다, 쓰다 | | advantage | 이익, 이점; 이롭게 하다 |
| | in between | 중간에, 틈에, 중간적인 | | come along | 나타나다, 동행하다 |
| 20 | psychologist | 심리학자 | | infected | 감염된 |
| | figure out | 산출[계산]하다, 알아내다 | | advantageous | 유리한, 이로운 |
| | employee | 직원, 종업원 | | continue to V | 계속 ~하다 |
| | empathize | 공감하다, 감정 이입을 하다 | | generation | 세대, 일족, 발생 |
| | in order to V | ~하기 위해, ~하려고 | | sprout | 싹을 틔우다 |
| | point of view | 관점, 견해, 전망, 경치 | | diversity | 다양(성) |

(.hwp) (.pdf) → www.englishjmygod.com

# Voca

| ❶ voca | ❷ text | ❸ [ / ] | ❹ _____ | ❺ quiz 1 | ❻ quiz 2 | ❼ quiz 3 | ❽ quiz 4 | ❾ quiz 5 |

| | | | | | | |
|---|---|---|---|---|---|---|
| | security | 안전, 안심, 보안, 보증 | | obstacle | 장애물, 난관 |
| | dependent on | ~에 의존하는 | | arise | 생기다, 일어나다, 유발되다 |
| | stable | 안정된, 지속성이 있는; 마구간, 외양간 | | principle | 원칙, 원리 |
| | support | 지지[지원]하다, 부양하다; 지지, 후원 | | hold true | 사실이다, 유효하다 |
| | underground | 지하의, 비밀의; 지하, 지하철 | | undercut | 싸게 팔다, 약화시키다, 밑을 잘라내다 |
| | complete | 완성[완료]하다; 완전한 | | put ~ in ... | ~을 ...에 넣다 |
| | collapse | 붕괴 | | temporary | 일시적인, 임시의 |
| | ensure | 확실하게 하다, 보장하다 | | inactivity | 비활동, 휴지, 무기력 |
| | manage to | (힘든 일을) 간신히 해내다 | 23 | identity | 정체성 |
| | dominate | 우세하다 | | anthropologist | 인류학자 |
| 22 | remarkable | 놀랄 만한, 주목할 만한, 훌륭한 | | stand to reason | 당연하다, 도리에 맞다, 합리적이다 |
| | extent | 정도, 규모, 범위 | | decline | 하락[감소]하다, 거절하다; 감소, 하락 |
| | show up | 나타나다, 등장하다 | | consequence | 결과, 영향(력), 중요성 |
| | physiological | 생리적인, 생리학(상)의 | | outsource | 외주 제작하다, 외부에서 조달하다 |
| | unwind | 풀다, 펴다, 긴장을 풀다 | | corporation | (규모가 큰) 기업, 회사, 법인 |
| | go for | ~을 위해 가다, ~에 해당되다, 선택하다 | | relieve | 완화[안도]시키다, 구제하다 |
| | outcome | 결과(물) | | traditionally | 전통적으로 |
| | objective | 목표, 목적, 객관적인 | | exclusive | 배타적인, 독점적인; 독점 기사 |
| | relaxed | 느긋한, 여유 있는 | | feed | 먹이를 주다, 먹이다; 먹이 |
| | energize | 기운 나게 하다, 격려하다 | | head off | ~을 막다 |
| | get off | 내리다, 떠나다, 퇴근하다 | | domestic | 국내의, 가정(용)의, 길들여진 |
| | pound | 빻다, 두드리다; (단위) 파운드, 동물 수용소 | | conflict | 갈등 |
| | motivate | 자극[유발]하다, 동기를 주다 | | shift | 변화, 이동, 교대; 바꾸다, 이동하다 |
| | engage | 참여[관여]하다, 약속[약혼]하다, 사로잡다 | | dynamics | 힘, 역학, 역학 관계 |
| | inevitable | 불가피한, 필연적인 | | bound | 묶인, 꼭 ~하는; 인접하다, 껑충 달리다 |

# Voca

|  |  |  |  |  |  |
|---|---|---|---|---|---|
|  | spark | 촉발시키다, 유발하다; 불꽃, 불똥 |  | survey | 조사하다, 둘러보다; 조사 |
|  | pressure | 압력, 압박, 스트레스; 압력을 가하다 |  | respondent | 응답자; 반응하는 |
|  | household | 가족, 가정; 가족의, 가정의 |  | access | 접속하다 |
|  | include | 포함하다, 포괄하다 |  | decrease | 감소; 감소하다 |
|  | workday | 근무일 |  | via | 경유하여, ~을 거쳐, ~에 의해 |
|  | invest | 투자하다, (시간, 노력 등을) 들이다 |  | compared to | ~에 비해, ~와 비교하여 |
|  | pursuit | 추구, 뒤쫓음, 추적, 일 |  | previous | 이전의, 사전의 |
|  | diversify | 변화시키다, 다양화하다 | 26 | astronomy | 천문학 |
|  | substantially | 충분히, 상당히, 실질적으로, 대체로 |  | manuscript | (자필) 원고, 사본, 필사본 |
|  | cuisine | 요리 |  | come to V | ~이 되다, ~에 이르다 |
| 24 | company | 친구, 동료, 회사, 교제; 회사의 |  | observatory | 관측소, 천문대, 기상대 |
|  | mindful | 의식하는, 염두에 두는 |  | assistant | 보조의; 조수 |
|  | deserve | ~ 받을 가치가 있다, ~할 만하다 |  | inhabit | 살다, 거주[서식]하다 |
|  | commit to V | ~하겠다고 약속하다 |  | claim | 주장[요구]하다, 차지하다; 요구, 주장 |
|  | instance | 사례, 경우 |  | astronomical | 천문학의, 천문학적인 |
|  | conscience | 양심, (양심의) 가책 |  | serve as | ~의 역할을 하다 |
|  | contribute | 공헌하다, 기여[기부]하다 |  | publication | 출판(물), 발행 |
|  | genuinely | 진정으로, 순수[성실]하게 | 27 | virtual | 사실상의, 실질상의, 가상의 |
|  | corporate | 회사의, 기업의, 법인의 |  | athletic | 운동 경기의 |
|  | build on | ~을 발판으로 삼다, ~을 의지하다 |  | participate in | ~에 참여[참가]하다 |
|  | consumer | 소비자 |  | submit | 제출하다, 복종시키다 |
|  | encourage | 장려[격려]하다, 촉구하다 |  | entry | 참가, 출품(작), 입구, 참가자 |
|  | embrace | 포옹하다, 수용하다; 포옹, 수용 |  | exceed | 초과하다 |
|  | sustainable | 지속 가능한 | 28 | be held | 열리다, 개최되다 |
| 25 | finding | 결과, 결론 |  | rain or shine | 날씨와 관계없이, 어떤 일이 있더라도 |

| ❶ voca | ❷ text | ❸ [ / ] | ❹ ___ | ❺ quiz 1 | ❻ quiz 2 | ❼ quiz 3 | ❽ quiz 4 | ❾ quiz 5 |
|---|---|---|---|---|---|---|---|---|
| | participation | 참여, 참가 | | base ~ on ... | ~을 ...에 근거하다 | | | |
| | requirement | 요건, 필요조건 | | efficient | 유능한, 능률적인, 효율적인 | | | |
| | resident | 거주자, 주민; 거주하는, 고유의 | | rapidly | 빠르게, 급히 | | | |
| | valid | 유효한, 타당한, 근거가 있는 | | eliminate | 제거하다 | | | |
| | basis | 토대, 기초, 근거, 이유 | | as a result | 그 결과 | | | |
| | city council | 시의회 | | sensitive | 민감한, 신경 과민의, 감수성이 풍부한 | | | |
| 29 | go into | 투입되다, 시작하다, 논의하다 | | effect | 결과, 영향, 효과; 초래하다, 이루다 | | | |
| | stream | 흐름, 개울, 경향; 흐르다, 흘러나오다 | | aging | 노화; 늙어 가는 | | | |
| | carbon | 탄소 | | alter | 바꾸다, 변경하다, 고치다 | | | |
| | bring up | ~을 제기하다, 제시하다 | 31 | rebel | 반항자 | | | |
| | terrible | 끔찍한, 무서운, 심한 | | look for | ~을 찾다, ~을 모집하다 | | | |
| | caution | 조심, 주의, 신중; 주의하다 | | alternative | 대안 | | | |
| | by the time | ~할 때까지 | | in favor of | ~에 우호적인, ~을 지지하여 | | | |
| | reasonably | 합리적으로, 타당하게, 적정하게 | | maintain | 유지하다, 주장하다 | | | |
| | consume | 소비하다, 섭취하다, 먹다 | | uniqueness | 독특함, 유일함, 유례없는 일 | | | |
| | toxic | 유독한, 치명적인, 중독(성)의 | | majority | 가장 많은 수, 다수 | | | |
| | individual | 개인; 개인의, 개별적인, 독특한 | | trick | 속임수, 재주, 비결; 속임수의; 속이다 | | | |
| | make sense | 말이 되다, 타당하다, 의미가 통하다 | | reversal | 전환, 반전, 좌절 | | | |
| | perishable | 상하기 쉬운 | | suit | 정장, 소송; 적합하다, (알)맞다 | | | |
| | goods | 상품 | | purpose | 목적, 의도; 의도하다 | | | |
| 30 | wear off | 사라지다, 없어지다, 닳게 하다 | | mainstream | 주류, 대세; 주류의 | | | |
| | remove | 제거하다, 없애다, 옮기다 | | loyalty | 충성(도), 충의 | | | |
| | liver | 간 | 32 | abstract | 추상적인; 추상, 요약; 요약[추출]하다 | | | |
| | gradually | 서서히, 점차 | | complex | 복잡한, 복합의; 복합체, 콤플렉스 | | | |
| | degrade | 저하[악화]시키다, 비하하다, 분해하다 | | recreate | 기분 전환을 하다, 기운을 회복시키다 | | | |

# Voca

| ❶ voca | ❷ text | ❸ [ / ] | ❹ ＿＿ | ❺ quiz 1 | ❻ quiz 2 | ❼ quiz 3 | ❽ quiz 4 | ❾ quiz 5 |

|  |  |  |  |  |  |
|---|---|---|---|---|---|
|  | psychology | 심리, 심리학 |  | prevent | 막다, 예방하다 |
|  | speculate | 사색하다, 추측하다, 투기하다 |  | bounce | 튀다, 뛰어오르다; 튀어오름 |
|  | plot | 음모, 줄거리, 작은 토지; 음모[줄거리]를 짜다 |  | material | 재료, 물질; 물질의, 육체의, 중요한 |
|  | considerable | 상당한, 많은 | 34 | sort | 분류하다, 구분하다; 종류 |
|  | with ease | 쉽게 |  | manageable | 관리[처리]할 수 있는 |
|  | cope with | ~에 대처[대응]하다, 극복하다 |  | overwhelming | 압도적인, 너무도 강력한 |
|  | abstraction | 추상적 개념, 관념 |  | enormous | 엄청난, 거대한, 막대한 |
|  | framework | 하부 구조, 체계, 뼈대, 틀 |  | impression | 인상, 감명, 흔적 |
| 33 | prey | (동물의) 먹이, 희생자; 포식하다 |  | be vital to | ~에 중요하다 |
|  | be engaged in | ~으로 바쁘다, ~에 종사[관여]하다 |  | relevant to | ~에 관련된 |
|  | sensory | 감각의, 지각의 |  | organize | 조직하다, 정리하다, 개최하다 |
|  | arms race | 군비 경쟁 |  | stock | 재고(품), 저장, 주식; 비축하다, 저장하다 |
|  | moth | 나방 |  | accomplish | 달성하다, 성취하다, 이루다 |
|  | specifically | 특별히, 구체적으로, 명확하게 |  | irrelevant | 무관한, 상관없는, 부적절한 |
|  | in response to | ~에 반응[응답]하여 |  | contradiction | 모순, 반박 |
|  | threat | 협박, 위협, 조짐 |  | steady | 한결같은, 확고한, 안정된, 착실한 |
|  | evolve | 진화하다, (서서히) 발전하다 |  | elimination | 제거, 삭제 |
|  | detect | 알아내다, 감지하다, 탐지하다 |  | fraction | 부분, 분수, 아주 조금 |
|  | frequency | 빈번함, 빈도, 진동수 |  | retrieve | 되찾다, 구하다, 회상하다, 검색하다 |
|  | vocalization | 발성, 발성법 | 35 | thrive | 번성[번영]하다, 잘 자라다 |
|  | acoustic | 청각의, 음향의 |  | prosper | 번영하다, 번성하다, 성공하다 |
|  | camouflage | 위장하다, 감추다; 위장, 기만 |  | precisely | 정확히, 바로 |
|  | absorb | 흡수하다, 몰두[열중]시키다 |  | ruler | 통치자, 지배자, (도구) 자 |
|  | emit | 내뿜다, 방출하다, 내다 |  | remarkably | 놀라울 정도로, 뚜렷하게, 몹시 |
|  | thereby | 그렇게 함으로써, 그것 때문에 |  | assess | (자질 등을) 재다, 평가[가늠]하다 |

| ❶ voca | | ❷ text | ❸ [ / ] | ❹ _____ | ❺ quiz 1 | ❻ quiz 2 | ❼ quiz 3 | ❽ quiz 4 | ❾ quiz 5 |
|---|---|---|---|---|---|---|---|---|---|

| | voca | text | | | voca | text |
|---|---|---|---|---|---|---|
| | substantial | 상당한 | 37 | architect | 건축가, 설계자 |
| | base on | ~에 근거하다 | | impressive | 인상적인, 감명 깊은 |
| | strike | 치다, 떠오르다, 노력하다; 타격, 공격, 파업 | | contain | 포함[함유]하다, 억누르다, 억제하다 |
| | illustrate | 보여 주다, 예증하다, 삽화를 넣다 | | auditorium | 강당, 청중석 |
| | weakness | 약점, 결점 | | composed of | ~으로 구성된 |
| | revenue | 수입, 수익, 세입 | | instinctively | 본능적으로, 무의식적으로 |
| | medieval | 중세의, 중세풍의 | | refined | 정제된, 세련된 |
| | extract | 추출(물); 추출하다, 끄집어내다 | | sensibility | 감각, 감성, 감수성, 민감 |
| | more of ~ than ... | ...이라기보다는 ~ | | at that | 그것도, 게다가 |
| | exception | 예외(사항), 제외 | | aesthetically | 미학적으로 |
| 36 | compete | 다투다, 겨루다, 경쟁하다 | | known as | ~으로 알려진 |
| | right next to | ~바로 옆에 | | parametric design | 파라메트릭 디자인(알고리즘 프로세스에 따라 특징을 형성시키는 디자인 방법) |
| | in search of | ~을 추구하여, ~을 찾아서 | | a set of | 일련의, 일습의 |
| | firm | 확고한, 고정된; 회사 | | criteria | 기준, 표준 ((단수형 criterion)) |
| | advertise | 광고하다, 선전하다 | | generate | 발생시키다, 만들어내다, (감정을) 일으키다 |
| | temptation | 유혹, 충동 | | used to V | ~하곤 했다, ~이었다[했다] |
| | advertising | 광고, 광고업 | | lightweight | 가벼운, 경량의 |
| | benefit | 이익, 이득; 이익이 되다 | | blindly | 맹목적으로 |
| | misconception | 잘못된 생각, 오해 | | vary | 다르다, 바꾸다, 변하다 |
| | account for | (~의 비율을) 차지하다, 설명하다 | 38 | merely | 그저, 단지 |
| | differentiated | 차별화된 | | incredibly | 놀라울 정도로, 엄청나게 |
| | enable A to V | A가 ~할 수 있게 하다 | | adaptive | 적응하는, 적응할 수 있는 |
| | benefit from | ~로부터 혜택[이익]을 얻다 | | economize | 경제적으로 사용하다 |
| | variety | 변화, 다양(성), 품종 | | resource | 수단, 기지 (-s) 자원, 소질; 자원을 제공하다 |
| | structure | 구조, 조직, 체계; 구성하다, 조직화하다 | | analysis | 분석 ((복수형 analyses)) |

**❶ voca　❷ text　❸ [ / ]　❹ _____　❺ quiz 1　❻ quiz 2　❼ quiz 3　❽ quiz 4　❾ quiz 5**

| | | | | | |
|---|---|---|---|---|---|
| | singular | 뛰어난, 비범한, 특이한, 단일의 | | employ | 고용하다, 사용[이용]하다 |
| | at hand | 당면한, 처리해야 하는, 가까이에 | | align with | ~에 부합하다, 맞추다 |
| | devote ~ to ... | ~을 ...에 쏟다[바치다] | 40 | conduct | ~을 하다, 지휘하다, (전기 등을) 전도하다; 행동 |
| 39 | carry out | ~을 수행하다, 실행하다 | | motivation | 동기 (부여) |
| | engagement | 참여, 약속, 약혼, 고용 | | attack | 공격하다; 공격, 발작 |
| | theoretical | 이론의, 이론상의 | | assistance | 도움, 지원 |
| | practical | 실용적인, 실제의 | | motive | 동기; 원동력이 되는 |
| | standpoint | 견지, 관점, 견해 | | reduce | 줄이다, 낮추다, 감소하다 |
| | identify | 알아보다, 확인하다, 동일시하다 | | discomfort | 불편, 불쾌, 가벼운 통증 |
| | fall into | ~안으로 떨어지다 | | distress | 고민, 고통, 빈곤; ~을 괴롭히다 |
| | influential | 영향력 있는, 영향력이 큰 | | stem from | ~에서 기인하다, 유래하다 |
| | the latter | (둘 중에서) 후자 | | arousal | 흥분, 각성 |
| | be responsible for | ~에 책임이 있다 | | affected | 가장된, 꾸민, 감염된 |
| | indeed | 실제로, 사실 | | discharge | 해소하다 |
| | constructive | 건설적인, 발전적인 | | victim | 희생(자), 피해자 |
| | performance | 수행, 성과, 성적, 공연 | 41 ~ 42 | unusual | 보통이 아닌, 이상한, 유별난 |
| | provide ~ with ... | ~에게 ...을 제공하다 | | spread | 펴다, 퍼뜨리다, 퍼지다; 확장, 유포, 보급 |
| | necessary | 필요한, 필연적인; (-s) 필수품 | | widely | 널리, 크게 |
| | noteworthy | 주목할 가치가 있는, 현저한 | | pass down | ~을 물려주다, 전해주다 |
| | in other words | 즉, 다시 말해서 | | oral tradition | 구전 |
| | expectation | 기대, 요구, 예상, 가망 | | accumulate | 축적하다 |
| | ambition | 포부, 야망 | | norm | 표준, 기준, (-s) 규범, 모범, 평균 |
| | achievement | 업적, 성취 | | perception | 인식, 인지, 지각 |
| | meaningful | 의미 있는, 중요한 | | advent | 출현, 등장, 도래 |
| | evident | 분명한, 명백한, 뚜렷한 | | literacy | 읽고 쓸 줄 아는 능력, 교양 있음 |

# Voca

| ❶ voca | ❷ text | ❸ [ / ] | ❹ _____ | ❺ quiz 1 | ❻ quiz 2 | ❼ quiz 3 | ❽ quiz 4 | ❾ quiz 5 |

| | | | | | |
|---|---|---|---|---|---|
| | transfer | 옮기다, 전하다; 이동, 환승 | flourish | 번성[번창]하다, 잘 자라다 | |
| | fade | 바래다, 희미해지다, 서서히 사라지다 | lead to | ~을 낳다, ~으로 이어지다 | |
| | fad | 일시적 유행 | nursing home | 요양원, 양로원 | |
| | no longer | 더 이상 ~아닌[하지 않는] | in turn | 결과적으로, 차례차례 | |
| | signify | 의미하다, 중요하다 | fundraising | 모금(의) | |
| | chronological | 발생 순서대로 된, 연대순의 | lay | (물건을) 놓다, (알을) 낳다 | |
| | struggle to V | ~하려고 애쓰다 | stepping stone | 디딤돌, 발판 | |
| | formerly | 이전에, 예전에 | courageous | 용감한, 용기 있는 | |
| | association | 연관(성), 연상, 협회 | orphan | 고아; 고아로 만들다 | |
| | retire | 물러나다, 은퇴하다 | threaten to V | ~하겠다고 위협하다 | |
| | stereotype | 고정 관념, 전형; 정형화하다 | adoption | 채택 | |
| | updated | 최신의 | racial | 인종의, 민족의 | |
| 43 ~45 | dye | 염료; 염색하다 | richness | 풍성함, 풍부함, 풍요로움 | |
| | aspect | 측면, 면, 양상, 관점 | | | |
| | approach | 접근하다; 접근(법) | | | |
| | express | 표현하다, 나타내다; 급행의 | | | |
| | intention | 의도, 의향 | | | |
| | anticipate | 예상하다, 기대하다 | | | |
| | rage | 격노, 분노; 몹시 화를 내다 | | | |
| | accuse A of B | A를 B라는 이유로 비난하다 | | | |
| | ungrateful | 은혜를 모르는, 고마워할 줄 모르는 | | | |
| | in the face of | ~에 직면하여 | | | |
| | confusion | 혼란 | | | |
| | resolve | 결심[결정]하다, 해결하다, 용해하다 | | | |
| | following | 다음(의); 다음에 계속되는 | | | |

# Voca Test

영 ▶ 한

| ❶ voca | ❷ text | ❸ [ / ] | ❹ ___ | ❺ quiz 1 | ❻ quiz 2 | ❼ quiz 3 | ❽ quiz 4 | ❾ quiz 5 |
|---|---|---|---|---|---|---|---|---|
| 18 | draw | | | deal with | | | | |
| | attention | | | in particular | | | | |
| | frequently | | | exhibit | | | | |
| | be supposed to V | | | avoid | | | | |
| | unaware | | | suggestion | | | | |
| | grateful | | | trait | | | | |
| | remind ~ that ... | | | suggest | | | | |
| | look forward to | | | acceptable | | | | |
| | improvement | | | perform | | | | |
| | faithfully | | | focus on | | | | |
| 19 | desperate | | | unreliability | | | | |
| | border on | | 21 | suspect | | | | |
| | irritation | | | fungi | | | | |
| | bother | | | forward | | | | |
| | trivial | | | species | | | | |
| | glance | | | assume | | | | |
| | statue | | | emerge | | | | |
| | inscribe | | | advantage | | | | |
| | in between | | | come along | | | | |
| 20 | psychologist | | | infected | | | | |
| | figure out | | | advantageous | | | | |
| | employee | | | continue to V | | | | |
| | empathize | | | generation | | | | |
| | in order to V | | | sprout | | | | |
| | point of view | | | diversity | | | | |

(.hwp) (.pdf) → www.englishjmygod.com

# Voca Test

영 ◇ 한

| ❶ voca | ❷ text | ❸ [ / ] | ❹ ____ | ❺ quiz 1 | ❻ quiz 2 | ❼ quiz 3 | ❽ quiz 4 | ❾ quiz 5 |
|---|---|---|---|---|---|---|---|---|

|  | security |  |  | | | obstacle |  |  |
|---|---|---|---|---|---|---|---|---|
|  | dependent on |  |  | | | arise |  |  |
|  | stable |  |  | | | principle |  |  |
|  | support |  |  | | | hold true |  |  |
|  | underground |  |  | | | undercut |  |  |
|  | complete |  |  | | | put ~ in ... |  |  |
|  | collapse |  |  | | | temporary |  |  |
|  | ensure |  |  | | | inactivity |  |  |
|  | manage to |  |  | 23 | | identity |  |  |
|  | dominate |  |  | | | anthropologist |  |  |
| 22 | remarkable |  |  | | | stand to reason |  |  |
|  | extent |  |  | | | decline |  |  |
|  | show up |  |  | | | consequence |  |  |
|  | physiological |  |  | | | outsource |  |  |
|  | unwind |  |  | | | corporation |  |  |
|  | go for |  |  | | | relieve |  |  |
|  | outcome |  |  | | | traditionally |  |  |
|  | objective |  |  | | | exclusive |  |  |
|  | relaxed |  |  | | | feed |  |  |
|  | energize |  |  | | | head off |  |  |
|  | get off |  |  | | | domestic |  |  |
|  | pound |  |  | | | conflict |  |  |
|  | motivate |  |  | | | shift |  |  |
|  | engage |  |  | | | dynamics |  |  |
|  | inevitable |  |  | | | bound |  |  |

# Voca Test

영 > 한

| ❶ voca | ❷ text | ❸ [ / ] | ❹ ____ | ❺ quiz 1 | ❻ quiz 2 | ❼ quiz 3 | ❽ quiz 4 | ❾ quiz 5 |
|---|---|---|---|---|---|---|---|---|

| | | | | |
|---|---|---|---|---|
| | spark | | survey | |
| | pressure | | respondent | |
| | household | | access | |
| | include | | decrease | |
| | workday | | via | |
| | invest | | compared to | |
| | pursuit | | previous | |
| | diversify | 26 | astronomy | |
| | substantially | | manuscript | |
| | cuisine | | come to V | |
| 24 | company | | observatory | |
| | mindful | | assistant | |
| | deserve | | inhabit | |
| | commit to V | | claim | |
| | instance | | astronomical | |
| | conscience | | serve as | |
| | contribute | | publication | |
| | genuinely | 27 | virtual | |
| | corporate | | athletic | |
| | build on | | participate in | |
| | consumer | | submit | |
| | encourage | | entry | |
| | embrace | | exceed | |
| | sustainable | 28 | be held | |
| 25 | finding | | rain or shine | |

(.hwp) (.pdf) → www.englishjmygod.com

# Voca Test

영 한

| ❶ voca | ❷ text | ❸ [ / ] | ❹ ____ | ❺ quiz 1 | ❻ quiz 2 | ❼ quiz 3 | ❽ quiz 4 | ❾ quiz 5 |
|---|---|---|---|---|---|---|---|---|
| | participation | | | | base ~ on ... | | | |
| | requirement | | | | efficient | | | |
| | resident | | | | rapidly | | | |
| | valid | | | | eliminate | | | |
| | basis | | | | as a result | | | |
| | city council | | | | sensitive | | | |
| 29 | go into | | | | effect | | | |
| | stream | | | | aging | | | |
| | carbon | | | | alter | | | |
| | bring up | | | 31 | rebel | | | |
| | terrible | | | | look for | | | |
| | caution | | | | alternative | | | |
| | by the time | | | | in favor of | | | |
| | reasonably | | | | maintain | | | |
| | consume | | | | uniqueness | | | |
| | toxic | | | | majority | | | |
| | individual | | | | trick | | | |
| | make sense | | | | reversal | | | |
| | perishable | | | | suit | | | |
| | goods | | | | purpose | | | |
| 30 | wear off | | | | mainstream | | | |
| | remove | | | | loyalty | | | |
| | liver | | | 32 | abstract | | | |
| | gradually | | | | complex | | | |
| | degrade | | | | recreate | | | |

# Voca Tes

영 ▶ 한

| ❶ voca | ❷ text | ❸ [ / ] | ❹ ＿＿ | ❺ quiz 1 | ❻ quiz 2 | ❼ quiz 3 | ❽ quiz 4 | ❾ quiz 5 |
|---|---|---|---|---|---|---|---|---|
| | psychology | | | prevent | | | | |
| | speculate | | | bounce | | | | |
| | plot | | | material | | | | |
| | considerable | | 34 | sort | | | | |
| | with ease | | | manageable | | | | |
| | cope with | | | overwhelming | | | | |
| | abstraction | | | enormous | | | | |
| | framework | | | impression | | | | |
| 33 | prey | | | be vital to | | | | |
| | be engaged in | | | relevant to | | | | |
| | sensory | | | organize | | | | |
| | arms race | | | stock | | | | |
| | moth | | | accomplish | | | | |
| | specifically | | | irrelevant | | | | |
| | in response to | | | contradiction | | | | |
| | threat | | | steady | | | | |
| | evolve | | | elimination | | | | |
| | detect | | | fraction | | | | |
| | frequency | | | retrieve | | | | |
| | vocalization | | 35 | thrive | | | | |
| | acoustic | | | prosper | | | | |
| | camouflage | | | precisely | | | | |
| | absorb | | | ruler | | | | |
| | emit | | | remarkably | | | | |
| | thereby | | | assess | | | | |

(.hwp) (.pdf) → www.englishjmygod.com

# Voca Test

영 › 한

| ❶ voca | ❷ text | ❸ [ / ] | ❹ ____ | ❺ quiz 1 | ❻ quiz 2 | ❼ quiz 3 | ❽ quiz 4 | ❾ quiz 5 |
|---|---|---|---|---|---|---|---|---|
| | substantial | | | 37 | architect | | | |
| | base on | | | | impressive | | | |
| | strike | | | | contain | | | |
| | illustrate | | | | auditorium | | | |
| | weakness | | | | composed of | | | |
| | revenue | | | | instinctively | | | |
| | medieval | | | | refined | | | |
| | extract | | | | sensibility | | | |
| | more of ~ than ... | | | | at that | | | |
| | exception | | | | aesthetically | | | |
| 36 | compete | | | | known as | | | |
| | right next to | | | | parametric design | | | |
| | in search of | | | | a set of | | | |
| | firm | | | | criteria | | | |
| | advertise | | | | generate | | | |
| | temptation | | | | used to V | | | |
| | advertising | | | | lightweight | | | |
| | benefit | | | | blindly | | | |
| | misconception | | | | vary | | | |
| | account for | | | 38 | merely | | | |
| | differentiated | | | | incredibly | | | |
| | enable A to V | | | | adaptive | | | |
| | benefit from | | | | economize | | | |
| | variety | | | | resource | | | |
| | structure | | | | analysis | | | |

# Voca Test

영 > 한

| | ❶ voca | ❷ text | ❸ [ / ] | ❹ ____ | ❺ quiz 1 | ❻ quiz 2 | ❼ quiz 3 | ❽ quiz 4 | ❾ quiz 5 |
|---|---|---|---|---|---|---|---|---|---|

| | | | | |
|---|---|---|---|---|
| | singular | | employ | |
| | at hand | | align with | |
| | devote ~ to … | 40 | conduct | |
| 39 | carry out | | motivation | |
| | engagement | | attack | |
| | theoretical | | assistance | |
| | practical | | motive | |
| | standpoint | | reduce | |
| | identify | | discomfort | |
| | fall into | | distress | |
| | influential | | stem from | |
| | the latter | | arousal | |
| | be responsible for | | affected | |
| | indeed | | discharge | |
| | constructive | | victim | |
| | performance | 41 ~42 | unusual | |
| | provide ~ with … | | spread | |
| | necessary | | widely | |
| | noteworthy | | pass down | |
| | in other words | | oral tradition | |
| | expectation | | accumulate | |
| | ambition | | norm | |
| | achievement | | perception | |
| | meaningful | | advent | |
| | evident | | literacy | |

(.hwp) (.pdf) → www.englishjmygod.com

# Voca Test

영 ○ 한

| ❶ voca | ❷ text | ❸ [ / ] | ❹ ___ | ❺ quiz 1 | ❻ quiz 2 | ❼ quiz 3 | ❽ quiz 4 | ❾ quiz 5 |
|---|---|---|---|---|---|---|---|---|
| | transfer | | | flourish | | | | |
| | fade | | | lead to | | | | |
| | fad | | | nursing home | | | | |
| | no longer | | | in turn | | | | |
| | signify | | | fundraising | | | | |
| | chronological | | | lay | | | | |
| | struggle to V | | | stepping stone | | | | |
| | formerly | | | courageous | | | | |
| | association | | | orphan | | | | |
| | retire | | | threaten to V | | | | |
| | stereotype | | | adoption | | | | |
| | updated | | | racial | | | | |
| 43~45 | dye | | | richness | | | | |
| | aspect | | | | | | | |
| | approach | | | | | | | |
| | express | | | | | | | |
| | intention | | | | | | | |
| | anticipate | | | | | | | |
| | rage | | | | | | | |
| | accuse A of B | | | | | | | |
| | ungrateful | | | | | | | |
| | in the face of | | | | | | | |
| | confusion | | | | | | | |
| | resolve | | | | | | | |
| | following | | | | | | | |

# Voca Test

영 ▶ 한

| ❶ voca | ❷ text | ❸ [ / ] | ❹ ___ | ❺ quiz 1 | ❻ quiz 2 | ❼ quiz 3 | ❽ quiz 4 | ❾ quiz 5 |
|---|---|---|---|---|---|---|---|---|
| 18 | 끌다, 그리다, 비기다; 끌기, 제비(뽑기) | | | | ~을 처리[해결]하다, 다루다 | | | |
| | 주의(력), 집중(력), 관심 | | | | 특히, 특별히 | | | |
| | 자주, 흔히, 빈번히 | | | | 전시하다, 보여 주다, 드러내다; 전시(품) | | | |
| | ~을 해야 하다, ~을 하기로 되어 있다 | | | | 피하다, 막다 | | | |
| | 알아채지 못하는, 모르는, 부주의한 | | | | 제안, 암시, 시사 | | | |
| | 고마워하는, 감사하는 | | | | 특성, 특색, 특징 | | | |
| | ~에게 ...을 상기시키다 | | | | 제안하다, 암시하다, 시사하다 | | | |
| | ~을 고대하다 | | | | 받아들일 만한, 용인되는 | | | |
| | 개선, 향상 | | | | 수행하다, 행동하다, 공연[연주]하다 | | | |
| | 충실하게 | | | | ~에 집중하다, 초점을 맞추다 | | | |
| 19 | 필사적인, 간절한, 절망적인 | | | | 신뢰할 수 없음 | | | |
| | ~에 가깝다 | 21 | | | 의심하다, 수상히 여기다; 용의자 | | | |
| | 짜증, 화, 따끔거림, 염증 | | | | 균, 곰팡이류, 세균 | | | |
| | 괴롭히다, 성가시게 하다, 신경 쓰다 | | | | 전달하다, 전송하다; 앞으로 | | | |
| | 사소한, 하찮은, 평범한 | | | | (분류상의) 종(種) | | | |
| | 흘긋 보다, 대강 훑어보다; 흘긋 봄 | | | | 추정하다, (태도 등을) 취하다, 맡다 | | | |
| | 상(像), 조각상 | | | | 나오다, 나타나다, 드러나다 | | | |
| | (이름 등을) 새기다, 쓰다 | | | | 이익, 이점; 이롭게 하다 | | | |
| | 중간에, 틈에, 중간적인 | | | | 나타나다, 동행하다 | | | |
| 20 | 심리학자 | | | | 감염된 | | | |
| | 산출[계산]하다, 알아내다 | | | | 유리한, 이로운 | | | |
| | 직원, 종업원 | | | | 계속 ~하다 | | | |
| | 공감하다, 감정 이입을 하다 | | | | 세대, 일족, 발생 | | | |
| | ~하기 위해, ~하려고 | | | | 싹을 틔우다 | | | |
| | 관점, 견해, 전망, 경치 | | | | 다양(성) | | | |

# Voca Test

영 · 한

| ❶ voca | ❷ text | ❸ [ / ] | ❹ ____ | ❺ quiz 1 | ❻ quiz 2 | ❼ quiz 3 | ❽ quiz 4 | ❾ quiz 5 |
|---|---|---|---|---|---|---|---|---|
| | | 안전, 안심, 보안, 보증 | | | 장애물, 난관 | | | |
| | | ~에 의존하는 | | | 생기다, 일어나다, 유발되다 | | | |
| | | 안정된, 지속성이 있는; 마구간, 외양간 | | | 원칙, 원리 | | | |
| | | 지지[지원]하다, 부양하다; 지지, 후원 | | | 사실이다, 유효하다 | | | |
| | | 지하의, 비밀의; 지하, 지하철 | | | 싸게 팔다, 약화시키다, 밑을 잘라내다 | | | |
| | | 완성[완료]하다; 완전한 | | | ~을 ...에 넣다 | | | |
| | | 붕괴 | | | 일시적인, 임시의 | | | |
| | | 확실하게 하다, 보장하다 | | | 비활동, 휴지, 무기력 | | | |
| | | (힘든 일을) 간신히 해내다 | 23 | | 정체성 | | | |
| | | 우세하다 | | | 인류학자 | | | |
| 22 | | 놀랄 만한, 주목할 만한, 훌륭한 | | | 당연하다, 도리에 맞다, 합리적이다 | | | |
| | | 정도, 규모, 범위 | | | 하락[감소]하다, 거절하다; 감소, 하락 | | | |
| | | 나타나다, 등장하다 | | | 결과, 영향(력), 중요성 | | | |
| | | 생리적인, 생리학(상)의 | | | 외주 제작하다, 외부에서 조달하다 | | | |
| | | 풀다, 펴다, 긴장을 풀다 | | | (규모가 큰) 기업, 회사, 법인 | | | |
| | | ~을 위해 가다, ~에 해당되다, 선택하다 | | | 완화[안도]시키다, 구제하다 | | | |
| | | 결과(물) | | | 전통적으로 | | | |
| | | 목표, 목적, 객관적인 | | | 배타적인, 독점적인; 독점 기사 | | | |
| | | 느긋한, 여유 있는 | | | 먹이를 주다, 먹이다; 먹이 | | | |
| | | 기운 나게 하다, 격려하다 | | | ~을 막다 | | | |
| | | 내리다, 떠나다, 퇴근하다 | | | 국내의, 가정(용)의, 길들여진 | | | |
| | | 빻다, 두드리다; (단위) 파운드, 동물 수용소 | | | 갈등 | | | |
| | | 자극[유발]하다, 동기를 주다 | | | 변화, 이동, 교대; 바꾸다, 이동하다 | | | |
| | | 참여[관여]하다, 약속[약혼]하다, 사로잡다 | | | 힘, 역학, 역학 관계 | | | |
| | | 불가피한, 필연적인 | | | 묶인, 꼭 ~하는; 인접하다, 껑충 달리다 | | | |

# Voca Test

| ❶ voca | ❷ text | ❸ [ / ] | ❹ ____ | ❺ quiz 1 | ❻ quiz 2 | ❼ quiz 3 | ❽ quiz 4 | ❾ quiz 5 |
|---|---|---|---|---|---|---|---|---|
| | | 촉발시키다, 유발하다;<br>불꽃, 불똥 | | | 조사하다, 둘러보다; 조사 | | | |
| | | 압력, 압박, 스트레스;<br>압력을 가하다 | | | 응답자; 반응하는 | | | |
| | | 가족, 가정; 가족의,<br>가정의 | | | 접속하다 | | | |
| | | 포함하다, 포괄하다 | | | 감소; 감소하다 | | | |
| | | 근무일 | | | 경유하여, ~을 거쳐, ~에<br>의해 | | | |
| | | 투자하다, (시간, 노력<br>등을) 들이다 | | | ~에 비해, ~와 비교하여 | | | |
| | | 추구, 뒤쫓음, 추적, 일 | | | 이전의, 사전의 | | | |
| | | 변화시키다, 다양화하다 | 26 | | 천문학 | | | |
| | | 충분히, 상당히,<br>실질적으로, 대체로 | | | (자필) 원고, 사본, 필사본 | | | |
| | | 요리 | | | ~이 되다, ~에 이르다 | | | |
| 24 | | 친구, 동료, 회사, 교제;<br>회사의 | | | 관측소, 천문대, 기상대 | | | |
| | | 의식하는, 염두에 두는 | | | 보조의; 조수 | | | |
| | | ~ 받을 가치가 있다,<br>~할 만하다 | | | 살다, 거주[서식]하다 | | | |
| | | ~하겠다고 약속하다 | | | 주장[요구]하다, 차지하다;<br>요구, 주장 | | | |
| | | 사례, 경우 | | | 천문학의, 천문학적인 | | | |
| | | 양심, (양심의) 가책 | | | ~의 역할을 하다 | | | |
| | | 공헌하다,<br>기여[기부]하다 | | | 출판(물), 발행 | | | |
| | | 진정으로,<br>순수[성실]하게 | 27 | | 사실상의, 실질상의, 가상의 | | | |
| | | 회사의, 기업의, 법인의 | | | 운동 경기의 | | | |
| | | ~을 발판으로 삼다, ~을<br>의지하다 | | | ~에 참여[참가]하다 | | | |
| | | 소비자 | | | 제출하다, 복종시키다 | | | |
| | | 장려[격려]하다,<br>촉구하다 | | | 참가, 출품(작), 입구, 참가자 | | | |
| | | 포옹하다, 수용하다;<br>포옹, 수용 | | | 초과하다 | | | |
| | | 지속 가능한 | 28 | | 열리다, 개최되다 | | | |
| 25 | | 결과, 결론 | | | 날씨와 관계없이, 어떤 일이<br>있더라도 | | | |

(.hwp) (.pdf) → www.englishjmygod.com

# Voca Test

| ❶ voca | ❷ text | ❸ [ / ] | ❹ ____ | ❺ quiz 1 | ❻ quiz 2 | ❼ quiz 3 | ❽ quiz 4 | ❾ quiz 5 |
|---|---|---|---|---|---|---|---|---|
| | | | 참여, 참가 | | | ~을 ...에 근거하다 | | |
| | | | 요건, 필요조건 | | | 유능한, 능률적인, 효율적인 | | |
| | | | 거주자, 주민; 거주하는, 고유의 | | | 빠르게, 급히 | | |
| | | | 유효한, 타당한, 근거가 있는 | | | 제거하다 | | |
| | | | 토대, 기초, 근거, 이유 | | | 그 결과 | | |
| 29 | | | 시의회 | | | 민감한, 신경 과민의, 감수성이 풍부한 | | |
| | | | 투입되다, 시작하다, 논의하다 | | | 결과, 영향, 효과; 초래하다, 이루다 | | |
| | | | 흐름, 개울, 경향; 흐르다, 흘러나오다 | | | 노화; 늙어 가는 | | |
| | | | 탄소 | | | 바꾸다, 변경하다, 고치다 | | |
| | | | ~을 제기하다, 제시하다 | 31 | | 반항자 | | |
| | | | 끔찍한, 무서운, 심한 | | | ~을 찾다, ~을 모집하다 | | |
| | | | 조심, 주의, 신중; 주의하다 | | | 대안 | | |
| | | | ~할 때까지 | | | ~에 우호적인, ~을 지지하여 | | |
| | | | 합리적으로, 타당하게, 적정하게 | | | 유지하다, 주장하다 | | |
| | | | 소비하다, 섭취하다, 먹다 | | | 독특함, 유일함, 유례없는 일 | | |
| | | | 유독한, 치명적인, 중독(성)의 | | | 가장 많은 수, 다수 | | |
| | | | 개인; 개인의, 개별적인, 독특한 | | | 속임수, 재주, 비결; 속임수의; 속이다 | | |
| | | | 말이 되다, 타당하다, 의미가 통하다 | | | 전환, 반전, 좌절 | | |
| | | | 상하기 쉬운 | | | 정장, 소송; 적합하다, (알)맞다 | | |
| | | | 상품 | | | 목적, 의도; 의도하다 | | |
| 30 | | | 사라지다, 없어지다, 닳게 하다 | | | 주류, 대세; 주류의 | | |
| | | | 제거하다, 없애다, 옮기다 | | | 충성(도), 충의 | | |
| | | | 간 | 32 | | 추상적인; 추상, 요약; 요약[추출]하다 | | |
| | | | 서서히, 점차 | | | 복잡한, 복합의; 복합체, 콤플렉스 | | |
| | | | 저하[악화]시키다, 비하하다, 분해하다 | | | 기분 전환을 하다, 기운을 회복시키다 | | |

# Voca Test

| ❶ voca | ❷ text | ❸ [ / ] | ❹ ___ | ❺ quiz 1 | ❻ quiz 2 | ❼ quiz 3 | ❽ quiz 4 | ❾ quiz 5 |
|---|---|---|---|---|---|---|---|---|
| | 심리, 심리학 | | | | | | | 막다, 예방하다 |
| | 사색하다, 추측하다, 투기하다 | | | | | | | 튀다, 뛰어오르다; 튀어오름 |
| | 음모, 줄거리, 작은 토지; 음모[줄거리]를 짜다 | | | | | | | 재료, 물질; 물질의, 육체의, 중요한 |
| | 상당한, 많은 | | | 34 | | | | 분류하다, 구분하다; 종류 |
| | 쉽게 | | | | | | | 관리[처리]할 수 있는 |
| | ~에 대처[대응]하다, 극복하다 | | | | | | | 압도적인, 너무도 강력한 |
| | 추상적 개념, 관념 | | | | | | | 엄청난, 거대한, 막대한 |
| | 하부 구조, 체계, 뼈대, 틀 | | | | | | | 인상, 감명, 흔적 |
| 33 | (동물의) 먹이, 희생자; 포식하다 | | | | | | | ~에 중요하다 |
| | ~으로 바쁘다, ~에 종사[관여]하다 | | | | | | | ~에 관련된 |
| | 감각의, 지각의 | | | | | | | 조직하다, 정리하다, 개최하다 |
| | 군비 경쟁 | | | | | | | 재고(품), 저장, 주식; 비축하다, 저장하다 |
| | 나방 | | | | | | | 달성하다, 성취하다, 이루다 |
| | 특별히, 구체적으로, 명확하게 | | | | | | | 무관한, 상관없는, 부적절한 |
| | ~에 반응[응답]하여 | | | | | | | 모순, 반박 |
| | 협박, 위협, 조짐 | | | | | | | 한결같은, 확고한, 안정된, 착실한 |
| | 진화하다, (서서히) 발전하다 | | | | | | | 제거, 삭제 |
| | 알아내다, 감지하다, 탐지하다 | | | | | | | 부분, 분수, 아주 조금 |
| | 빈번함, 빈도, 진동수 | | | | | | | 되찾다, 구하다, 회상하다, 검색하다 |
| | 발성, 발성법 | | | 35 | | | | 번성[번영]하다, 잘 자라다 |
| | 청각의, 음향의 | | | | | | | 번영하다, 번성하다, 성공하다 |
| | 위장하다, 감추다; 위장, 기만 | | | | | | | 정확히, 바로 |
| | 흡수하다, 몰두[열중]시키다 | | | | | | | 통치자, 지배자, (도구) 자 |
| | 내뿜다, 방출하다, 내다 | | | | | | | 놀라울 정도로, 뚜렷하게, 몹시 |
| | 그렇게 함으로써, 그것 때문에 | | | | | | | (자질 등을) 재다, 평가[가늠]하다 |

# Voca Test

| ❶ voca | ❷ text | ❸ [ / ] | ❹ _____ | ❺ quiz 1 | ❻ quiz 2 | ❼ quiz 3 | ❽ quiz 4 | ❾ quiz 5 |
|---|---|---|---|---|---|---|---|---|
| | | 상당한 | 37 | | | | 건축가, 설계자 | |
| | | ~에 근거하다 | | | | | 인상적인, 감명 깊은 | |
| | | 치다, 떠오르다, 노력하다; 타격, 공격, 파업 | | | | | 포함[함유]하다, 억누르다, 억제하다 | |
| | | 보여 주다, 예증하다, 삽화를 넣다 | | | | | 강당, 청중석 | |
| | | 약점, 결점 | | | | | ~으로 구성된 | |
| | | 수입, 수익, 세입 | | | | | 본능적으로, 무의식적으로 | |
| | | 중세의, 중세풍의 | | | | | 정제된, 세련된 | |
| | | 추출(물); 추출하다, 끄집어내다 | | | | | 감각, 감성, 감수성, 민감 | |
| | | ...이라기보다는 ~ | | | | | 그것도, 게다가 | |
| | | 예외(사항), 제외 | | | | | 미학적으로 | |
| 36 | | 다투다, 겨루다, 경쟁하다 | | | | | ~으로 알려진 | |
| | | ~바로 옆에 | | | | | 파라메트릭 디자인(알고리즘 프로세스에 따라 특징을 형성시키는 디자인 방법) | |
| | | ~을 추구하여, ~을 찾아서 | | | | | 일련의, 일습의 | |
| | | 확고한, 고정된; 회사 | | | | | 기준, 표준 ((단수형 criterion)) | |
| | | 광고하다, 선전하다 | | | | | 발생시키다, 만들어내다, (감정을) 일으키다 | |
| | | 유혹, 충동 | | | | | ~하곤 했다, ~이었다[했다] | |
| | | 광고, 광고업 | | | | | 가벼운, 경량의 | |
| | | 이익, 이득; 이익이 되다 | | | | | 맹목적으로 | |
| | | 잘못된 생각, 오해 | | | | | 다르다, 바꾸다, 변하다 | |
| | | (~의 비율을) 차지하다, 설명하다 | 38 | | | | 그저, 단지 | |
| | | 차별화된 | | | | | 놀라울 정도로, 엄청나게 | |
| | | A가 ~할 수 있게 하다 | | | | | 적응하는, 적응할 수 있는 | |
| | | ~로부터 혜택[이익]을 얻다 | | | | | 경제적으로 사용하다 | |
| | | 변화, 다양(성), 품종 | | | | | 수단, 기지 (-s) 자원, 소질; 자원을 제공하다 | |
| | | 구조, 조직, 체계; 구성하다, 조직화하다 | | | | | 분석 ((복수형 analyses)) | |

# Voca Test

| ❶ voca | ❷ text | ❸ [ / ] | ❹ ____ | ❺ quiz 1 | ❻ quiz 2 | ❼ quiz 3 | ❽ quiz 4 | ❾ quiz 5 |

| | | | | | |
|---|---|---|---|---|---|
| | | 뛰어난, 비범한, 특이한, 단일의 | | | 고용하다, 사용[이용]하다 |
| | | 당면한, 처리해야 하는, 가까이에 | | | ~에 부합하다, 맞추다 |
| | | ~을 ...에 쏟다[바치다] | 40 | | ~을 하다, 지휘하다, (전기 등을) 전도하다; 행동 |
| 39 | | ~을 수행하다, 실행하다 | | | 동기 (부여) |
| | | 참여, 약속, 약혼, 고용 | | | 공격하다; 공격, 발작 |
| | | 이론의, 이론상의 | | | 도움, 지원 |
| | | 실용적인, 실제의 | | | 동기; 원동력이 되는 |
| | | 견지, 관점, 견해 | | | 줄이다, 낮추다, 감소하다 |
| | | 알아보다, 확인하다, 동일시하다 | | | 불편, 불쾌, 가벼운 통증 |
| | | ~안으로 떨어지다 | | | 고민, 고통, 빈곤; ~을 괴롭히다 |
| | | 영향력 있는, 영향력이 큰 | | | ~에서 기인하다, 유래하다 |
| | | (둘 중에서) 후자 | | | 흥분, 각성 |
| | | ~에 책임이 있다 | | | 가장된, 꾸민, 감염된 |
| | | 실제로, 사실 | | | 해소하다 |
| | | 건설적인, 발전적인 | | | 희생(자), 피해자 |
| | | 수행, 성과, 성적, 공연 | 41 ~42 | | 보통이 아닌, 이상한, 유별난 |
| | | ~에게 ...을 제공하다 | | | 펴다, 퍼뜨리다, 퍼지다; 확장, 유포, 보급 |
| | | 필요한, 필연적인; (-s) 필수품 | | | 널리, 크게 |
| | | 주목할 가치가 있는, 현저한 | | | ~을 물려주다, 전해주다 |
| | | 즉, 다시 말해서 | | | 구전 |
| | | 기대, 요구, 예상, 가망 | | | 축적하다 |
| | | 포부, 야망 | | | 표준, 기준, (-s) 규범, 모범, 평균 |
| | | 업적, 성취 | | | 인식, 인지, 지각 |
| | | 의미 있는, 중요한 | | | 출현, 등장, 도래 |
| | | 분명한, 명백한, 뚜렷한 | | | 읽고 쓸 줄 아는 능력, 교양 있음 |

(.hwp) (.pdf) → www.englishjmygod.com

# Voca Test

❶ voca    ❷ text    ❸ [ / ]    ❹ _____    ❺ quiz 1    ❻ quiz 2    ❼ quiz 3    ❽ quiz 4    ❾ quiz 5

| | | | | | | | | |
|---|---|---|---|---|---|---|---|---|
| | | 옮기다, 전하다; 이동, 환승 | | | 번성[번창]하다, 잘 자라다 | | | |
| | | 바래다, 희미해지다, 서서히 사라지다 | | | ~을 낳다, ~으로 이어지다 | | | |
| | | 일시적 유행 | | | 요양원, 양로원 | | | |
| | | 더 이상 ~아닌[하지 않는] | | | 결과적으로, 차례차례 | | | |
| | | 의미하다, 중요하다 | | | 모금(의) | | | |
| | | 발생 순서대로 된, 연대순의 | | | (물건을) 놓다, (알을) 낳다 | | | |
| | | ~하려고 애쓰다 | | | 디딤돌, 발판 | | | |
| | | 이전에, 예전에 | | | 용감한, 용기 있는 | | | |
| | | 연관(성), 연상, 협회 | | | 고아; 고아로 만들다 | | | |
| | | 물러나다, 은퇴하다 | | | ~하겠다고 위협하다 | | | |
| | | 고정 관념, 전형; 정형화하다 | | | 채택 | | | |
| | | 최신의 | | | 인종의, 민족의 | | | |
| 43 ~45 | | 염료; 염색하다 | | | 풍성함, 풍부함, 풍요로움 | | | |
| | | 측면, 면, 양상, 관점 | | | | | | |
| | | 접근하다; 접근(법) | | | | | | |
| | | 표현하다, 나타내다; 급행의 | | | | | | |
| | | 의도, 의향 | | | | | | |
| | | 예상하다, 기대하다 | | | | | | |
| | | 격노, 분노; 몹시 화를 내다 | | | | | | |
| | | A를 B라는 이유로 비난하다 | | | | | | |
| | | 은혜를 모르는, 고마워할 줄 모르는 | | | | | | |
| | | ~에 직면하여 | | | | | | |
| | | 혼란 | | | | | | |
| | | 결심[결정]하다, 해결하다, 용해하다 | | | | | | |
| | | 다음(의); 다음에 계속되는 | | | | | | |

## 2023 고2 9월 모의고사

❶ voca    ❷ text    ❸ [ / ]    ❹ ____    ❺ quiz 1    ❻ quiz 2    ❼ quiz 3    ❽ quiz 4    ❾ quiz 5

# 18 목적

❶ To whom it may concern,

I would like to draw your attention to a problem that frequently occurs with the No. 35 buses.

관계자분께, 35번 버스에서 자주 발생하는 문제에 대해 귀하의 주의를 환기하고 싶습니다.

❷ There is a bus stop about halfway along Fenny Road, at which the No.35 buses are supposed to stop.

Fenny Road를 따라 중간쯤 버스 정류장이 있고, 그곳에서 35번 버스가 정차하게 되어 있습니다.

❸ It would appear, however, that some of your drivers are either unaware of this bus stop or for some reason choose to ignore it, driving past even though the buses are not full.

그러나 버스 기사들 중 일부는 이 버스 정류장을 인식하지 못하거나 어떤 이유에서인지 그것을 무시하기로 선택하여 버스가 꽉 차지 않았음에도 운전해 지나쳐가는 것으로 보입니다.

❹ I would be grateful if you could remind your drivers that this bus stop exists and that they should be prepared to stop at it.

기사들에게 이 버스 정류장이 존재하고 그곳에 정차할 준비가 되어 있어야 한다는 것을 상기시켜 주시면 감사하겠습니다.

❺ I look forward to seeing an improvement in this service soon.

곧 이 서비스가 개선되기를 기대합니다.

❻ Yours faithfully, John Williams

진심을 담아, John Williams 드림

# 19 심경

❶ My 10-year-old appeared, in desperate need of a quarter.

내 열 살짜리 아이가 나타났고, 25센트 동전을 절실히 필요로 했다.

❷ "A quarter? What on earth do you need a quarter for?" My tone bordered on irritation.

"25센트 동전? 도대체 25센트 동전이 왜 필요하지?" 나의 말투는 거의 짜증에 가까웠다.

❸ I didn't want to be bothered with such a trivial demand.

나는 그런 사소한 요구에 방해받고 싶지 않았다.

❹ "There's a garage sale up the street, and there's something I just gotta have! It only costs a quarter.

Please?" I placed a quarter in my son's hand.

"거리 위쪽에서 중고 물품 판매 행사를 하는데, 제가 꼭 사야 할 게 있어요! 25센트밖에 안 해요. 네?" 나는 아들의 손에 25센트 동전을 쥐여 주었다.

❺ Moments later, a little voice said, "Here, Mommy, this is for you."

잠시 후 작은 목소리가 "여기요, 엄마, 이거 엄마를 위한 거예요."라고 말했다.

❻ I glanced down at the hands of my little son and saw a four-inch cream-colored statue of two small

children hugging one another.

나는 내 어린 아들의 손을 힐끗 내려다보았고, 두 어린아이가 서로 껴안고 있는 4인치짜리 크림색의 조각상을 보았다.

❼ Inscribed at their feet were words that read *It starts with 'L' ends with 'E' and in between are 'O' and 'V.'*

그들의 발밑에는 'L'로 시작하여 'E'로 끝나고 그 사이에 'O'와 'V'가 있다는 말이 새겨져 있었다.

❽ As I watched him race back to the garage sale, I smiled with a heart full of happiness.

아이가 중고 물품 판매 행사로 서둘러 돌아가는 모습을 바라보며 나는 행복이 가득한 마음으로 미소를 지었다.

❾ That 25-cent garage sale purchase brought me a lot of joy.

그 25센트짜리 중고 물품 판매 행사 구입품은 나에게 큰 기쁨을 가져다 주었다.

## 20 요지

❶ Managers frequently try to play psychologist, to "figure out" why an employee has acted in a certain way.

관리자들은 직원이 왜 특정한 방식으로 행동했는지를 '파악하기' 위해 심리학자 역할을 하려고 자주 노력한다.

❷ Empathizing with employees in order to understand their point of view can be very helpful.

그들의 관점을 이해하기 위해 직원들과 공감하는 것은 매우 도움이 될 수 있다.

❸ However, when dealing with ㅋa problem area, in particular, remember that it is not the person who is bad, but the actions exhibited on the job.

하지만, 특히 문제 영역을 다룰 때, 그것은 잘하지 못하는 사람이 아니라 근무 중에 보여지는 행동이라는 것을 기억하라.

❹ Avoid making suggestions to employees about personal traits they should change; instead suggest more acceptable ways of performing.

직원들에게 그들이 바꿔야 할 인격적 특성에 대해 제안하는 것을 피하라.; 대신에 더 용인되는 수행 방법을 제안하라..

❺ For example, instead of focusing on a person's "unreliability," a manager might focus on the fact that the employee "has been late to work seven times this month."

예를 들어, 관리자는 어떤 사람의 '신뢰할 수 없음'에 초점을 맞추는 대신, 그 직원이 '이번 달에 회사에 일곱 번 지각했다'는 사실에 초점을 맞출 수도 있을 것이다.

❻ It is difficult for employees to change who they are; it is usually much easier for them to change how they act.

직원들은 자신이 어떤 사람인지를 바꾸기는 어렵다. 일반적으로 자신이 행동하는 방식을 바꾸기가 훨씬 쉽다.

# 21 주장

**❶** I suspect fungi are a little more forward "thinking" than their larger partners.

나는 균류가 자신의 더 큰 상대보다 조금 더 앞서 '생각한다'고 짐작한다.

**❷** Among trees, each species fights other species.

나무들 사이에서 각 종은 다른 종들과 싸운다.

**❸** Let's assume the beeches native to Central Europe could emerge victorious in most forests there.

중부 유럽 태생의 너도밤나무가 그곳의 숲 대부분에서 우세하게 나타날 수 있다고 가정해 보자.

**❹** Would this really be an advantage? What would happen if a new pathogen came along that infected most of the beeches and killed them? In that case, wouldn't it be more advantageous if there were a certain number of other species around — oaks, maples, or firs — that would continue to grow and provide the shade needed for a new generation of young beeches to sprout and grow up? Diversity provides security for ancient forests.

이게 정말 이점일까? 만약 대부분의 너도밤나무를 감염시켜 죽게 만드는 새로운 병원균이 나타나면 어떻게 될까? 그런 경우, 주변에 참나무, 단풍나무 또는 전나무와 같은 일정한 수의 다른 종이 계속 자라서 새로운 세대의 어린 너도밤나무가 싹을 틔우고 자라는 데 필요한 그늘을 제공한다면 더 유리하지 않을까? 다양성은 오래된 숲에 안전을 제공한다.

**❺** Because fungi are also very dependent on stable conditions, they support other species underground and protect them from complete collapse to ensure that one species of tree doesn't manage to dominate.

균류도 또한 안정적인 조건에 매우 의존하기 때문에, 그들은 한 종의 나무가 우세해지지 않도록 확실히 하기 위해 땅 속에서 다른 종을 지원하고 그것들을 완전한 붕괴로부터 보호한다.

## 22 의미

❶ It's remarkable that positive fantasies help us relax to such an extent that it shows up in physiological tests.

낙관적인 상상이 생리학적 검사에서 나타날 정도로 우리가 긴장을 푸는 데 도움이 된다는 것은 주목할 만하다.

❷ If you want to unwind, you can take some deep breaths, get a massage, or go for a walk — but you can also try simply closing your eyes and fantasizing about some future outcome that you might enjoy.

만약 여러분이 긴장을 풀고 싶다면, 심호흡하거나, 마사지를 받거나, 산책을 할 수도 있지만, 단순히 눈을 감고 여러분이 누릴지도 모를 미래의 결과에 대해 상상해 볼 수도 있다.

❸ But what about when your objective is to make your wish a reality? The *last* thing you want to be is relaxed.

하지만 여러분의 목표가 소망을 실현하는 것인 경우라면 어떨까? 여러분이 '가장 피해야 할' 상태는 긴장이 풀려 있는 것이다.

❹ You want to be energized enough to get off the couch and lose those pounds or find that job or study for that test, and you want to be motivated enough to stay engaged even when the inevitable obstacles or challenges arise.

여러분은 소파에서 일어나 체중을 감량하거나 직업을 찾거나 시험공부를 할 수 있을 만큼 충분히 활력을 얻어야 하고, 피할 수 없는 장애물이나 문제가 발생할 때도 계속 전념할 수 있도록 충분히 동기 부여 되어야 한다.

❺ The principle of "Dream it. Wish it. Do it." does not hold true, and now we know why: in dreaming it, you undercut the energy you need to do it.

'그것을 꿈꿔라. 그것을 소망하라. 그것을 실행하라.'라는 원칙은 사실이 아니며, 우리는 이제 그 이유를 안다.

❻ You put yourself in a temporary state of complete happiness, calmness — and inactivity.

그것을 꿈꾸는 중에, 여러분은 그것을 하는 데 필요한 에너지를 약화시킨다. 여러분은 스스로를 완전한 행복, 고요, 그리고 비활동의 일시적인 상태에 빠지게 한다.

# 23 주제

❶ If cooking is as central to human identity, biology, and culture as the biological anthropologist Richard Wrangham suggests, it stands to reason that the decline of cooking in our time would have serious consequences for modern life, and so it has.

생물인류학자인 Richard Wrangham이 말하는 것만큼 요리가 인간의 정체성, 생물학 및 문화에 중요하다면, 우리 시대의 요리 감소가 현대 생활에 심각한 결과들을 초래한다고 추론하는 것은 당연하고, 실제로 그래왔다.

❷ Are they all bad? Not at all.

그것들이 모두 나쁜가? 전혀 그렇지 않다.

❸ The outsourcing of much of the work of cooking to corporations has relieved women of what has traditionally been their exclusive responsibility for feeding the family, making it easier for them to work outside the home and have careers.

요리하는 일의 많은 부분을 기업에 아웃소싱하는 것은 전통적으로 여성들에게 한정된, 가족들을 먹여야 하는 책임이었던 것에서 여성들을 벗어나게 했고, 그들이 집 밖에서 일하고 직업을 갖는 것을 더 쉽게 했다.

❹ It has headed off many of the domestic conflicts that such a large shift in gender roles and family dynamics was bound to spark.

그것은 성 역할과 가족 역학의 그렇게 큰 변화가 촉발할 많은 가정 내 갈등을 막아냈다.

❺ It has relieved other pressures in the household, including longer workdays and overscheduled children, and saved us time that we can now invest in other pursuits.

그것은 더 긴 근무일과 분주한 자녀를 포함하여 가정의 다른 곤란을 덜어주었고, 이제 우리가 다른 일에 투자할 수 있도록 시간을 절약해 주었다.

❻ It has also allowed us to diversify our diets substantially, making it possible even for people with no cooking skills and little money to enjoy a whole different cuisine.

그것은 또한 우리의 식단을 상당히 다양하게 해주었고, 요리 기술이 없고 돈이 거의 없는 사람들까지도 완전히 색다른 요리를 즐길 수 있게 해 주었다.

❼ All that's required is a microwave.

필요한 것이라곤 전자레인지뿐이다.

## 24 제목

❶ As you may already know, what and how you buy can be political.

이미 알고 있겠지만, 여러분이 무엇을 어떻게 구매하는지는 정치적일 수 있다.

❷ To whom do you want to give your money? Which companies and corporations do you value and respect? Be mindful about every purchase by carefully researching the corporations that are taking our money to decide if they deserve our support.

여러분은 여러분의 돈을 누구에게 주고 싶은가? 여러분은 어떤 회사와 기업을 가치 있게 여기고 존중하는가? 우리의 지원을 받을 자격이 있는지를 결정하기 위해 우리의 돈을 가져가는 기업들을 면밀히 조사함으로써 모든 구매에 주의를 기울여라.

❸ Do they have a record of polluting the environment, or do they have fair-trade practices and an end-of-life plan for the products they make? Are they committed to bringing about good in the world? For instance, my family has found a company producing recycled, plastic-packaging-free toilet paper with a social conscience.

그들은 환경을 오염시킨 기록이 있는가, 아니면 그들이 만든 제품에 대한 공정 거래 관행과 제품 수명 종료 계획이 있는가? 그들은 세상에 득이 되는 것에 헌신하고 있는가? 예를 들어, 우리 가족은 사회적 양심을 가지고 재활용되고 플라스틱 포장이 없는 화장지를 생산하는 회사를 발견했다.

❹ They contribute 50 percent of their profits to the construction of toilets around the world, and we're genuinely happy to spend our money on this special toilet paper each month.

그들은 수익의 50%를 전 세계 화장실 건설에 기부하고 우리는 이 특별한 화장지에 매달 돈을 쓸 수 있어서 정말 기쁘다.

❺ Remember that the corporate world is built on consumers, so as a consumer you have the power to vote with your wallet and encourage companies to embrace healthier and more sustainable practices with every purchase you choose to make.

기업의 세계는 소비자를 기반으로 구축되므로, 소비자로서 여러분은 지갑으로 투표하고 여러분이 선택한 모든 구매를 통해 회사들이 더 건강하고 더 지속 가능한 관행을 받아들이도록 장려할 힘이 있다는 것을 기억하라.

# 26 일치

❶ Camille Flammarion was born at Montigny-le-Roi, France.

Camille Flammarion은 프랑스 Montigny-le-Roi에서 태어났다.

❷ He became interested in astronomy at an early age, and when he was only sixteen he wrote a book on the origin of the world.

그는 어린 나이에 천문학에 흥미가 생겼고, 불과 16세에 그는 세상의 기원에 관한 책을 썼다.

❸ The manuscript was not published at the time, but it came to the attention of Urbain Le Verrier, the director of the Paris Observatory.

그 원고는 그 당시 출판되지 않았지만, Paris Observatory의 관리자인 Urbain Le Verrier의 관심을 끌게 되었다.

❹ He became an assistant to Le Verrier in 1858 and worked as a calculator.

그는 1858년에 Le Verrier의 조수가 되었고 계산원으로 일했다.

❺ At nineteen, he wrote another book called *The Plurality of Inhabited Worlds*, in which he passionately claimed that life exists outside the planet Earth.

19세에 그는 The Plurality of Inhabited Worlds라는 또 다른 책을 썼는데, 이 책에서 그는 외계에 생명체가 존재한다고 열정적으로 주장했다.

❻ His most successful work, *Popular Astronomy*, was published in 1880, and eventually sold 130,000 copies.

그의 가장 성공적인 저서인 Popular Astronomy는 1880년에 출판되었고, 결국 130,000부가 판매되었다.

❼ With his own funds, he built an observatory at Juvisy and spent May to November of each year there.

자신의 자금으로 그는 Juvisy에 천문대를 세웠고, 매년 5월에서 11월까지 그곳에서 지냈다.

❽ In 1887, he founded the French Astronomical Society and served as editor of its monthly publication.

1887년에 그는 French Astronomical Society를 설립했고 그것의 월간 간행물의 편집자로 일했다.

# 29 어법

❶ There is little doubt that we are driven by the sell-by date.

우리가 판매 유효 기한에 따라 움직인다는 것은 의심할 여지가 거의 없다.

❷ Once an item is past that date it goes into the waste stream, further increasing its carbon footprint.

일단 어떤 품목이 그 기한을 지나면 폐기물 흐름으로 들어가고, 이는 그것의 탄소 발자국을 더욱더 증가시킨다.

❸ Remember those items have already travelled hundreds of miles to reach the shelves and once they go into waste they start a new carbon mile journey.

그러한 품목들이 선반에 도달하기 위해 이미 수백 마일을 이동했고 일단 그것들이 버려지게 되면 그것들은 새로운 탄소 마일 여정을 시작한다는 것을 기억하라.

❹ But we all make our own judgement about sell-by dates; those brought up during the Second World War are often scornful of the terrible waste they believe such caution encourages.

그러나 우리 모두는 판매 유효 기한에 대해 자신만의 판단을 내린다. 가령, 제2차 세계 대전 중에 자란 사람들은 그들이 생각하기에 그러한 경고가 조장하는 끔찍한 낭비를 자주 경멸한다.

❺ The manufacturer of the food has a view when making or growing something that by the time the product reaches the shelves it has already been travelling for so many days and possibly many miles.

식품 제조업자는 무엇인가를 만들거나 재배할 때 제품이 선반에 도달할 때에는 그것은 이미 매우 오랫동안 그리고 아마도 상당한 거리를 이동해 왔다는 관점을 가지고 있다.

❻ The manufacturer then decides that a product can reasonably be consumed within say 90 days and 90 days minus so many days for travelling gives the sell-by date.

그래서 제조업자는 제품이 이를테면 90일 이내에는 무리 없이 소비될 수 있고 90일에서 이동에 필요한 많은 날들을 뺀 것이 판매 유효 기한이 된다고 결정한다.

❼ But whether it becomes toxic is something each individual can decide.

그러나 그것이 유독해지는지는 각 개인이 결정할 수 있는 것이다.

❽ It would seem to make sense not to buy large packs of perishable goods but non-perishable items may become cost-effective.

큰 묶음의 상하기 쉬운 제품을 사지 않는 것이 이치에 맞는 것으로 보이겠지만, 상하지 않는 품목들의 경우에는 비용 효율이 높아질 수도 있다.

(.hwp) (.pdf) → www.englishjmygod.com

# 30 어휘

❶ The "jolt" of caffeine does wear off.

카페인의 '충격'은 확실히 점차 사라진다.

❷ Caffeine is removed from your system by an enzyme within your liver, which gradually degrades it over time.

카페인은 여러분의 간 안에 있는 효소에 의해 여러분의 신체로부터 제거되는데, 이 효소는 시간이 지남에 따라 그것을 점진적으로 분해한다.

❸ Based in large part on genetics, some people have a more efficient version of the enzyme that degrades caffeine, allowing the liver to rapidly clear it from the bloodstream.

대체로 유전적 특징 때문에, 어떤 사람들은 카페인을 분해하는 더 효율적인 형태의 효소를 갖고 있는데, 이는 간이 그것을 혈류로부터 더 빠르게 제거할 수 있도록 한다.

❹ These rare individuals can drink an espresso with dinner and fall fast asleep at midnight without a problem.

이 몇 안 되는 사람들은 저녁과 함께 에스프레소를 마시고도 아무 문제 없이 한밤중에 깊이 잠들 수 있다.

❺ Others, however, have a slower-acting version of the enzyme.

그러나 다른 사람들은 더 느리게 작용하는 형태의 효소를 가지고 있다.

❻ It takes far longer for their system to eliminate the same amount of caffeine.

그들의 신체가 같은 양의 카페인을 제거하는 데 훨씬 더 오랜 시간이 걸린다.

❼ As a result, they are very sensitive to caffeine's effects.

결과적으로, 그들은 카페인의 효과에 매우 민감하다.

❽ One cup of tea or coffee in the morning will last much of the day, and should they have a second cup, even early in the afternoon, they will find it difficult to fall asleep in the evening.

아침에 마시는 한 잔의 차나 커피는 그날 대부분 동안 지속될 것이고, 심지어 이른 오후라도, 두 번째 잔을 마신다면, 그들은 저녁에 잠드는 것이 어렵다는 것을 알 것이다.

❾ Aging also alters the speed of caffeine clearance: the older we are, the longer it takes our brain and body to remove caffeine, and thus the more sensitive we become in later life to caffeine's sleep-disrupting influence.

노화는 또한 카페인 제거 속도를 변화시킨다. 즉, 우리가 나이가 들수록 우리의 뇌와 신체가 카페인을 제거하는 것이 더 오래 걸리고, 따라서 우리는 노후에 카페인의 수면을 방해하는 효과에 더 민감해진다.

# 31 빈칸

❶ Rebels may think they're rebels, but clever marketers influence them just like the rest of us.

반항자들은 자신들이 반항자라고 생각할지도 모르지만, 영리한 마케터들은 나머지 우리에게 그러듯이 그들에게 영향을 준다.

❷ Saying, "Everyone is doing it" may turn some people off from an idea.

"모두가 그것을 하고 있다."라고 말하는 것은 일부 사람들로 하여금 어떠한 생각에 대해 흥미를 잃게 할지도 모른다.

❸ These people will look for alternatives, which (if cleverly planned) can be exactly what a marketer or persuader wants you to believe.

이 사람들은 대안을 찾을 것이고, 그것은 (만약 영리하게 계획된다면) 정확히 마케터나 설득자가 여러분이 믿기를 원하는 것일 수 있다.

❹ If I want you to consider an idea, and know you strongly reject popular opinion in favor of maintaining your independence and uniqueness, I would present the majority option first, which you would reject in favor of my actual preference.

만약 내가 여러분이 한 아이디어를 고려하길 바라고, 여러분의 독립성과 유일성을 유지하기 위해 대중적인 의견을 강하게 거부한다는 것을 안다면, 나는 대다수가 선택하는 것을 먼저 제시할 것이고, 여러분은 내가 실제로 선호하는 것에 맞게 그것을 거부할 것이다.

❺ We are often tricked when we try to maintain a position of defiance.

우리는 반항의 입장을 유지하려고 할 때 종종 속는다.

❻ People use this reversal to make us "independently" choose an option which suits their purposes.

사람들은 우리가 그들의 목적에 맞는 선택지를 '독자적으로' 택하도록 만들기 위해 이러한 반전을 사용한다.

❼ Some brands have taken full effect of our defiance towards the mainstream and positioned themselves as rebels; which has created even stronger brand loyalty.

일부 브랜드들은 주류에 대한 우리의 반항을 완전히 활용하여 스스로를 반항자로 자리매김해 왔고, 이는 훨씬 더 강력한 브랜드 충성도를 만들어 왔다.

# 32 빈칸

❶ A typical soap opera creates an abstract world, in which a highly complex web of relationships connects fictional characters that exist first only in the minds of the program's creators and are then recreated in the minds of the viewer.

전형적인 드라마는 추상적인 세계를 만들어내며, 그 세계에서는 프로그램 제작자들의 마음속에만 먼저 존재하고 그러고 나서 시청자의 마음속에 재현되는 허구의 캐릭터들을 매우 복잡한 관계망이 연결한다.

❷ If you were to think about how much human psychology, law, and even everyday physics the viewer must know in order to follow and speculate about the plot, you would discover it is considerable — at least as much as the knowledge required to follow and speculate about a piece of modern mathematics, and in most cases, much more.

만약 줄거리를 따라가고 그것에 대해 추측하기 위해 시청자가 얼마나 많은 인간 심리학, 법, 그리고 심지어 일상에서의 물리학을 알아야 하는지에 대해 생각한다면, 여러분은 그것이 상당하다는 것을, 즉 적어도 현대 수학의 한 부분을 따라가고 그것에 대해 추측하는 데 필요한 지식만큼이라는 것, 그리고 대부분의 경우 훨씬 더 많다는 것을 발견할 것이다.

❸ Yet viewers follow soap operas with ease.

하지만 시청자들은 드라마를 쉽게 따라간다.

❹ How are they able to cope with such abstraction? Because, of course, the abstraction is built on an extremely familiar framework.

그들은 어떻게 그런 추상에 대처할 수 있을까? 왜냐하면, 당연하게도, 그 추상은 매우 친숙한 틀 위에서 만들어졌기 때문이다.

❺ The characters in a soap opera and the relationships between them are very much like the real people and relationships we experience every day.

드라마 속 인물들과 그들 사이의 관계는 우리가 매일 경험하는 실제 사람들 및 관계와 매우 흡사하다.

❻ The abstraction of a soap opera is only a step removed from the real world.

드라마의 추상은 현실 세계에서 불과 한 걸음 떨어져 있다.

❼ The mental "training" required to follow a soap opera is provided by our everyday lives.

드라마를 따라가기 위해 필요한 정신적 '훈련'은 우리의 일상에 의해 제공된다.

# 33 빈칸

❶ As always happens with natural selection, bats and their prey have been engaged in a life-or-death sensory arms race for millions of years.

　자연 선택에서 항상 그렇듯이, 박쥐와 그 먹잇감은 수백만 년 동안 생사를 가르는 감각 군비 경쟁에 참여해 왔다.

❷ It's believed that hearing in moths arose specifically in response to the threat of being eaten by bats. (Not all insects can hear.)

　나방의 청력은 특히 박쥐에게 잡아먹히는 위협에 대한 반응으로 생겨난 것으로 여겨진다. (모든 곤충이 들을 수 있는 것은 아니다.)

❸ Over millions of years, moths have evolved the ability to detect sounds at ever higher frequencies, and, as they have, the frequencies of bats' vocalizations have risen, too.

　수백만 년 동안, 나방은 계속 더 높아진 주파수의 소리를 감지하는 능력을 진화시켰고, 그것들이 그렇게 함에 따라 박쥐의 발성 주파수도 높아졌다.

❹ Some moth species have also evolved scales on their wings and a fur-like coat on their bodies; both act as "acoustic camouflage," by absorbing sound waves in the frequencies emitted by bats, thereby preventing those sound waves from bouncing back.

　수백만 년 동안, 나방은 계속 더 높아진 주파수의 소리를 감지하는 능력을 진화시켰고, 그것들이 그렇게 함에 따라 박쥐의 발성 주파수도 높아졌다. 둘 다 '음향 위장'의 역할을 하는데, 박쥐에 의해 방출되는 주파수의 음파를 흡수함으로써, 그것으로 음파가 되돌아가는 것을 방지한다.

❺ The B-2 bomber and other "stealth" aircraft have fuselages made of materials that do something similar with radar beams.

　B-2 폭격기와 그 밖의 '스텔스' 항공기는 레이더 전파에 대해 유사한 것을 하는 재료로 만들어진 기체를 가지고 있다.

# 34 빈칸

❶ Much of human thought is designed to screen out information and to sort the rest into a manageable condition.

인간 사고의 많은 부분은 정보를 걸러내고 나머지는 처리하기 쉬운 상태로 분류하도록 설계된다.

❷ The inflow of data from our senses could create an overwhelming chaos, especially given the enormous amount of information available in culture and society.

특히 문화와 사회에서 이용할 수 있는 엄청난 양의 정보를 고려할 때, 우리의 감각에서 오는 데이터의 유입은 압도적인 혼란을 야기할 수 있다.

❸ Out of all the sensory impressions and possible information, it is vital to find a small amount that is most relevant to our individual needs and to organize that into a usable stock of knowledge.

모든 감각적 인상과 가능한 정보 중에서, 우리의 개인적인 필요와 가장 관련이 있는 소량을 찾고 그것을 사용 가능한 지식체로 구성하는 것이 중요하다.

❹ Expectancies accomplish some of this work, helping to screen out information that is irrelevant to what is expected, and focusing our attention on clear contradictions.

예상들은 이 작업의 일부를 수행하여 예상되는 것과 무관한 정보를 걸러내는 데 도움이 되고, 명확한 모순에 우리의 주의를 집중시킨다.

❺ The processes of learning and memory are marked by a steady elimination of information.

학습과 기억의 과정은 정보의 지속적인 제거로 특징지어진다.

❻ People notice only a part of the world around them.

사람들은 그들 주변 세계의 일부분만을 인지한다.

❼ Then, only a fraction of what they notice gets processed and stored into memory.

그런 다음, 그들이 알아차린 것의 일부만 처리되어 기억에 저장된다.

❽ And only part of what gets committed to memory can be retrieved.

그리고 기억에 넘겨진 것의 일부만 생각해 낼 수 있다.

## 35 무관

❶ The irony of early democracy in Europe is that it thrived and prospered precisely because European rulers for a very long time were remarkably weak.

유럽 초기 민주주의의 아이러니는 바로 유럽의 통치자들이 매우 오랫동안 현저하게 약했기 때문에 그것이 번성하고 번영했다는 것이다.

❷ For more than a millennium after the fall of Rome, European rulers lacked the ability to assess what their people were producing and to levy substantial taxes based on this.

로마의 멸망 후 천 년 넘게, 유럽의 통치자들은 백성들이 생산하고 있었던 것을 평가하고 이를 바탕으로 상당한 세금을 부과할 능력이 부족했다.

❸ The most striking way to illustrate European weakness is to show how little revenue they collected.

유럽의 약함을 설명하는 가장 눈에 띄는 방법은 그들이 거둔 세입이 얼마나 적은지를 보여주는 것이다.

❹ Europeans would eventually develop strong systems of revenue collection, but it took them an awfully long time to do so.

유럽인들은 결국 강력한 세입 징수 시스템을 개발했지만, 그렇게 하는 데는 엄청나게 오랜 시간이 걸렸다.

❺ In medieval times, and for part of the early modern era, Chinese emperors and Muslim caliphs were able to extract much more of economic production than any European ruler with the exception of small city-states.

중세와 초기 근대의 일부 동안, 중국의 황제들과 이슬람 문명의 칼리프들은 작은 도시 국가들을 제외한 어떤 유럽 통치자들보다 경제적 생산물에서 훨씬 더 많은 것을 얻어낼 수 있었다.

# 36 순서

❶ If you drive down a busy street, you will find many competing businesses, often right next to one another.

만약 여러분이 번화한 거리를 운전한다면, 여러분은 자주 서로의 바로 옆에서 경쟁하는 많은 업체들을 발견할 것이다.

❷ For example, in most places a consumer in search of a quick meal has many choices, and more fast-food restaurants appear all the time.

예를 들어, 대부분의 장소에서 빠른 식사를 찾는 소비자는 많은 선택권을 가지고 있고, 더 많은 패스트푸드 식당들이 항상 나타난다.

❸ These competing firms advertise heavily.

이 경쟁하는 회사들은 광고를 많이 한다.

❹ The temptation is to see advertising as driving up the price of a product without any benefit to the consumer.

광고를 소비자에게 어떤 혜택도 없이 제품의 가격을 올리는 것으로 보기 쉽다.

❺ However, this misconception doesn't account for why firms advertise.

그러나 이러한 오해는 회사들이 광고하는 이유를 설명하지 않는다.

❻ In markets where competitors sell slightly differentiated products, advertising enables firms to inform their customers about new products and services.

경쟁사들이 약간 차별화된 제품들을 판매하는 시장에서, 광고는 회사들이 그들의 소비자들에게 새로운 제품과 서비스를 알릴 수 있게 해 준다.

❼ Yes, costs rise, but consumers also gain information to help make purchasing decisions.

물론 가격이 상승하기는 하지만, 소비자들은 구매 결정을 내리는 데 도움이 되는 정보도 얻는다.

❽ Consumers also benefit from added variety, and we all get a product that's pretty close to our vision of a perfect good — and no other market structure delivers that outcome.

소비자들은 또한 추가된 다양성으로부터 혜택을 얻고, 우리 모두는 완벽한 제품에 대한 우리의 상상에 매우 근접한 제품을 얻는데, 다른 어떤 시장 구조도 그러한 결과를 제공하지 않는다.

# 37 순서

❶ Architects might say a machine can never design an innovative or impressive building because a computer cannot be "creative."

건축가들은 컴퓨터가 '창의적'일 수 없기 때문에 기계는 결코 혁신적이거나 인상적인 건물을 디자인할 수 없다고 말할지도 모른다.

❷ Yet consider the Elbphilharmonie, a new concert hall in Hamburg, which contains a remarkably beautiful auditorium composed of ten thousand interlocking acoustic panels.

그러나 Hamburg에 있는, 1만 개의 서로 맞물리는 음향 패널로 구성된 놀랍도록 아름다운 강당을 포함하는 새로운 콘서트 홀인 Elbphilharmonie를 생각해보라.

❸ It is the sort of space that makes one instinctively think that only a human being — and a human with a remarkably refined creative sensibility, at that — could design something so aesthetically impressive.

그것은 인간만이, 그리고 그것도 놀랍도록 세련된 창의적 감수성을 가진 인간만이, 그토록 미적으로 인상적인 것을 디자인할 수 있다고 본능적으로 생각하게 만드는 종류의 공간이다.

❹ Yet the auditorium was, in fact, designed algorithmically, using a technique known as "parametric design."

그러나 실제로 그 강당은 '파라메트릭 디자인'이라고 알려진 기술을 사용하여 알고리즘에 의한 방식으로 디자인되었다.

❺ The architects gave the system a set of criteria, and it generated a set of possible designs for the architects to choose from.

건축가들은 그 시스템에 일련의 기준을 부여했고, 그것은 그 건축가들이 선택할 수 있는 일련의 가능한 디자인을 만들어냈다.

❻ Similar software has been used to design lightweight bicycle frames and sturdier chairs, among much else.

유사한 소프트웨어가 다른 많은 것들 중에서도 경량 자전거 프레임과 더 튼튼한 의자를 디자인하는 데 사용되어 왔다.

❼ Are these systems behaving "creatively"? No, they are using lots of processing power to blindly generate varied possible designs, working in a very different way from a human being.

이러한 시스템들은 '창의적으로' 작동하고 있는가? 아니다, 그것들은 인간과는 매우 다른 방식으로 작동하면서 다양한 가능한 디자인을 닥치는 대로 만들기 위해 많은 처리 능력을 사용하고 있다.

(.hwp) (.pdf) → www.englishjmygod.com

# 38 삽입

❶ The brain is a high-energy consumer of glucose, which is its fuel.

뇌는 그것의 연료인 포도당의 고에너지 소비자이다.

❷ Although the brain accounts for merely 3 percent of a person's body weight, it consumes 20 percent of the available fuel.

비록 뇌는 사람 체중의 단지 3퍼센트를 차지하지만, 사용 가능한 연료의 20퍼센트를 소비한다.

❸ Your brain can't store fuel, however, so it has to "pay as it goes."

그러나 여러분의 뇌는 연료를 저장할 수 없고, 따라서 '활동하는 대로 대가를 지불'해야 한다.

❹ Since your brain is incredibly adaptive, it economizes its fuel resources.

여러분의 뇌는 놀라울 정도로 적응력이 뛰어나기 때문에, 그것의 연료 자원을 경제적으로 사용한다.

❺ Thus, during a period of high stress, it shifts away from the analysis of the nuances of a situation to a singular and fixed focus on the stressful situation at hand.

따라서, 극심한 스트레스를 받는 기간 동안, 뇌는 상황의 미묘한 차이의 분석에서 당면한 스트레스 상황에 대한 단일하고 고정된 초점으로 이동한다.

❻ You don't sit back and speculate about the meaning of life when you are stressed.

여러분은 스트레스를 받을 때 앉아서 삶의 의미에 대해 사색하지 않는다.

❼ Instead, you devote all your energy to trying to figure out what action to take.

대신에, 여러분은 어떤 행동을 취해야 할지 알아내려고 노력하는 데 모든 에너지를 쏟는다.

❽ Sometimes, however, this shift from the higher-thinking parts of the brain to the automatic and

reflexive parts of the brain can lead you to do something too quickly, without thinking.

그러나 때때로 뇌의 고차원적 사고 영역에서 자동적이고 반사적인 영역으로의 이러한 이동은 여러분이 무언가를 생각 없이 너무 빨리하도록 이끌 수 있다.

# 39 삽입

❶ Much research has been carried out on the causes of engagement, an issue that is important from both a theoretical and practical standpoint: identifying the drivers of work engagement may enable us to manipulate or influence it.

몰입의 원인에 대한 많은 연구가 수행되어왔는데, 이는 이론적 그리고 실제적 둘 다의 관점에서 중요한 문제이다. 업무 몰입의 동기를 알아내는 것은 우리가 그것을 조작하거나 그것에 영향을 주는 것을 가능하게 할지도 모른다.

❷ The causes of engagement fall into two major camps: situational and personal.

몰입의 원인은 상황적인 것과 개인적인 것 두 가지 주요한 분야로 나뉜다.

❸ The most influential situational causes are job resources, feedback and leadership, the latter, of course, being responsible for job resources and feedback.

가장 영향력 있는 상황적 원인은 직무 자원, 피드백, 그리고 리더십이며, 후자는 물론 직무 자원과 피드백에 대한 책임이 있다.

❹ Indeed, leaders influence engagement by giving their employees honest and constructive feedback on their performance, and by providing them with the necessary resources that enable them to perform their job well.

실제로 리더들은 직원들에게 그들의 수행에 대한 솔직하고 건설적인 피드백을 제공하고 직원들이 자신의 직무를 잘 수행할 수 있도록 필요한 자원을 제공함으로써 몰입에 영향을 미친다.

❺ It is, however, noteworthy that although engagement drives job performance, job performance also drives engagement.

그러나 주목할 점은 몰입이 직무 수행의 동기가 되지만, 직무 수행도 몰입의 동기가 된다는 것이다.

❻ In other words, when employees are able to do their jobs well — to the point that they match or exceed their own expectations and ambitions — they will engage more, be proud of their achievements, and find work more meaningful.

즉, 직원들이 그들 자신의 기대와 포부에 부합하거나 그것을 능가할 정도로 그들의 직무를 잘 수행할 수 있을 때 직원들은 더 많이 몰입하고, 그들의 성과를 자랑스러워하며, 업무를 더 의미 있게 생각할 것이다.

❼ This is especially evident when people are employed in jobs that align with their values.

이것은 사람들이 그들의 가치와 일치하는 직무에 종사했을 때 특히 분명하다.

(.hwp) (.pdf) → www.englishjmygod.com

# 40 요약

❶ In 2006, researchers conducted a study on the motivations for helping after the September 11th terrorist attacks against the United States.

2006년에 연구자들은 미국을 향한 9.11 테러 공격 이후에 도움을 주려는 동기에 대한 연구를 수행했다.

❷ In the study, they found that individuals who gave money, blood, goods, or other forms of assistance because of other-focused motives (giving to reduce another's discomfort) were almost four times more likely to still be giving support one year later than those whose original motivation was to reduce personal distress.

그 연구에서, 그들은 타인에게 초점을 맞춘 동기(다른 사람의 곤란을 줄이기 위해 베푸는 것) 때문에 돈, 혈액, 물품, 또는 다른 형태의 도움을 주었던 사람들이 자신의 고통을 줄이는 것이 원래 동기였던 사람들보다 일 년 후에도 여전히 지원을 제공할 가능성이 거의 네 배 더 높다는 것을 발견했다.

❸ This effect likely stems from differences in emotional arousal.

이 결과는 감정적 자극의 차이에서 비롯된 것 같다.

❹ The events of September 11th emotionally affected people throughout the United States.

9.11의 사건들은 미국 전역의 사람들에게 감정적으로 영향을 미쳤다.

❺ Those who gave to reduce their own distress reduced their emotional arousal with their initial gift, discharging that emotional distress.

자기 자신의 고통을 줄이기 위해 베푼 사람들은 초기의 베풂을 통해 그 감정적 고통을 해소하면서 감정적 자극을 줄였다.

❻ However, those who gave to reduce others' distress did not stop empathizing with victims who continued to struggle long after the attacks.

하지만, 다른 사람들의 고통을 줄이기 위해 베푼 사람들은 공격 이후 오랫동안 계속해서 고군분투하는 피해자들에게 공감하기를 멈추지 않았다.

# 41~42 제목, 어휘

❶ In England in the 1680s, it was unusual to live to the age of fifty.

1680년대 영국에서는 50세까지 사는 것은 이례적인 일이었다.

❷ This was a period when knowledge was not spread widely, there were few books and most people could not read.

이 시기는 지식이 널리 보급되지 않았고, 책이 거의 없었으며, 대부분의 사람들이 읽을 수 없었던 때였다.

❸ As a consequence, knowledge passed down through the oral traditions of stories and shared experiences.

결과적으로, 지식은 이야기와 공유된 경험이라는 구전 전통을 통해 전수되었다.

❹ And since older people had accumulated more knowledge, the social norm was that to be over fifty was to be wise.

그리고 더 나이 든 사람들이 더 많은 지식을 축적했기 때문에 사회적 규범은 50세가 넘으면 지혜롭다는 것이었다.

❺ This social perception of age began to shift with the advent of new technologies such as the printing press.

나이에 대한 이런 사회적 인식은 인쇄기와 같은 새로운 기술의 출현으로 변화하기 시작했다.

❻ Over time, as more books were printed, literacy increased, and the oral traditions of knowledge transfer began to fade.

시간이 지나면서 더 많은 책이 인쇄됨에 따라 문해력이 증가했고, 지식 전달의 구전 전통이 사라지기 시작했다.

❼ With the fading of oral traditions, the wisdom of the old became less important and as a consequence being over fifty was no longer seen as signifying wisdom.

구전 전통이 사라지면서 노인들의 지혜는 덜 중요해졌고, 결과적으로 50세가 넘은 것은 더 이상 지혜로움을 의미하는 것으로 여겨지지 않았다.

❽ We are living in a period when the gap between chronological and biological age is changing fast and where social norms are struggling to adapt.

우리는 생활 연령과 생물학적 연령 사이의 격차가 빠르게 변하고 사회적 규범이 적응하기 위해 분투하는 시기에 살고 있다.

❾ In a video produced by the AARP (formerly the American Association of Retired Persons), young people were asked to do various activities 'just like an old person'.

AARP(이전의 American Association of Retired Persons)에 의해 제작된 영상에서 젊은이들은 다양한 활동을 '마치 꼭 노인처럼' 하도록 요청받았다.

❿ When older people joined them in the video, the gap between the stereotype and the older people's actual behaviour was striking. It is clear that in today's world our social norms need to be updated quickly.

영상에서 노인들이 그들에 합류했을 때, 고정관념과 노인들의 실제 행동 사이의 격차는 두드러졌다. 오늘날의 세상에서 우리의 사회적 규범은 신속하게 최신화되어야 한다는 것이 분명하다.

# 43~45 순서, 지칭, 세부 내용

❶ When Jack was a young man in his early twenties during the 1960s, he had tried to work in his father's insurance business, as was expected of him.

Jack은 1960년대에 20대 초반의 청년이었을 때, 그에게 기대됐던 대로 그의 아버지의 보험 회사에서 일하려고 노력했다.

❷ His two older brothers fit in easily and seemed to enjoy their work. But Jack was bored with the insurance industry. "It was worse than being bored," he said. "I felt like I was dying inside."

그의 두 형은 쉽게 적응했고 자신들의 일을 즐기는 것처럼 보였다. 그러나 Jack은 보험 업계에 싫증이 났다. "그것은 지루한 것보다 더 나빴다."라고 그는 말했다. "나는 내면이 죽어가는 것 같았다."

❸ Jack felt drawn to hair styling and dreamed of owning a hair shop with a lively environment. He was sure that he would enjoy the creative and social aspects of it and that he'd be successful.

Jack은 미용에 매력을 느꼈고 활기찬 분위기의 미용실을 갖는 것을 꿈꿨다. 그는 자신이 그것의 창의적이고 사교적인 측면을 즐길 것이고 성공할 것이라고 확신했다.

❹ When he was twenty-six, Jack approached his father and expressed his intentions of leaving the business to become a hairstylist. As Jack anticipated, his father raged and accused Jack of being selfish, ungrateful, and unmanly.

26세가 되었을 때, Jack은 아버지에게 가서 미용사가 되기 위해 회사를 떠나겠다는 의사를 밝혔다. Jack이 예상했던 대로, 그의 아버지는 화를 내며 Jack이 이기적이고, 배은망덕하며 남자답지 못하다고 비난했다.

❺ In the face of his father's fury, Jack felt confusion and fear. His resolve became weak. But then a force filled his chest and he stood firm in his decision.

아버지의 분노 앞에서, Jack은 혼란과 두려움을 느꼈다. 그의 결심은 약해졌다. 그러나 그때 어떤 힘이 그의 가슴을 채웠고 그는 자신의 결정에 확고했다.

❻ In following his path, Jack not only ran three flourishing hair shops, but also helped his clients experience their inner beauty by listening and encouraging them when they faced dark times.

자신의 길을 가면서, Jack은 세 개의 번창하는 미용실을 운영했을 뿐만 아니라, 또한 고객들이 어두운 시기에 직면했을 때 그들의 말을 듣고 격려함으로써 그들이 가진 내면의 아름다움을 경험하도록 도왔다.

❼ His love for his work led to donating time and talent at nursing homes, which in turn led to becoming a hospice volunteer, and eventually to starting fundraising efforts for the hospice program in his community. And all this laid a strong stepping stone for another courageous move in his life.

그의 일에 대한 사랑은 요양원에서 시간과 재능을 기부하는 것으로 이어졌고, 이는 결과적으로 호스피스 자원봉사자가 되고, 마침내는 그의 지역사회에서 호스피스 프로그램을 위한 기금 모금 운동을 시작하는 것으로 이어졌다. 그리고 이 모든 것은 그의 삶에서 또 다른 용기 있는 움직임을 위한 견고한 디딤돌을 놓았다.

❽ When, after having two healthy children of their own, Jack and his wife, Michele, decided to bring an orphaned child into their family, his father threatened to disown them. Jack understood that his father feared adoption, in this case especially because the child was of a different racial background than their family.

Jack과 그의 아내 Michele이 두 명의 건강한 아이를 낳은 후, 고아가 된 아이를 그들의 가정에 데려오기로 결정했을 때, 그의 아버지는 그들과 의절하겠다고 위협했다. Jack은 자신의 아버지가 입양을 두려워한다는 것을, 이 경우에는 특히 그 아이가 그들의 가족과 다른 인종적 배경을 가지고 있었기 때문임을 이해했다.

❾ Jack and Michele risked rejection and went ahead with the adoption. It took years but eventually Jack's father loved the little girl and accepted his son's independent choices.

Jack과 Michele은 거부의 위험을 무릅쓰고 입양을 진행했다. 몇 년이 걸렸지만, 결국 Jack의 아버지는 그 어린 여자아이를 사랑했고 자기 아들의 독립적인 선택을 받아들였다.

❿ Jack realized that, although he often felt fear and still does, he has always had courage. In fact, courage was the scaffolding around which he had built richness into his life.

Jack은 비록 자주 두려움을 느꼈고 여전히 그렇지만, 자신이 항상 용기가 있다는 것을 깨달았다. 사실, 용기는 그가 자신의 삶에 풍요로움을 쌓아온 발판이었다.

2023 고2 9월 모의고사 ❶ 회차 : 점 / 235점

❶ voca ❷ text ❸ [ / ] ❹ ____ ❺ quiz 1 ❻ quiz 2 ❼ quiz 3 ❽ quiz 4 ❾ quiz 5

## 18

To whom it may concern,

I would like to draw your attention to a problem that frequently occurs with the No. 35 buses. There is a bus stop about halfway along Fenny Road, [ **which / at which** ]1) the No.35 buses are supposed to stop. It would appear, however, [ **that / which** ]2) some of your drivers are [ **either / neither** ]3) unaware of this bus stop or for some reason choose to ignore it, driving past even though the buses are not full. I would be [ **graceful / grateful** ]4) if you could [ **mind / remind** ]5) your drivers that this bus stop [ **is existed / exists** ]6) and [ **that / what** ]7) they should be prepared to stop at it. I look forward to [ **see / seeing** ]8) an improvement in this service soon.

Yours faithfully, John Williams

관계자분께, 35번 버스에서 자주 발생하는 문제에 대해 귀하의 주의를 환기하고 싶습니다. Fenny Road를 따라 중간쯤 버스 정류장이 있고, 그곳에서 35번 버스가 정차하게 되어 있습니다. 그러나 버스 기사들 중 일부는 이 버스 정류장을 인식하지 못하거나 어떤 이유에서인지 그것을 무시하기로 선택하여 버스가 꽉 차지 않았음에도 운전해 지나쳐가는 것으로 보입니다. 기사들에게 이 버스 정류장이 존재하고 그곳에 정차할 준비가 되어 있어야 한다는 것을 상기시켜 주시면 감사하겠습니다. 곧 이 서비스가 개선되기를 기대합니다.
진심을 담아, John Williams 드림

## 19

My 10-year-old appeared, in [ **desperate / separate** ]9) need of a quarter. "A quarter? What on earth do you need a quarter for?" My tone [ **boarded / bordered** ]10) on irritation . I didn't want to be [ **bothering / bothered** ]11) with such a [ **tribal / trivial** ]12) demand. "There's a garage sale up the street, and there's something I just gotta have! It only costs a quarter. Please?" I placed a quarter in my son's hand. Moments later, a little voice said, "Here, Mommy, this is for you." I glanced down at the hands of my little son and saw a four-inch cream-colored [ **state / statue** ]13) of two small children [ **hug / hugging** ]14) one another. [ **Inscribed / Subscribed** ]15) at their feet [ **was / were** ]16) words that read *It starts with 'L' ends with 'E' and in between are 'O' and 'V.'* As I watched him [ **race / raced** ]17) back to the garage sale, I smiled with a heart full of happiness. That 25-cent garage sale purchase brought me a lot of joy.

내 열 살짜리 아이가 나타났고, 25센트 동전을 절실히 필요로 했다. "25센트 동전? 도대체 25센트 동전이 왜 필요하지?" 나의 말투는 거의 짜증에 가까웠다. 나는 그런 사소한 요구에 방해받고 싶지 않았다. "거리 위쪽에서 중고 물품 판매 행사를 하는데, 제가 꼭 사야 할 게 있어요! 25센트밖에 안 해요. 네?" 나는 아들의 손에 25센트 동전을 쥐여 주었다. 잠시 후 작은 목소리가 "여기요, 엄마, 이거 엄마를 위한 거예요."라고 말했다. 나는 내 어린 아들의 손을 힐끗 내려다보았고, 두 어린아이가 서로 껴안고 있는 4인치짜리 크림색의 조각상을 보았다. 그들의 발밑에는 'L'로 시작하여 'E'로 끝나고 그 사이에 'O'와 'V'가 있다는 말이 새겨져 있었다. 아이가 중고 물품 판매 행사로 서둘러 돌아가는 모습을 바라보며 나는 행복이 가득한 마음으로 미소를 지었다. 그 25센트짜리 중고 물품 판매 행사 구입품은 나에게 큰 기쁨을 가져다 주었다.

(.hwp) (.pdf) → www.englishjmygod.com

## 20

Managers frequently try to play psychologist, to "figure out" why an employee has acted in a certain way. [ **Empathizing / Sympathizing** ]18) with employees in order to understand their point of view can be very helpful. However, when [ **deals / dealing** ]19) with a problem area, in particular, remember [ **that / which** ]20) it is not the person who is bad, but the actions [ **exhibited / were exhibited** ]21) on the job. Avoid [ **making / to make** ]22) suggestions to employees about personal [ **behavior / traits** ]23) they should change; instead suggest more acceptable ways of [ **performing / characteristic** ]24) . For example, instead of focusing on a person's "unreliability," a manager might focus on the fact that the employee "has been [ **late / lately** ]25) to work seven times this month." It is difficult for employees to change who they [ **are / do** ]26) ; it is usually [ **much / very** ]27) easier for them to change [ **how / why** ]28) they act.

관리자들은 직원이 왜 특정한 방식으로 행동했는지를 '파악하기' 위해 심리학자 역할을 하려고 자주 노력한다. 그들의 관점을 이해하기 위해 직원들과 공감하는 것은 매우 도움이 될 수 있다. 하지만, 특히 문제 영역을 다룰 때, 그것은 잘하지 못하는 사람이 아니라 근무 중에 보여지는 행동이라는 것을 기억하라. 직원들에게 그들이 바꿔야 할 인격적 특성에 대해 제안하는 것을 피하라. 대신에 더 용인되는 수행 방법을 제안하라. 예를 들어, 관리자는 어떤 사람의 '신뢰할 수 없음'에 초점을 맞추는 대신, 그 직원이 '이번 달에 회사에 일곱 번 지각했다'는 사실에 초점을 맞출 수도 있을 것이다. 직원들은 자신이 어떤 사람인지를 바꾸기는 어렵다. 일반적으로 자신이 행동하는 방식을 바꾸기가 훨씬 쉽다.

## 21

I suspect fungi are a [ **little / few** ]29) more forward "thinking" [ **than / as** ]30) their larger partners. Among trees, each species [ **fight / fights** ]31) other species. Let's assume the beeches native to Central Europe could [ **emerge / submerge** ]32) victorious in most forests there. Would this really be an advantage? What would happen if a new pathogen came along that [ **perfected / infected** ]33) most of the beeches and killed them? In that case, wouldn't it be more advantageous if there [ **was / were** ]34) a certain number of other species around — oaks, maples, or firs — that would continue to grow and provide the shade [ **to need / needed** ]35) for a new generation of young beeches to sprout and grow up? [ **Predominance / Diversity** ]36) provides security for ancient forests. Because fungi are also very [ **dependent on / independent from** ]37) stable conditions, they support other species underground and protect them from complete [ **collaboration / collapse** ]38) to ensure that one species of tree doesn't manage to [ **dominate / eliminate** ]39) .

나는 균류가 자신의 더 큰 상대보다 조금 더 앞서 '생각한다'고 짐작한다. 나무들 사이에서 각 종은 다른 종들과 싸운다. 중부 유럽 태생의 너도밤나무가 그곳의 숲 대부분에서 우세하게 나타날 수 있다고 가정해 보자. 이게 정말 이점일까? 만약 대부분의 너도밤나무를 감염시켜 죽게 만드는 새로운 병원균이 나타나면 어떻게 될까? 그런 경우, 주변에 참나무, 단풍나무 또는 전나무와 같은 일정한 수의 다른 종이 계속 자라서 새로운 세대의 어린 너도밤나무가 싹을 틔우고 자라는 데 필요한 그늘을 제공한다면 더 유리하지 않을까? 다양성은 오래된 숲에 안전을 제공한다. 균류도 또한 안정적인 조건에 매우 의존하기 때문에, 그들은 한 종의 나무가 우세해지지 않도록 확실히 하기 위해 땅 속에서 다른 종을 지원하고 그것들을 완전한 붕괴로부터 보호한다.

## 22

It's remarkable that [ **positive / negative** ]⁴⁰⁾ fantasies help us [ **relax / relaxing** ]⁴¹⁾ to such an extent [ **that / what** ]⁴²⁾ it shows up in physiological tests. If you want to [ **wind / unwind** ]⁴³⁾ , you can take some deep breaths, get a massage, or go for a walk — but you can also try simply closing your eyes and fantasizing about some future [ **income / outcome** ]⁴⁴⁾ that you might enjoy. But what about when your [ **objective / subjective** ]⁴⁵⁾ is to make your wish a reality? The [ **first / last** ]⁴⁶⁾ thing you want to be is [ **relaxing / relaxed** ]⁴⁷⁾ . You want to be energized enough to get off the couch and lose those pounds or find that job or study for that test, and you want to be [ **motivation / motivated** ]⁴⁸⁾ enough to stay engaged even when the [ **evitable / inevitable** ]⁴⁹⁾ obstacles or challenges [ **arise / raise** ]⁵⁰⁾ . The principle of "Dream it. Wish it. Do it." does not hold [ **true / truly** ]⁵¹⁾ , and now we know why: in dreaming it, you [ **reinforce / undercut** ]⁵²⁾ the energy you need to do it. You put yourself in a temporary state of complete happiness, calmness — and [ **activity / inactivity** ]⁵³⁾ .

낙관적인 상상이 생리학적 검사에서 나타날 정도로 우리가 긴장을 푸는 데 도움이 된다는 것은 주목할 만하다. 만약 여러분이 긴장을 풀고 싶다면, 심호흡하거나, 마사지를 받거나, 산책을 할 수도 있지만, 단순히 눈을 감고 여러분이 누릴지도 모를 미래의 결과에 대해 상상해 볼 수도 있다. 하지만 여러분의 목표가 소망을 실현하는 것인 경우라면 어떨까? 여러분이 '가장 피해야 할' 상태는 긴장이 풀려 있는 것이다. 여러분은 소파에서 일어나 체중을 감량하거나 직업을 찾거나 시험공부를 할 수 있을 만큼 충분히 활력을 얻어야 하고, 피할 수 없는 장애물이나 문제가 발생할 때도 계속 전념할 수 있도록 충분히 동기 부여 되어야 한다. '그것을 꿈꿔라. 그것을 소망하라. 그것을 실행하라.'라는 원칙은 사실이 아니며, 우리는 이제 그 이유를 안다. 그것을 꿈꾸는 중에, 여러분은 그것을 하는 데 필요한 에너지를 약화시킨다. 여러분은 스스로를 완전한 행복, 고요, 그리고 비활동의 일시적인 상태에 빠지게 한다.

## 23

If cooking is as central to human [ **identity / identification** ]⁵⁴⁾ , biology, and culture as the biological anthropologist Richard Wrangham suggests, it stands to [ **reason / reasoning** ]⁵⁵⁾ that the [ **increase / decline** ]⁵⁶⁾ of cooking in our time would have serious consequences for modern life, and so it has. Are they all bad? Not at all. The outsourcing of much of the work of cooking to corporations has [ **relieved / been relieved** ]⁵⁷⁾ women of what has traditionally been their [ **exclusive / inclusive** ]⁵⁸⁾ responsibility for [ **feeding / feeding on** ]⁵⁹⁾ the family, making [ **it / them** ]⁶⁰⁾ easier for [ **it / them** ]⁶¹⁾ to work outside the home and have careers. It has headed off many of the domestic conflicts that such a large [ **adhesion / shift** ]⁶²⁾ in gender roles and family dynamics was bound to spark. It has relieved other pressures in the household, [ **including / excluding** ]⁶³⁾ longer workdays and overscheduled children, and saved us time that we can now invest in other pursuits. It has also allowed us [ **to diversify / diversifying** ]⁶⁴⁾ our diets substantially, making it possible even for people with no cooking skills and [ **few / little** ]⁶⁵⁾ money to enjoy a whole different cuisine. All that's required is a microwave.

생물인류학자인 Richard Wrangham이 말하는 것만큼 요리가 인간의 정체성, 생물학 및 문화에 중요하다면, 우리 시대의 요리 감소가 현대 생활에 심각한 결과들을 초래한다고 추론하는 것은 당연하고, 실제로 그래왔다. 그것들이 모두 나쁜가? 전혀 그렇지 않다. 요리하는 일의 많은 부분을 기업에 아웃소싱하는 것은 전통적으로 여성들에게 한정된, 가족들을 먹여야 하는 책임이었던 것에서 여성들을 벗어나게 했고; 그들이 집 밖에서 일하고 직업을 갖는 것을 더 쉽게 했다. 그것은 성 역할과 가족 역학의 그렇게 큰 변화가 촉발할 많은 가정 내 갈등을 막아냈다. 그것은 더 긴 근무일과 분주한 자녀를 포함하여 가정의 다른 곤란을 덜어주었고, 이제 우리가 다른 일에 투자할 수 있도록 시간을 절약해 주었다. 그것은 또한 우리의 식단을 상당히 다양하게 해주었고, 요리 기술이 없고 돈이 거의 없는 사람들까지도 완전히 색다른 요리를 즐길 수 있게 해주었다. 필요한 것이라곤 전자레인지뿐이다.

(.hwp) (.pdf) → www.englishjmygod.com

# 24

As you may already know, what and how you buy can be [ **environmental / political** ]⁶⁶⁾ . To whom do you want to give your money? Which companies and [ **cooperations / corporations** ]⁶⁷⁾ do you value and respect? Be mindful about every [ **purchase / purchases** ]⁶⁸⁾ by carefully researching the corporations that are taking our money to decide if they [ **deserve / preserve** ]⁶⁹⁾ our support. Do they have a record of polluting the environment, or do they have fair-trade practices and an end-of-life plan for the products they make? Are they [ **committed / deserved** ]⁷⁰⁾ to bringing about good in the world? For instance, my family has found a company [ **produces / producing** ]⁷¹⁾ recycled, plastic-packaging-free toilet paper with a social conscience. They contribute 50 percent of their profits to the [ **construction / destruction** ]⁷²⁾ of toilets around the world, and we're genuinely happy to spend our money on this special toilet paper each month. Remember that the corporate world is built on consumers, so as a consumer you have the power to vote with your wallet and [ **encourage / discourage** ]⁷³⁾ companies [ **to / from** ]⁷⁴⁾ embrace healthier and more [ **attainable / sustainable** ]⁷⁵⁾ practices with every purchase you choose to make.

이미 알고 있겠지만, 여러분이 무엇을 어떻게 구매하는지는 정치적일 수 있다. 여러분은 여러분의 돈을 누구에게 주고 싶은가? 여러분은 어떤 회사와 기업을 가치 있게 여기고 존중하는가? 우리의 지원을 받을 자격이 있는지를 결정하기 위해 우리의 돈을 가져가는 기업들을 면밀히 조사함으로써 모든 구매에 주의를 기울여라. 그들은 환경을 오염시킨 기록이 있는가, 아니면 그들이 만든 제품에 대한 공정 거래 관행과 제품 수명 종료 계획이 있는가? 그들은 세상에 득이 되는 것에 헌신하고 있는가? 예를 들어, 우리 가족은 사회적 양심을 가지고 재활용되고 플라스틱 포장이 없는 화장지를 생산하는 회사를 발견했다. 그들은 수익의 50%를 전 세계 화장실 건설에 기부하고 우리는 이 특별한 화장지에 매달 돈을 쓸 수 있어서 정말 기쁘다. 기업의 세계는 소비자를 기반으로 구축되므로, 소비자로서 여러분은 지갑으로 투표하고 여러분이 선택한 모든 구매를 통해 회사들이 더 건강하고 더 지속 가능한 관행을 받아들이도록 장려할 힘이 있다는 것을 기억하라.

# 26

Camille Flammarion was born at Montigny-le-Roi, France. He became [ **interesting / interested** ]⁷⁶⁾ in [ **anatomy / astronomy** ]⁷⁷⁾ at an early age, and when he was only sixteen he wrote a book on the origin of the world. The manuscript was not published at the time, but it came to the attention of Urbain Le Verrier, the director of the Paris [ **Observation / Observatory** ]⁷⁸⁾ . He became an [ **assistant / assistance** ]⁷⁹⁾ to Le Verrier in 1858 and worked as a calculator. At nineteen, he wrote another book called *The Plurality of Inhabited Worlds*, [ **which / in which** ]⁸⁰⁾ he passionately claimed that life exists outside the planet Earth. His most [ **successful / successive** ]⁸¹⁾ work, *Popular Astronomy*, was published in 1880, and eventually sold 130,000 copies. With his own funds, he built an observatory at Juvisy and spent May to November of each [ **year / years** ]⁸²⁾ there. In 1887, he founded the French Astronomical Society and [ **served / serving** ]⁸³⁾ as editor of its monthly publication.

Camille Flammarion은 프랑스 Montigny-le-Roi에서 태어났다. 그는 어린 나이에 천문학에 흥미가 생겼고, 불과 16세에 그는 세상의 기원에 관한 책을 썼다. 그 원고는 그 당시 출판되지 않았지만, Paris Observatory의 관리자인 Urbain Le Verrier의 관심을 끌게 되었다. 그는 1858년에 Le Verrier의 조수가 되었고 계산원으로 일했다. 19세에 그는 The Plurality of Inhabited Worlds라는 또 다른 책을 썼는데, 이 책에서 그는 외계에 생명체가 존재한다고 열정적으로 주장했다. 그의 가장 성공적인 저서인 Popular Astronomy는 1880년에 출판되었고, 결국 130,000부가 판매되었다. 자신의 자금으로 그는 Juvisy에 천문대를 세웠고, 매년 5월에서 11월까지 그곳에서 지냈다. 1887년에 그는 French Astronomical Society를 설립했고 그것의 월간 간행물의 편집자로 일했다.

## 29

There is [ **few / little** ]84) doubt [ **that / which** ]85) we are driven by the sell-by date. Once an item is past [ **that / those** ]86) date it goes into the waste stream, [ **farther / further** ]87) [ **increasing / increased** ]88) its carbon footprint. Remember those items have already travelled hundreds of miles to [ **arrive / reach** ]89) the shelves and once they go into waste they start a new carbon mile journey. But we all make our own [ **judge / judgement** ]90) about sell-by dates; those [ **brought / are brought** ]91) up [ **during / while** ]92) the Second World War are often [ **fond / scornful** ]93) of the terrible waste they believe such [ **cause / caution** ]94) encourages. The manufacturer of the food has a view when making or growing something [ **that / which** ]95) [ **at / by** ]96) the time the product reaches the shelves it has already been [ **travelling / travelled** ]97) for so many days and possibly many miles. The manufacturer then decides that a product can reasonably be [ **consuming / consumed** ]98) within say 90 days and 90 days minus so many days for travelling [ **gives / to give** ]99) the sell-by date. But whether it becomes toxic is something each [ **individual / individuals** ]100) can decide. It would seem to [ **make / be made** ]101) sense not to buy large packs of [ **perishable / non-perishable** ]102) goods but [ **perishable / non-perishable** ]103) items may become cost-effective.

우리가 판매 유효 기한에 따라 움직인다는 것은 의심할 여지가 거의 없다. 일단 어떤 품목이 그 기한을 지나면 폐기물 흐름으로 들어가고, 이는 그것의 탄소 발자국을 더욱더 증가시킨다. 그러한 품목들이 선반에 도달하기 위해 이미 수백 마일을 이동했고 일단 그것들이 버려지게 되면 그것들은 새로운 탄소 마일 여정을 시작한다는 것을 기억하라. 그러나 우리 모두는 판매 유효 기한에 대해 자신만의 판단을 내린다. 가령, 제2차 세계 대전 중에 자란 사람들은 그들이 생각하기에 그러한 경고가 조장하는 끔찍한 낭비를 자주 경멸한다. 식품 제조업자는 무엇인가를 만들거나 재배할 때 제품이 선반에 도달할 때에는 그것은 이미 매우 오랫동안 그리고 아마도 상당한 거리를 이동해 왔다는 관점을 가지고 있다. 그래서 제조업자는 제품이 이를테면 90일 이내에는 무리 없이 소비될 수 있고 90일에서 이동에 필요한 많은 날들을 뺀 것이 판매 유효 기한이 된다고 결정한다. 그러나 그것이 유독해지는지는 각 개인이 결정할 수 있는 것이다. 큰 묶음의 상하기 쉬운 제품을 사지 않는 것이 이치에 맞는 것으로 보이겠지만, 상하지 않는 품목들의 경우에는 비용 효율이 높아질 수도 있다.

## 30

The "jolt" of caffeine does wear off. Caffeine is removed from your system by an enzyme within your liver, [ **that / which** ]104) gradually [ **upgrades / degrades** ]105) it over time. Based in large part on genetics, some people have a more efficient version of the enzyme that [ **degrades / upgrades** ]106) caffeine, [ **allowing / allowed** ]107) the liver to rapidly [ **clear / pile** ]108) it from the bloodstream. These rare individuals can drink an espresso with dinner and fall fast [ **asleep / sleep** ]109) at midnight without a problem. Others, however, have a [ **slower-acting / fast-acting** ]110) version of the enzyme. It takes [ **far / very** ]111) longer for their system to [ **eliminate / reach** ]112) the same amount of caffeine. As a result, they are very [ **sensible / sensitive** ]113) to caffeine's effects. One cup of tea or coffee in the morning will last much of the day, and [ **they should / should they** ]114) have a second cup, even early in the afternoon, they [ **will / would** ]115) find it difficult to fall asleep in the evening. Aging also [ **alters / keeps** ]116) the speed of caffeine clearance: the older we are, the [ **longer / shorter** ]117) it takes our brain and body to [ **add / remove** ]118) caffeine, and thus the more [ **sensible / sensitive** ]119) we become in later life to caffeine's sleep-disrupting influence.

카페인의 '충격'은 확실히 점차 사라진다. 카페인은 여러분의 간 안에 있는 효소에 의해 여러분의 신체로부터 제거되는데, 이 효소는 시간이 지남에 따라 그것을 점진적으로 분해한다. 대체로 유전적 특징 때문에, 어떤 사람들은 카페인을 분해하는 더 효율적인 형태의 효소를 갖고 있는데, 이는 간이 그것을 혈류로부터 더 빠르게 제거할 수 있도록 한다. 이 몇 안 되는 사람들은 저녁과 함께 에스프레소를 마시고도 아무 문제 없이 한밤중에 깊이 잠들 수 있다. 그러나 다른 사람들은 더 느리게 작용하는 형태의 효소를 가지고 있다. 그들의 신체가 같은 양의 카페인을 제거하는 데 훨씬 더 오랜 시간이 걸린다. 결과적으로, 그들은 카페인의 효과에 매우 민감하다. 아침에 마시는 한 잔의 차나 커피는 그날 대부분 동안 지속될 것이고, 심지어 이른 오후라도, 두 번째 잔을 마신다면, 그들은 저녁에 잠드는 것이 어렵다는 것을 알 것이다. 노화는 또한 카페인 제거 속도를 변화시킨다. 즉, 우리가 나이가 들수록 우리의 뇌와 신체가 카페인을 제거하는 것이 더 오래 걸리고, 따라서 우리는 노후에 카페인의 수면을 방해하는 효과에 더 민감해진다.

(.hwp) (.pdf) → www.englishjmygod.com

# 31

Rebels may think they're rebels, but clever marketers [ **effect / influence** ]120) them just like the rest of us. Saying, "Everyone is doing it" may [ **keep / turn** ]121) some people off from an idea. These people will look for [ **alternatives / conventions** ]122) , [ **that / which** ]123) (if cleverly planned) can be exactly [ **that / what** ]124) a marketer or persuader wants you to believe. If I want you to consider an idea, and know you strongly [ **accept / reject** ]125) popular opinion in [ **favor / denial** ]126) of maintaining your [ **dependence / independence** ]127) and uniqueness, I would present the [ **majority / minority** ]128) option first, which you would reject in favor of my actual [ **preference / recommendation** ]129) . We are often tricked when we try to maintain a position of [ **agreement / defiance** ]130) . People use this [ **alignment / reversal** ]131) to make us "independently" choose an option which suits their purposes. Some brands have taken full effect of our [ **alignment / defiance** ]132) towards the mainstream and positioned themselves as [ **majority / rebels** ]133) ; which has created even stronger brand [ **loyalty / royalty** ]134) .

반항자들은 자신들이 반항자라고 생각할지도 모르지만, 영리한 마케터들은 나머지 우리에게 그러듯이 그들에게 영향을 준다. "모두가 그것을 하고 있다."라고 말하는 것은 일부 사람들로 하여금 어떠한 생각에 대해 흥미를 잃게 할지도 모른다. 이 사람들은 대안을 찾을 것이고, 그것은 (만약 영리하게 계획된다면) 정확히 마케터나 설득자가 여러분이 믿기를 원하는 것일 수 있다. 만약 내가 여러분이 한 아이디어를 고려하길 바라고, 여러분의 독립성과 유일성을 유지하기 위해 대중적인 의견을 강하게 거부한다는 것을 안다면, 나는 대다수가 선택하는 것을 먼저 제시할 것이고, 여러분은 내가 실제로 선호하는 것에 맞게 그것을 거부할 것이다. 우리는 반항의 입장을 유지하려고 할 때 종종 속는다. 사람들은 우리가 그들의 목적에 맞는 선택지를 '독자적으로' 택하도록 만들기 위해 이러한 반전을 사용한다. 일부 브랜드들은 주류에 대한 우리의 반항을 완전히 활용하여 스스로를 반항자로 자리매김해 왔고, 이는 훨씬 더 강력한 브랜드 충성도를 만들어 왔다.

# 32

A typical soap opera creates an [ **abstract / concrete** ]135) world, in which a highly complex web of relationships [ **connect / connects** ]136) fictional characters that [ **exist / exists** ]137) first only in the minds of the program's creators and are then recreated in the minds of the viewer. If you [ **were / had been** ]138) to think about how much human psychology, law, and even everyday physics the viewer must know in order to follow and [ **articulate / speculate** ]139) about the plot, you would discover it is [ **considerate / considerable** ]140) — at least as [ **many / much** ]141) as the knowledge required to follow and speculate about a piece of modern mathematics, and in most cases, much more. Yet viewers follow soap operas with [ **ease / challenge** ]142) . How are they able to cope with such [ **abstraction / specification** ]143) ? Because, of course, the abstraction is built on an extremely [ **familiar / strange** ]144) framework. The characters in a soap opera and the relationships between them [ **is / are** ]145) very much like the real people and relationships we experience every day. The abstraction of a soap opera is only a step [ **added / removed** ]146) from the real world. The mental "training" required to follow a soap opera is provided by our everyday lives.

전형적인 드라마는 추상적인 세계를 만들어내며, 그 세계에서는 프로그램 제작자들의 마음속에만 먼저 존재하고 그러고 나서 시청자의 마음속에 재현되는 허구의 캐릭터들을 매우 복잡한 관계망이 연결한다. 만약 줄거리를 따라가고 그것에 대해 추측하기 위해 시청자가 얼마나 많은 인간 심리학, 법, 그리고 심지어 일상에서의 물리학을 알아야 하는지에 대해 생각한다면, 여러분은 그것이 상당하다는 것을, 즉 적어도 현대 수학의 한 부분을 따라가고 그것에 대해 추측하는 데 필요한 지식만큼이라는 것, 그리고 대부분의 경우 훨씬 더 많다는 것을 발견할 것이다. 하지만 시청자들은 드라마를 쉽게 따라간다. 그들은 어떻게 그런 추상에 대처할 수 있을까? 왜냐하면, 당연하게도, 그 추상은 매우 친숙한 틀 위에서 만들어졌기 때문이다. 드라마 속 인물들과 그들 사이의 관계는 우리가 매일 경험하는 실제 사람들 및 관계와 매우 흡사하다. 드라마의 추상은 현실 세계에서 불과 한 걸음 떨어져 있다. 드라마를 따라가기 위해 필요한 정신적 '훈련'은 우리의 일상에 의해 제공된다.

## 33

As always happens with natural selection, bats and their prey have [ **engaged / been engaged** ]147) in a life-or-death [ **sensible / sensory** ]148) arms race for millions of years. It's believed that hearing in moths [ **arose / rose** ]149) specifically in response to the threat of [ **eating / being eaten by** ]150) bats. (Not all insects can hear.) Over millions of years, moths have evolved the ability to [ **detect / protect** ]151) sounds at ever higher frequencies, and, as they have, the frequencies of bats' vocalizations have [ **raised / risen** ]152) , too. Some moth species have also evolved scales on their wings and a fur-like coat on their bodies; both act as "acoustic camouflage," by absorbing sound waves in the frequencies [ **emitted / omitted** ]153) by bats, thereby preventing those sound waves [ **from / to** ]154) bouncing back. The B-2 bomber and other "stealth" aircraft have fuselages [ **make / made** ]155) of materials that do something similar with radar beams.

자연 선택에서 항상 그렇듯이, 박쥐와 그 먹잇감은 수백만 년 동안 생사를 가르는 감각 군비 경쟁에 참여해 왔다. 나방의 청력은 특히 박쥐에게 잡아먹히는 위협에 대한 반응으로 생겨난 것으로 여겨진다. (모든 곤충이 들을 수 있는 것은 아니다.) 수백만 년 동안, 나방은 계속 더 높아진 주파수의 소리를 감지하는 능력을 진화시켰고, 그것들이 그렇게 함에 따라 박쥐의 발성 주파수도 높아졌다. 일부 나방 종은 또한 날개의 비늘과 몸에 모피와 같은 외피를 진화시켰다. 둘 다 '음향 위장'의 역할을 하는데, 박쥐에 의해 방출되는 주파수의 음파를 흡수함으로써, 그것으로 음파가 되돌아가는 것을 방지한다. B-2 폭격기와 그 밖의 '스텔스' 항공기는 레이더 전파에 대해 유사한 것을 하는 재료로 만들어진 기체를 가지고 있다.

## 34

Much of human thought is designed to screen out information and to sort the rest into [ **overwhelming / overwhelmed** ]156) chaos, especially given the enormous amount of information available in culture and society. Out of all the sensory impressions and possible information, it is vital to find a small amount that is most [ **relevant / respective** ]157) to our individual needs and to organize that into a usable stock of knowledge. Expectancies accomplish some of this work, helping to screen out information that is [ **relevant / irrelevant** ]158) to what is expected, and focusing our attention on clear [ **alignments / contradictions** ]159) . The processes of learning and memory are marked by a steady [ **absorption / elimination** ]160) of information. People notice only a part of the world around them. Then, only a fraction of what they notice gets processed and stored into memory. And only part of what gets committed to memory can be [ **relieved / retrieved** ]161) .

인간 사고의 많은 부분은 정보를 걸러내고 나머지는 처리하기 쉬운 상태로 분류하도록 설계된다. 특히 문화와 사회에서 이용할 수 있는 엄청난 양의 정보를 고려할 때, 우리의 감각에서 오는 데이터의 유입은 압도적인 혼란을 야기할 수 있다. 모든 감각적 인상과 가능한 정보 중에서, 우리의 개인적인 필요와 가장 관련이 있는 소량을 찾고 그것을 사용 가능한 지식체로 구성하는 것이 중요하다. 예상들은 이 작업의 일부를 수행하여 예상되는 것과 무관한 정보를 걸러내는 데 도움이 되고, 명확한 모순에 우리의 주의를 집중시킨다. 학습과 기억의 과정은 정보의 지속적인 제거로 특징지어진다. 사람들은 그들 주변 세계의 일부분만을 인지한다. 그런 다음, 그들이 알아차린 것의 일부만 처리되어 기억에 저장된다. 그리고 기억에 넘겨진 것의 일부만 생각해 낼 수 있다.

(.hwp) (.pdf) → www.englishjmygod.com

## 35

The irony of early democracy in Europe is [ **that** / **what** ]<sup>162)</sup> it thrived and prospered precisely because European rulers for a very long time were remarkably [ **strong** / **weak** ]<sup>163)</sup> . For more than a millennium after the fall of Rome, European rulers [ **had** / **lacked** ]<sup>164)</sup> the ability to [ **assess** / **access** ]<sup>165)</sup> what their people were producing and to levy [ **substantial** / **substantive** ]<sup>166)</sup> taxes based on this. The most striking way to illustrate European [ **power** / **weakness** ]<sup>167)</sup> is to show how [ **few** / **little** ]<sup>168)</sup> revenue they collected. Europeans would eventually develop strong systems of [ **avenue** / **revenue** ]<sup>169)</sup> collection, but it took them an awfully long time to do so. In medieval times, and for part of the early modern era, Chinese emperors and Muslim caliphs were able to [ **extract** / **subtract** ]<sup>170)</sup> much more of economic production than any European ruler with the exception of small city-states.

유럽 초기 민주주의의 아이러니는 바로 유럽의 통치자들이 매우 오랫동안 현저하게 약했기 때문에 그것이 번성하고 번영했다는 것이다. 로마의 멸망 후 천 년 넘게, 유럽의 통치자들은 백성들이 생산하고 있었던 것을 평가하고 이를 바탕으로 상당한 세금을 부과할 능력이 부족했다. 유럽의 약함을 설명하는 가장 눈에 띄는 방법은 그들이 거둔 세입이 얼마나 적은지를 보여주는 것이다. 유럽인들은 결국 강력한 세입 징수 시스템을 개발했지만, 그렇게 하는 데는 엄청나게 오랜 시간이 걸렸다. 중세와 초기 근대의 일부 동안, 중국의 황제들과 이슬람 문명의 칼리프들은 작은 도시 국가들을 제외한 어떤 유럽 통치자들보다 경제적 생산물에서 훨씬 더 많은 것을 얻어낼 수 있었다.

## 36

If you drive down a busy street, you will find many [ **compete** / **competing** ]<sup>171)</sup> businesses, often right next to one another. For example, in most places a consumer in search of a quick meal has many choices, and more fast-food restaurants appear all the time. These competing [ **firms** / **forms** ]<sup>172)</sup> advertise heavily. The temptation is to see advertising as driving [ **down** / **up** ]<sup>173)</sup> the price of a product without any benefit to the consumer. However, this misconception doesn't account for [ **why** / **which** ]<sup>174)</sup> firms advertise. In markets [ **which** / **where** ]<sup>175)</sup> competitors sell slightly differentiated products, advertising enables firms to [ **inform** / **deform** ]<sup>176)</sup> their customers about new products and services. Yes, costs rise, but consumers also [ **gain** / **lose** ]<sup>177)</sup> information to help make purchasing decisions. Consumers also benefit from [ **added** / **lost** ]<sup>178)</sup> variety, and we all get a product that's pretty close to our vision of a perfect good — and no other market structure delivers that [ **income** / **outcome** ]<sup>179)</sup> .

만약 여러분이 번화한 거리를 운전한다면, 여러분은 자주 서로의 바로 옆에서 경쟁하는 많은 업체들을 발견할 것이다. 예를 들어, 대부분의 장소에서 빠른 식사를 찾는 소비자는 많은 선택권을 가지고 있고, 더 많은 패스트푸드 식당들이 항상 나타난다. 이 경쟁하는 회사들은 광고를 많이 한다. 광고를 소비자에게 어떤 혜택도 없이 제품의 가격을 올리는 것으로 보기 쉽다. 그러나 이러한 오해는 회사들이 광고하는 이유를 설명하지 않는다. 경쟁사들이 약간 차별화된 제품들을 판매하는 시장에서, 광고는 회사들이 그들의 소비자들에게 새로운 제품과 서비스를 알릴 수 있게 해 준다. 물론 가격이 상승하기는 하지만, 소비자들은 구매 결정을 내리는 데 도움이 되는 정보도 얻는다. 소비자들은 또한 추가된 다양성으로부터 혜택을 얻고, 우리 모두는 완벽한 제품에 대한 우리의 상상에 매우 근접한 제품을 얻는데, 다른 어떤 시장 구조도 그러한 결과를 제공하지 않는다.

## 37

Architects might say a machine can never design an innovative or impressive building because a computer cannot be "creative." **[ So / Yet ]**[180] consider the Elbphilharmonie, a new concert hall in Hamburg, which contains a remarkably beautiful auditorium **[ consisted / composed ]**[181] of ten thousand interlocking acoustic panels. It is the sort of space that makes one instinctively **[ think / to think ]**[182] that only a human being — and a human with a remarkably **[ refining / refined ]**[183] creative sensibility, at that — could design something so aesthetically impressive. Yet the auditorium was, in fact, designed algorithmically, using a technique known **[ as / for ]**[184] "parametric design." The architects gave the system a set of criteria, and it generated a set of possible designs for the architects to **[ choose / choose from ]**[185] . Similar software has been used to **[ design / designing ]**[186] lightweight bicycle frames and sturdier chairs, among much else. Are these systems behaving "creatively"? No, they are using lots of processing power to **[ blindly / creatively ]**[187] generate **[ singular / varied ]**[188] possible designs, working in a very **[ different / similar ]**[189] way from a human being.

건축가들은 컴퓨터가 '창의적'일 수 없기 때문에 기계는 결코 혁신적이거나 인상적인 건물을 디자인할 수 없다고 말할지도 모른다. 그러나 Hamburg에 있는, 1만 개의 서로 맞물리는 음향 패널로 구성된 놀랍도록 아름다운 강당을 포함하는 새로운 콘서트 홀인 Elbphilharmonie를 생각해보라. 그것은 인간만이, 그리고 그것도 놀랍도록 세련된 창의적 감수성을 가진 인간만이, 그토록 미적으로 인상적인 것을 디자인할 수 있다고 본능적으로 생각하게 만드는 종류의 공간이다. 그러나 실제로 그 강당은 '파라메트릭 디자인'이라고 알려진 기술을 사용하여 알고리즘에 의한 방식으로 디자인되었다. 건축가들은 그 시스템에 일련의 기준을 부여했고, 그것은 그 건축가들이 선택할 수 있는 일련의 가능한 디자인을 만들어냈다. 유사한 소프트웨어가 다른 많은 것들 중에서도 경량 자전거 프레임과 더 튼튼한 의자를 디자인하는 데 사용되어 왔다. 이러한 시스템들은 '창의적으로' 작동하고 있는가? 아니다, 그것들은 인간과는 매우 다른 방식으로 작동하면서 다양한 가능한 디자인을 닥치는 대로 만들기 위해 많은 처리 능력을 사용하고 있다.

## 38

The brain is a high-energy consumer of glucose, **[ that / which ]**[190] is its fuel. Although the brain **[ accounts / accounts for ]**[191] merely 3 percent of a person's body weight, it consumes 20 percent of the available fuel. Your brain can't store fuel, **[ moreover / however ]**[192] , so it has to "pay as it goes."  Since your brain is incredibly **[ adaptive / adoptive ]**[193] , it economizes its fuel resources. Thus, during a period of high stress, it shifts away from the analysis of the nuances of a situation to a **[ singular / multiple ]**[194] and **[ fixed / variable ]**[195] focus on the stressful situation at hand. You don't sit back and speculate about the meaning of life when you are stressed. **[ Instead / Additionally ]**[196] , you devote all your energy to **[ try / trying ]**[197] to figure out what action to take. Sometimes, however, this shift from the higher-thinking parts of the brain to the **[ automatic / manual ]**[198] and reflexive parts of the brain can lead you to do something too quickly, **[ with / without ]**[199] thinking.

뇌는 그것의 연료인 포도당의 고에너지 소비자이다. 비록 뇌는 사람 체중의 단지 3퍼센트를 차지하지만, 사용 가능한 연료의 20퍼센트를 소비한다. 그러나 여러분의 뇌는 연료를 저장할 수 없고, 따라서 '활동하는 대로 대가를 지불'해야 한다. 여러분의 뇌는 놀라울 정도로 적응력이 뛰어나기 때문에, 그것의 연료 자원을 경제적으로 사용한다. 따라서, 극심한 스트레스를 받는 기간 동안, 뇌는 상황의 미묘한 차이의 분석에서 당면한 스트레스 상황에 대한 단일하고 고정된 초점으로 이동한다. 여러분은 스트레스를 받을 때 앉아서 삶의 의미에 대해 사색하지 않는다. 대신에, 여러분은 어떤 행동을 취해야 할지 알아내려고 노력하는 데 모든 에너지를 쏟는다. 그러나 때때로 뇌의 고차원적 사고 영역에서 자동적이고 반사적인 영역으로의 이러한 이동은 여러분이 무언가를 생각 없이 너무 빨리하도록 이끌 수 있다.

# 39

Much research has been carried out on the [ **causes** / **results** ]200) of engagement, an issue that is important from both a theoretical and practical standpoint: [ **combining** / **identifying** ]201) the drivers of work engagement may [ **enable** / **hinder** ]202) us to manipulate or influence it. The causes of engagement fall into two major camps: situational and personal. The most influential situational causes are job resources, feedback and leadership, the latter, of course, being responsible for job resources and feedback. Indeed, leaders [ **effect** / **influence** ]203) engagement by giving their employees honest and constructive feedback on their performance, and by providing them [ **for** / **with** ]204) the necessary resources that [ **enable** / **force** ]205) them to perform their job well. It is, however, noteworthy that [ **although** / **because** ]206) engagement drives job performance, job performance also drives engagement. In other words, when employees are able to do their jobs well — to the point that they match or exceed their own expectations and ambitions — they will [ **engage** / **identify** ]207) more, be proud of their achievements, and find work more [ **meaningful** / **meaningfully** ]208) . This is especially evident when people are employed in jobs that align with their values.

몰입의 원인에 대한 많은 연구가 수행되어왔는데, 이는 이론적 그리고 실제적 둘 다의 관점에서 중요한 문제이다. 업무 몰입의 동기를 알아내는 것은 우리가 그것을 조작하거나 그것에 영향을 주는 것을 가능하게 할지도 모른다. 몰입의 원인은 상황적인 것과 개인적인 것 두 가지 주요한 분야로 나뉜다. 가장 영향력 있는 상황적 원인은 직무 자원, 피드백, 그리고 리더십이며, 후자는 물론 직무 자원과 피드백에 대한 책임이 있다. 실제로 리더들은 직원들에게 그들의 수행에 대한 솔직하고 건설적인 피드백을 제공하고 직원들이 자신의 직무를 잘 수행할 수 있도록 필요한 자원을 제공함으로써 몰입에 영향을 미친다. 그러나 주목할 점은 몰입이 직무 수행의 동기가 되지만, 직무 수행도 몰입의 동기가 된다는 것이다. 즉, 직원들이 그들 자신의 기대와 포부에 부합하거나 그것을 능가할 정도로 그들의 직무를 잘 수행할 수 있을 때 직원들은 더 많이 몰입하고, 그들의 성과를 자랑스러워하며, 업무를 더 의미 있게 생각할 것이다. 이것은 사람들이 그들의 가치와 일치하는 직무에 종사했을 때 특히 분명하다.

# 40

In 2006, researchers [ **conducting** / **conducted** ]209) a study on the motivations for helping after the September 11th terrorist attacks against the United States. In the study, they found that individuals who gave money, blood, goods, or other forms of assistance [ **because** / **because of** ]210) [ **self-focused** / **other-focused** ]211) motives (giving to reduce another's discomfort) were almost four times [ **more** / **less** ]212) likely to still be giving support one year later [ **as** / **than** ]213) those whose original motivation was to reduce personal distress. This effect likely stems from differences in emotional arousal. The events of September 11th emotionally affected people throughout the United States. Those who gave to reduce their own distress [ **reduced** / **was reduced by** ]214) their emotional arousal with their initial gift, [ **charging** / **discharging** ]215) that emotional distress. However, those who gave to reduce others' distress did not stop [ **empathizing** / **sympathizing** ]216) with victims who continued to struggle long after the attacks.

2006년에 연구자들은 미국을 향한 9.11 테러 공격 이후에 도움을 주려는 동기에 대한 연구를 수행했다. 그 연구에서, 그들은 타인에게 초점을 맞춘 동기(다른 사람의 곤란을 줄이기 위해 베푸는 것) 때문에 돈, 혈액, 물품, 또는 다른 형태의 도움을 주었던 사람들이 자신의 고통을 줄이는 것이 원래 동기였던 사람들보다 일 년 후에도 여전히 지원을 제공할 가능성이 거의 네 배 더 높다는 것을 발견했다. 이 결과는 감정적 자극의 차이에서 비롯된 것 같다. 9.11의 사건들은 미국 전역의 사람들에게 감정적으로 영향을 미쳤다. 자기 자신의 고통을 줄이기 위해 베푼 사람들은 초기의 베풂을 통해 그 감정적 고통을 해소하면서 감정적 자극을 줄였다. 하지만, 다른 사람들의 고통을 줄이기 위해 베푼 사람들은 공격 이후 오랫동안 계속해서 고군분투하는 피해자들에게 공감하기를 멈추지 않았다.

## 41 ~ 42

In England in the 1680s, it was [ **usual / unusual** ]217) to live to the age of fifty. This was a period when knowledge was not spread widely, there were [ **few / little** ]218) books and most people could not read. As a consequence, knowledge passed down through the oral traditions of stories and shared experiences. And since older people had [ **accumulated / been accumulated** ]219) more knowledge, the social norm was that to be over fifty was to be wise. This social perception of age began to [ **shift / stiffen** ]220) with the advent of new technologies such as the printing press. Over time, as more books were printed, [ **literacy / literature** ]221) increased, and the oral traditions of knowledge transfer began to fade. With the fading of oral traditions, the wisdom of the old became [ **less / more** ]222) important and as a consequence being over fifty was no longer seen as [ **signifying / magnifying** ]223) wisdom.

We are living in a period when the gap between chronological and biological age is changing fast and [ **which / where** ]224) social norms are struggling to [ **adapt / adopt** ]225) . In a video produced by the AARP (formerly the American Association of Retired Persons), young people were asked to do various activities 'just like an old person'. When older people [ **joined / joined to** ]226) them in the video, the gap between the stereotype and the older people's actual behaviour was [ **hidden / striking** ]227) . It is clear that in today's world our social norms need to be updated quickly.

1680년대 영국에서는 50세까지 사는 것은 이례적인 일이었다. 이 시기는 지식이 널리 보급되지 않았고, 책이 거의 없었으며, 대부분의 사람들이 읽을 수 없었던 때였다. 결과적으로, 지식은 이야기와 공유된 경험이라는 구전 전통을 통해 전수되었다. 그리고 더 나이 든 사람들이 더 많은 지식을 축적했기 때문에 사회적 규범은 50세가 넘으면 지혜롭다는 것이었다. 나이에 대한 이런 사회적 인식은 인쇄기와 같은 새로운 기술의 출현으로 변화하기 시작했다. 시간이 지나면서 더 많은 책이 인쇄됨에 따라 문해력이 증가했고, 지식 전달의 구전 전통이 사라지기 시작했다. 구전 전통이 사라지면서 노인들의 지혜는 덜 중요해졌고, 결과적으로 50세가 넘은 것은 더 이상 지혜로움을 의미하는 것으로 여겨지지 않았다.
우리는 생활 연령과 생물학적 연령 사이의 격차가 빠르게 변하고 사회적 규범이 적응하기 위해 분투하는 시기에 살고 있다. AARP(이전의 American Association of Retired Persons)에 의해 제작된 영상에서 젊은이들은 다양한 활동을 '마치 꼭 노인처럼' 하도록 요청받았다. 영상에서 노인들이 그들에 합류했을 때, 고정관념과 노인들의 실제 행동 사이의 격차는 두드러졌다. 오늘날의 세상에서 우리의 사회적 규범은 신속하게 최신화되어야 한다는 것이 분명하다.

# 43 ~ 45

When Jack was a young man in his early twenties during the 1960s, he had tried to work in his father's insurance business, as [ was / had ]²²⁸⁾ expected of him. His two older brothers fit in easily and seemed to enjoy their work. But Jack was bored with the insurance industry. "It was worse than being bored," he said. "I felt like I was dying inside." Jack felt drawn to hair styling and dreamed of owning a hair shop with a lively environment. He was sure that he would enjoy the creative and social aspects of it and that he'd be successful. When he was twenty-six, Jack [ approached / approached to ]²²⁹⁾ his father and expressed his intentions of leaving the business to become a hairstylist. As Jack anticipated, his father raged and accused Jack [ of / to ]²³⁰⁾ being selfish, ungrateful, and [ unman / unmanly ]²³¹⁾ . In the face of his father's fury, Jack felt confusion and fear. His resolve became weak. But then a force filled his chest and he stood firm in his decision. In following his path, Jack not only ran three flourishing hair shops, but also helped his clients experience their inner beauty by listening and encouraging them when they faced dark times. His love for his work led to donating time and talent at nursing homes, which in turn led to becoming a hospice volunteer, and eventually to starting fundraising efforts for the hospice program in his community. And all this [ lay / laid ]²³²⁾ a strong stepping stone for another courageous move in his life. When, after having two healthy children of their own, Jack and his wife, Michele, decided to bring an orphaned child into their family, his father threatened to disown them. Jack understood that his father feared [ adaptation / adoption ]²³³⁾ , in this case especially because the child was of a different racial background than their family. Jack and Michele risked rejection and went ahead with the adoption. It took years but eventually Jack's father loved the little girl and accepted his son's independent choices. Jack realized that, although he often felt fear and still [ is / does ]²³⁴⁾ , he has always had courage. In fact, courage was the scaffolding [ which / around which ]²³⁵⁾ he had built richness into his life.

Jack은 1960년대에 20대 초반의 청년이었을 때, 그에게 기대됐던 대로 그의 아버지의 보험 회사에서 일하려고 노력했다. 그의 두 형은 쉽게 적응했고 자신들의 일을 즐기는 것처럼 보였다. 그러나 Jack은 보험 업계에 싫증이 났다. "그것은 지루한 것보다 더 나빴다."라고 그는 말했다. "나는 내면이 죽어가는 것 같았다." Jack은 미용에 매력을 느꼈고 활기찬 분위기의 미용실을 갖는 것을 꿈꿨다. 그는 자신이 그것의 창의적이고 사교적인 측면을 즐길 것이고 성공할 것이라고 확신했다. 26세가 되었을 때, Jack은 아버지에게 가서 미용사가 되기 위해 회사를 떠나겠다는 의사를 밝혔다. Jack이 예상했던 대로, 그의 아버지는 화를 내며 Jack이 이기적이고, 배은망덕하며 남자답지 못하다고 비난했다. 아버지의 분노 앞에서, Jack은 혼란과 두려움을 느꼈다. 그의 결심은 약해졌다. 그러나 그때 어떤 힘이 그의 가슴을 채웠고 그는 자신의 결정에 확고했다. 자신의 길을 가면서, Jack은 세 개의 번창하는 미용실을 운영했을 뿐만 아니라, 또한 고객들이 어두운 시기에 직면했을 때 그들의 말을 듣고 격려함으로써 그들이 가진 내면의 아름다움을 경험하도록 도왔다. 그의 일에 대한 사랑은 요양원에서 시간과 재능을 기부하는 것으로 이어졌고, 이는 결과적으로 호스피스 자원봉사자가 되고, 마침내는 그의 지역사회에서 호스피스 프로그램을 위한 기금 모금 운동을 시작하는 것으로 이어졌다. 그리고 이 모든 것은 그의 삶에서 또 다른 용기 있는 움직임을 위한 견고한 디딤돌을 놓았다. Jack과 그의 아내 Michele이 두 명의 건강한 아이를 낳은 후, 고아가 된 아이를 그들의 가정에 데려오기로 결정했을 때, 그의 아버지는 그들과 의절하겠다고 위협했다. Jack은 자신의 아버지가 입양을 두려워한다는 것을, 이 경우에는 특히 그 아이가 그들의 가족과 다른 인종적 배경을 가지고 있었기 때문임을 이해했다. Jack과 Michele은 거부의 위험을 무릅쓰고 입양을 진행했다. 몇 년이 걸렸지만, 결국 Jack의 아버지는 그 어린 여자아이를 사랑했고 자기 아들의 독립적인 선택을 받아들였다. Jack은 비록 자주 두려움을 느꼈고 여전히 그렇지만, 자신이 항상 용기가 있다는 것을 깨달았다. 사실, 용기는 그가 자신의 삶에 풍요로움을 쌓아온 발판이었다.

## 18

To whom it may concern,

I would like to draw your attention to a problem that frequently occurs with the No. 35 buses. There is a bus stop about halfway along Fenny Road, [ **which / at which** ]¹⁾ the No.35 buses are supposed to stop. It would appear, however, [ **that / which** ]²⁾ some of your drivers are [ **either / neither** ]³⁾ unaware of this bus stop or for some reason choose to ignore it, driving past even though the buses are not full. I would be [ **graceful / grateful** ]⁴⁾ if you could [ **mind / remind** ]⁵⁾ your drivers that this bus stop [ **is existed / exists** ]⁶⁾ and [ **that / what** ]⁷⁾ they should be prepared to stop at it. I look forward to [ **see / seeing** ]⁸⁾ an improvement in this service soon.

Yours faithfully, John Williams

## 19

My 10-year-old appeared, in [ **desperate / separate** ]⁹⁾ need of a quarter. "A quarter? What on earth do you need a quarter for?" My tone [ **boarded / bordered** ]¹⁰⁾ on irritation . I didn't want to be [ **bothering / bothered** ]¹¹⁾ with such a [ **tribal / trivial** ]¹²⁾ demand. "There's a garage sale up the street, and there's something I just gotta have! It only costs a quarter. Please?" I placed a quarter in my son's hand. Moments later, a little voice said, "Here, Mommy, this is for you." I glanced down at the hands of my little son and saw a four-inch cream-colored [ **state / statue** ]¹³⁾ of two small children [ **hug / hugging** ]¹⁴⁾ one another. [ **Inscribed / Subscribed** ]¹⁵⁾ at their feet [ **was / were** ]¹⁶⁾ words that read *It starts with 'L' ends with 'E' and in between are 'O' and 'V.'* As I watched him [ **race / raced** ]¹⁷⁾ back to the garage sale, I smiled with a heart full of happiness. That 25-cent garage sale purchase brought me a lot of joy.

## 20

Managers frequently try to play psychologist, to "figure out" why an employee has acted in a certain way. [ **Empathizing / Sympathizing** ]¹⁸⁾ with employees in order to understand their point of view can be very helpful. However, when [ **deals / dealing** ]¹⁹⁾ with a problem area, in particular, remember [ **that / which** ]²⁰⁾ it is not the person who is bad, but the actions [ **exhibited / were exhibited** ]²¹⁾ on the job. Avoid [ **making / to make** ]²²⁾ suggestions to employees about personal [ **behavior / traits** ]²³⁾ they should change; instead suggest more acceptable ways of [ **performing / characteristic** ]²⁴⁾ . For example, instead of focusing on a person's "unreliability," a manager might focus on the fact that the employee "has been [ **late / lately** ]²⁵⁾ to work seven times this month." It is difficult for employees to change who they [ **are / do** ]²⁶⁾ ; it is usually [ **much / very** ]²⁷⁾ easier for them to change [ **how / why** ]²⁸⁾ they act.

## 21

I suspect fungi are a **[ little / few ]**²⁹⁾ more forward "thinking" **[ than / as ]**³⁰⁾ their larger partners. Among trees, each species **[ fight / fights ]**³¹⁾ other species. Let's assume the beeches native to Central Europe could **[ emerge / submerge ]**³²⁾ victorious in most forests there. Would this really be an advantage? What would happen if a new pathogen came along that **[ perfected / infected ]**³³⁾ most of the beeches and killed them? In that case, wouldn't it be more advantageous if there **[ was / were ]**³⁴⁾ a certain number of other species around — oaks, maples, or firs — that would continue to grow and provide the shade **[ to need / needed ]**³⁵⁾ for a new generation of young beeches to sprout and grow up? **[ Predominance / Diversity ]**³⁶⁾ provides security for ancient forests. Because fungi are also very **[ dependent on / independent from ]**³⁷⁾ stable conditions, they support other species underground and protect them from complete **[ collaboration / collapse ]**³⁸⁾ to ensure that one species of tree doesn't manage to **[ dominate / eliminate ]**³⁹⁾ .

## 22

It's remarkable that **[ positive / negative ]**⁴⁰⁾ fantasies help us **[ relax / relaxing ]**⁴¹⁾ to such an extent **[ that / what ]**⁴²⁾ it shows up in physiological tests. If you want to **[ wind / unwind ]**⁴³⁾ , you can take some deep breaths, get a massage, or go for a walk — but you can also try simply closing your eyes and fantasizing about some future **[ income / outcome ]**⁴⁴⁾ that you might enjoy. But what about when your **[ objective / subjective ]**⁴⁵⁾ is to make your wish a reality? The **[ first / *last* ]**⁴⁶⁾ thing you want to be is **[ relaxing / relaxed ]**⁴⁷⁾ . You want to be energized enough to get off the couch and lose those pounds or find that job or study for that test, and you want to be **[ motivation / motivated ]**⁴⁸⁾ enough to stay engaged even when the **[ evitable / inevitable ]**⁴⁹⁾ obstacles or challenges **[ arise / raise ]**⁵⁰⁾ . The principle of "Dream it. Wish it. Do it." does not hold **[ true / truly ]**⁵¹⁾ , and now we know why: in dreaming it, you **[ reinforce / undercut ]**⁵²⁾ the energy you need to do it. You put yourself in a temporary state of complete happiness, calmness — and **[ activity / inactivity ]**⁵³⁾ .

## 23

If cooking is as central to human **[ identity / identification ]**⁵⁴⁾ , biology, and culture as the biological anthropologist Richard Wrangham suggests, it stands to **[ reason / reasoning ]**⁵⁵⁾ that the **[ increase / decline ]**⁵⁶⁾ of cooking in our time would have serious consequences for modern life, and so it has. Are they all bad? Not at all. The outsourcing of much of the work of cooking to corporations has **[ relieved / been relieved ]**⁵⁷⁾ women of what has traditionally been their **[ exclusive / inclusive ]**⁵⁸⁾ responsibility for **[ feeding / feeding on ]**⁵⁹⁾ the family, making **[ it / them ]**⁶⁰⁾ easier for **[ it / them ]**⁶¹⁾ to work outside the home and have careers. It has headed off many of the domestic conflicts that such a large **[ adhesion / shift ]**⁶²⁾ in gender roles and family dynamics was bound to spark. It has relieved other pressures in the household, **[ including / excluding ]**⁶³⁾ longer workdays and overscheduled children, and saved us time that we can now invest in other pursuits. It has also allowed us **[ to diversify / diversifying ]**⁶⁴⁾ our diets substantially, making it possible even for people with no cooking skills and **[ few / little ]**⁶⁵⁾ money to enjoy a whole different cuisine. All that's required is a microwave.

## 24

As you may already know, what and how you buy can be [ **environmental / political** ]⁶⁶⁾ . To whom do you want to give your money? Which companies and [ **cooperations / corporations** ]⁶⁷⁾ do you value and respect? Be mindful about every [ **purchase / purchases** ]⁶⁸⁾ by carefully researching the corporations that are taking our money to decide if they [ **deserve / preserve** ]⁶⁹⁾ our support. Do they have a record of polluting the environment, or do they have fair-trade practices and an end-of-life plan for the products they make? Are they [ **committed / deserved** ]⁷⁰⁾ to bringing about good in the world? For instance, my family has found a company [ **produces / producing** ]⁷¹⁾ recycled, plastic-packaging-free toilet paper with a social conscience. They contribute 50 percent of their profits to the [ **construction / destruction** ]⁷²⁾ of toilets around the world, and we're genuinely happy to spend our money on this special toilet paper each month. Remember that the corporate world is built on consumers, so as a consumer you have the power to vote with your wallet and [ **encourage / discourage** ]⁷³⁾ companies [ **to / from** ]⁷⁴⁾ embrace healthier and more [ **attainable / sustainable** ]⁷⁵⁾ practices with every purchase you choose to make.

## 26

Camille Flammarion was born at Montigny-le-Roi, France. He became [ **interesting / interested** ]⁷⁶⁾ in [ **anatomy / astronomy** ]⁷⁷⁾ at an early age, and when he was only sixteen he wrote a book on the origin of the world. The manuscript was not published at the time, but it came to the attention of Urbain Le Verrier, the director of the Paris [ **Observation / Observatory** ]⁷⁸⁾ . He became an [ **assistant / assistance** ]⁷⁹⁾ to Le Verrier in 1858 and worked as a calculator. At nineteen, he wrote another book called *The Plurality of Inhabited Worlds*, [ **which / in which** ]⁸⁰⁾ he passionately claimed that life exists outside the planet Earth. His most [ **successful / successive** ]⁸¹⁾ work, *Popular Astronomy*, was published in 1880, and eventually sold 130,000 copies. With his own funds, he built an observatory at Juvisy and spent May to November of each [ **year / years** ]⁸²⁾ there. In 1887, he founded the French Astronomical Society and [ **served / serving** ]⁸³⁾ as editor of its monthly publication.

## 29

There is [ **few / little** ]⁸⁴⁾ doubt [ **that / which** ]⁸⁵⁾ we are driven by the sell-by date. Once an item is past [ **that / those** ]⁸⁶⁾ date it goes into the waste stream, [ **farther / further** ]⁸⁷⁾ [ **increasing / increased** ]⁸⁸⁾ its carbon footprint. Remember those items have already travelled hundreds of miles to [ **arrive / reach** ]⁸⁹⁾ the shelves and once they go into waste they start a new carbon mile journey. But we all make our own [ **judge / judgement** ]⁹⁰⁾ about sell-by dates; those [ **brought / are brought** ]⁹¹⁾ up [ **during / while** ]⁹²⁾ the Second World War are often [ **fond / scornful** ]⁹³⁾ of the terrible waste they believe such [ **cause / caution** ]⁹⁴⁾ encourages. The manufacturer of the food has a view when making or growing something [ **that / which** ]⁹⁵⁾ [ **at / by** ]⁹⁶⁾ the time the product reaches the shelves it has already been [ **travelling / travelled** ]⁹⁷⁾ for so many days and possibly many miles. The manufacturer then decides that a product can reasonably be [ **consuming / consumed** ]⁹⁸⁾ within say 90 days and 90 days minus so many days for travelling [ **gives / to give** ]⁹⁹⁾ the sell-by date. But whether it becomes toxic is something each [ **individual / individuals** ]¹⁰⁰⁾ can decide. It would seem to [ **make / be made** ]¹⁰¹⁾ sense not to buy large packs of [ **perishable / non-perishable** ]¹⁰²⁾ goods but [ **perishable / non-perishable** ]¹⁰³⁾ items may become cost-effective.

# 30

The "jolt" of caffeine does wear off. Caffeine is removed from your system by an enzyme within your liver, **[ that / which ]**<sup>104)</sup> gradually **[ upgrades / degrades ]**<sup>105)</sup> it over time. Based in large part on genetics, some people have a more efficient version of the enzyme that **[ degrades / upgrades ]**<sup>106)</sup> caffeine, **[ allowing / allowed ]**<sup>107)</sup> the liver to rapidly **[ clear / pile ]**<sup>108)</sup> it from the bloodstream. These rare individuals can drink an espresso with dinner and fall fast **[ asleep / sleep ]**<sup>109)</sup> at midnight without a problem. Others, however, have a **[ slower-acting / fast-acting ]**<sup>110)</sup> version of the enzyme. It takes **[ far / very ]**<sup>111)</sup> longer for their system to **[ eliminate / reach ]**<sup>112)</sup> the same amount of caffeine. As a result, they are very **[ sensible / sensitive ]**<sup>113)</sup> to caffeine's effects. One cup of tea or coffee in the morning will last much of the day, and **[ they should / should they ]**<sup>114)</sup> have a second cup, even early in the afternoon, they **[ will / would ]**<sup>115)</sup> find it difficult to fall asleep in the evening. Aging also **[ alters / keeps ]**<sup>116)</sup> the speed of caffeine clearance: the older we are, the **[ longer / shorter ]**<sup>117)</sup> it takes our brain and body to **[ add / remove ]**<sup>118)</sup> caffeine, and thus the more **[ sensible / sensitive ]**<sup>119)</sup> we become in later life to caffeine's sleep-disrupting influence.

# 31

Rebels may think they're rebels, but clever marketers **[ effect / influence ]**<sup>120)</sup> them just like the rest of us. Saying, "Everyone is doing it" may **[ keep / turn ]**<sup>121)</sup> some people off from an idea. These people will look for **[ alternatives / conventions ]**<sup>122)</sup> , **[ that / which ]**<sup>123)</sup> (if cleverly planned) can be exactly **[ that / what ]**<sup>124)</sup> a marketer or persuader wants you to believe. If I want you to consider an idea, and know you strongly **[ accept / reject ]**<sup>125)</sup> popular opinion in **[ favor / denial ]**<sup>126)</sup> of maintaining your **[ dependence / independence ]**<sup>127)</sup> and uniqueness, I would present the **[ majority / minority ]**<sup>128)</sup> option first, which you would reject in favor of my actual **[ preference / recommendation ]**<sup>129)</sup> . We are often tricked when we try to maintain a position of **[ agreement / defiance ]**<sup>130)</sup> . People use this **[ alignment / reversal ]**<sup>131)</sup> to make us "independently" choose an option which suits their purposes. Some brands have taken full effect of our **[ alignment / defiance ]**<sup>132)</sup> towards the mainstream and positioned themselves as **[ majority / rebels ]**<sup>133)</sup> ; which has created even stronger brand **[ loyalty / royalty ]**<sup>134)</sup> .

# 32

A typical soap opera creates an **[ abstract / concrete ]**<sup>135)</sup> world, in which a highly complex web of relationships **[ connect / connects ]**<sup>136)</sup> fictional characters that **[ exist / exists ]**<sup>137)</sup> first only in the minds of the program's creators and are then recreated in the minds of the viewer. If you **[ were / had been ]**<sup>138)</sup> to think about how much human psychology, law, and even everyday physics the viewer must know in order to follow and **[ articulate / speculate ]**<sup>139)</sup> about the plot, you would discover it is **[ considerate / considerable ]**<sup>140)</sup> — at least as **[ many / much ]**<sup>141)</sup> as the knowledge required to follow and speculate about a piece of modern mathematics, and in most cases, much more. Yet viewers follow soap operas with **[ ease / challenge ]**<sup>142)</sup> . How are they able to cope with such **[ abstraction / specification ]**<sup>143)</sup> ? Because, of course, the abstraction is built on an extremely **[ familiar / strange ]**<sup>144)</sup> framework. The characters in a soap opera and the relationships between them **[ is / are ]**<sup>145)</sup> very much like the real people and relationships we experience every day. The abstraction of a soap opera is only a step **[ added / removed ]**<sup>146)</sup> from the real world. The mental "training" required to follow a soap opera is provided by our everyday lives.

## 33

As always happens with natural selection, bats and their prey have **[ engaged / been engaged ]**<sup>147)</sup> in a life-or-death **[ sensible / sensory ]**<sup>148)</sup> arms race for millions of years. It's believed that hearing in moths **[ arose / rose ]**<sup>149)</sup> specifically in response to the threat of **[ eating / being eaten by ]**<sup>150)</sup> bats. (Not all insects can hear.) Over millions of years, moths have evolved the ability to **[ detect / protect ]**<sup>151)</sup> sounds at ever higher frequencies, and, as they have, the frequencies of bats' vocalizations have **[ raised / risen ]**<sup>152)</sup> , too. Some moth species have also evolved scales on their wings and a fur-like coat on their bodies; both act as "acoustic camouflage," by absorbing sound waves in the frequencies **[ emitted / omitted ]**<sup>153)</sup> by bats, thereby preventing those sound waves **[ from / to ]**<sup>154)</sup> bouncing back. The B-2 bomber and other "stealth" aircraft have fuselages **[ make / made ]**<sup>155)</sup> of materials that do something similar with radar beams.

## 34

Much of human thought is designed to screen out information and to sort the rest into **[ overwhelming / overwhelmed ]**<sup>156)</sup> chaos, especially given the enormous amount of information available in culture and society. Out of all the sensory impressions and possible information, it is vital to find a small amount that is most **[ relevant / respective ]**<sup>157)</sup> to our individual needs and to organize that into a usable stock of knowledge. Expectancies accomplish some of this work, helping to screen out information that is **[ relevant / irrelevant ]**<sup>158)</sup> to what is expected, and focusing our attention on clear **[ alignments / contradictions ]**<sup>159)</sup> . The processes of learning and memory are marked by a steady **[ absorption / elimination ]**<sup>160)</sup> of information. People notice only a part of the world around them. Then, only a fraction of what they notice gets processed and stored into memory. And only part of what gets committed to memory can be **[ relieved / retrieved ]**<sup>161)</sup> .

## 35

The irony of early democracy in Europe is **[ that / what ]**<sup>162)</sup> it thrived and prospered precisely because European rulers for a very long time were remarkably **[ strong / weak ]**<sup>163)</sup> . For more than a millennium after the fall of Rome, European rulers **[ had / lacked ]**<sup>164)</sup> the ability to **[ assess / access ]**<sup>165)</sup> what their people were producing and to levy **[ substantial / substantive ]**<sup>166)</sup> taxes based on this. The most striking way to illustrate European **[ power / weakness ]**<sup>167)</sup> is to show how **[ few / little ]**<sup>168)</sup> revenue they collected. Europeans would eventually develop strong systems of **[ avenue / revenue ]**<sup>169)</sup> collection, but it took them an awfully long time to do so. In medieval times, and for part of the early modern era, Chinese emperors and Muslim caliphs were able to **[ extract / subtract ]**<sup>170)</sup> much more of economic production than any European ruler with the exception of small city-states.

# 36

If you drive down a busy street, you will find many [ **compete / competing** ]171) businesses, often right next to one another. For example, in most places a consumer in search of a quick meal has many choices, and more fast-food restaurants appear all the time. These competing [ **firms / forms** ]172) advertise heavily. The temptation is to see advertising as driving [ **down / up** ]173) the price of a product without any benefit to the consumer. However, this misconception doesn't account for [ **why / which** ]174) firms advertise. In markets [ **which / where** ]175) competitors sell slightly differentiated products, advertising enables firms to [ **inform / deform** ]176) their customers about new products and services. Yes, costs rise, but consumers also [ **gain / lose** ]177) information to help make purchasing decisions. Consumers also benefit from [ **added / lost** ]178) variety, and we all get a product that's pretty close to our vision of a perfect good — and no other market structure delivers that [ **income / outcome** ]179) .

# 37

Architects might say a machine can never design an innovative or impressive building because a computer cannot be "creative." [ **So / Yet** ]180) consider the Elbphilharmonie, a new concert hall in Hamburg, which contains a remarkably beautiful auditorium [ **consisted / composed** ]181) of ten thousand interlocking acoustic panels. It is the sort of space that makes one instinctively [ **think / to think** ]182) that only a human being — and a human with a remarkably [ **refining / refined** ]183) creative sensibility, at that — could design something so aesthetically impressive. Yet the auditorium was, in fact, designed algorithmically, using a technique known [ **as / for** ]184) "parametric design." The architects gave the system a set of criteria, and it generated a set of possible designs for the architects to [ **choose / choose from** ]185) . Similar software has been used to [ **design / designing** ]186) lightweight bicycle frames and sturdier chairs, among much else. Are these systems behaving "creatively"? No, they are using lots of processing power to [ **blindly / creatively** ]187) generate [ **singular / varied** ]188) possible designs, working in a very [ **different / similar** ]189) way from a human being.

# 38

The brain is a high-energy consumer of glucose, [ **that / which** ]190) is its fuel. Although the brain [ **accounts / accounts for** ]191) merely 3 percent of a person's body weight, it consumes 20 percent of the available fuel. Your brain can't store fuel, [ **moreover / however** ]192) , so it has to "pay as it goes."  Since your brain is incredibly [ **adaptive / adoptive** ]193) , it economizes its fuel resources. Thus, during a period of high stress, it shifts away from the analysis of the nuances of a situation to a [ **singular / multiple** ]194) and [ **fixed / variable** ]195) focus on the stressful situation at hand. You don't sit back and speculate about the meaning of life when you are stressed. [ **Instead / Additionally** ]196) , you devote all your energy to [ **try / trying** ]197) to figure out what action to take. Sometimes, however, this shift from the higher-thinking parts of the brain to the [ **automatic / manual** ]198) and reflexive parts of the brain can lead you to do something too quickly, [ **with / without** ]199) thinking.

## 39

Much research has been carried out on the [ **causes / results** ]200) of engagement, an issue that is important from both a theoretical and practical standpoint: [ **combining / identifying** ]201) the drivers of work engagement may [ **enable / hinder** ]202) us to manipulate or influence it. The causes of engagement fall into two major camps: situational and personal. The most influential situational causes are job resources, feedback and leadership, the latter, of course, being responsible for job resources and feedback. Indeed, leaders [ **effect / influence** ]203) engagement by giving their employees honest and constructive feedback on their performance, and by providing them [ **for / with** ]204) the necessary resources that [ **enable / force** ]205) them to perform their job well. It is, however, noteworthy that [ **although / because** ]206) engagement drives job performance, job performance also drives engagement. In other words, when employees are able to do their jobs well — to the point that they match or exceed their own expectations and ambitions — they will [ **engage / identify** ]207) more, be proud of their achievements, and find work more [ **meaningful / meaningfully** ]208) . This is especially evident when people are employed in jobs that align with their values.

## 40

In 2006, researchers [ **conducting / conducted** ]209) a study on the motivations for helping after the September 11th terrorist attacks against the United States. In the study, they found that individuals who gave money, blood, goods, or other forms of assistance [ **because / because of** ]210) [ **self-focused / other-focused** ]211) motives (giving to reduce another's discomfort) were almost four times [ **more / less** ]212) likely to still be giving support one year later [ **as / than** ]213) those whose original motivation was to reduce personal distress. This effect likely stems from differences in emotional arousal. The events of September 11th emotionally affected people throughout the United States. Those who gave to reduce their own distress [ **reduced / was reduced by** ]214) their emotional arousal with their initial gift, [ **charging / discharging** ]215) that emotional distress. However, those who gave to reduce others' distress did not stop [ **empathizing / sympathizing** ]216) with victims who continued to struggle long after the attacks.

## 41 ~ 42

In England in the 1680s, it was [ **usual / unusual** ]217) to live to the age of fifty. This was a period when knowledge was not spread widely, there were [ **few / little** ]218) books and most people could not read. As a consequence, knowledge passed down through the oral traditions of stories and shared experiences. And since older people had [ **accumulated / been accumulated** ]219) more knowledge, the social norm was that to be over fifty was to be wise. This social perception of age began to [ **shift / stiffen** ]220) with the advent of new technologies such as the printing press. Over time, as more books were printed, [ **literacy / literature** ]221) increased, and the oral traditions of knowledge transfer began to fade. With the fading of oral traditions, the wisdom of the old became [ **less / more** ]222) important and as a consequence being over fifty was no longer seen as [ **signifying / magnifying** ]223) wisdom.

We are living in a period when the gap between chronological and biological age is changing fast and **[ which / where ]**224) social norms are struggling to **[ adapt / adopt ]**225) . In a video produced by the AARP (formerly the American Association of Retired Persons), young people were asked to do various activities 'just like an old person'. When older people **[ joined / joined to ]**226) them in the video, the gap between the stereotype and the older people's actual behaviour was **[ hidden / striking ]**227) . It is clear that in today's world our social norms need to be updated quickly.

## 43 ~ 45

When Jack was a young man in his early twenties during the 1960s, he had tried to work in his father's insurance business, as **[ was / had ]**228) expected of him. His two older brothers fit in easily and seemed to enjoy their work. But Jack was bored with the insurance industry. "It was worse than being bored," he said. "I felt like I was dying inside." Jack felt drawn to hair styling and dreamed of owning a hair shop with a lively environment. He was sure that he would enjoy the creative and social aspects of it and that he'd be successful. When he was twenty-six, Jack **[ approached / approached to ]**229) his father and expressed his intentions of leaving the business to become a hairstylist. As Jack anticipated, his father raged and accused Jack **[ of / to ]**230) being selfish, ungrateful, and **[ unman / unmanly ]**231) . In the face of his father's fury, Jack felt confusion and fear. His resolve became weak. But then a force filled his chest and he stood firm in his decision. In following his path, Jack not only ran three flourishing hair shops, but also helped his clients experience their inner beauty by listening and encouraging them when they faced dark times. His love for his work led to donating time and talent at nursing homes, which in turn led to becoming a hospice volunteer, and eventually to starting fundraising efforts for the hospice program in his community. And all this **[ lay / laid ]**232) a strong stepping stone for another courageous move in his life. When, after having two healthy children of their own, Jack and his wife, Michele, decided to bring an orphaned child into their family, his father threatened to disown them. Jack understood that his father feared **[ adaptation / adoption ]**233) , in this case especially because the child was of a different racial background than their family. Jack and Michele risked rejection and went ahead with the adoption. It took years but eventually Jack's father loved the little girl and accepted his son's independent choices. Jack realized that, although he often felt fear and still **[ is / does ]**234) , he has always had courage. In fact, courage was the scaffolding **[ which / around which ]**235) he had built richness into his life.

2023 고2 9월 모의고사 　　　❶ 회차 ：　　　　점 / 335점

❶ voca　　❷ text　　❸ [ / ]　　④ ＿＿＿　　❺ quiz 1　　❻ quiz 2　　❼ quiz 3　　❽ quiz 4　　❾ quiz 5

## 18

To whom it may concern,

I would like to **d**_____1) your **a**_____2) to a problem that **f**_____3) occurs with the No. 35 buses. There is a bus stop about **h**_____4) along Fenny Road, at which the No.35 buses are supposed to stop. It would appear, however, that some of your drivers are either **u**_____5) of this bus stop or for some reason choose to **i**_____6) it, driving **p**_____7) even though the buses are not full. I would be **g**_____8) if you could **r**_____9) your drivers that this bus stop exists and that they should be **p**_____10) to stop at it. I look forward to seeing an **i**_____11) in this service soon.

Yours **f**_____12) John Williams

관계자분께, 35번 버스에서 자주 발생하는 문제에 대해 귀하의 주의를 환기하고 싶습니다. Fenny Road를 따라 중간쯤 버스 정류장이 있고, 그곳에서 35번 버스가 정차하게 되어 있습니다. 그러나 버스 기사들 중 일부는 이 버스 정류장을 인식하지 못하거나 어떤 이유에서인지 그것을 무시하기로 선택하여 버스가 꽉 차지 않았음에도 운전해 지나쳐가는 것으로 보입니다. 기사들에게 이 버스 정류장이 존재하고 그곳에 정차할 준비가 되어 있어야 한다는 것을 상기시켜 주시면 감사하겠습니다. 곧 이 서비스가 개선되기를 기대합니다.
진심을 담아, John Williams 드림

## 19

My 10-year-old appeared, in **d**_____13) need of a **q**_____14) "A quarter? What on earth do you need a quarter for?" My tone bordered on **i**_____15) I didn't want to be bothered with such a **t**_____16) demand. "There's a **g**_____17) sale up the street, and there's something I just gotta have! It only costs a quarter. Please?" I **p**_____18) a quarter in my son's hand. Moments later, a little voice said, "Here, Mommy, this is for you." I **g**_____19) down at the hands of my little son and saw a four-inch cream-colored **s**_____20) of two small children hugging one another. **I**_____21) at their feet were words that read *It starts with 'L' ends with 'E' and in between are 'O' and 'V.'* As I watched him **r**_____22) back to the garage sale, I smiled with a heart full of happiness. That 25-cent garage sale **p**_____23) brought me a lot of joy.

내 열 살짜리 아이가 나타났고, 25센트 동전을 절실히 필요로 했다. "25센트 동전? 도대체 25센트 동전이 왜 필요하지?" 나의 말투는 거의 짜증에 가까웠다. 나는 그런 사소한 요구에 방해받고 싶지 않았다. "거리 위쪽에서 중고 물품 판매 행사를 하는데, 제가 꼭 사야 할 게 있어요! 25센트밖에 안 해요. 네?" 나는 아들의 손에 25센트 동전을 쥐여 주었다. 잠시 후 작은 목소리가 "여기요, 엄마, 이거 엄마를 위한 거예요."라고 말했다. 나는 내 어린 아들의 손을 힐끗 내려다보았고, 두 어린아이가 서로 껴안고 있는 4인치짜리 크림색의 조각상을 보았다. 그들의 발밑에는 'L'로 시작하여 'E'로 끝나고 그 사이에 'O'와 'V'가 있다는 말이 새겨져 있었다. 아이가 중고 물품 판매 행사로 서둘러 돌아가는 모습을 바라보며 나는 행복이 가득한 마음으로 미소를 지었다. 그 25센트짜리 중고 물품 판매 행사 구입품은 나에게 큰 기쁨을 가져다 주었다.

# 20

Managers f_____24) try to play psychologist, to "figure out" why an e_____25) has acted in a certain way. E_____26) with employees in order to understand their point of view can be very h_____27) However, when d_____28) with a problem area, in p_____29) remember that it is not the person who is bad, but the actions e_____30) on the job. A_____31) making s_____32) to employees about personal t_____33) they should change; instead suggest more a_____34) ways of performing. For example, instead of focusing on a person's " u_____35) ," a manager might focus on the fact that the employee "has been late to work seven times this month." It is difficult for employees to change who they are; it is usually much easier for them to change _____36) they act.

관리자들은 직원이 왜 특정한 방식으로 행동했는지를 '파악하기' 위해 심리학자 역할을 하려고 자주 노력한다. 그들의 관점을 이해하기 위해 직원들과 공감하는 것은 매우 도움이 될 수 있다. 하지만, 특히 문제 영역을 다룰 때, 그것은 잘하지 못하는 사람이 아니라 근무 중에 보여지는 행동이라는 것을 기억하라. 직원들에게 그들이 바꿔야 할 인격적 특성에 대해 제안하는 것을 피하라. 대신에 더 용인되는 수행 방법을 제안하라. 예를 들어, 관리자는 어떤 사람의 '신뢰할 수 없음'에 초점을 맞추는 대신, 그 직원이 '이번 달에 회사에 일곱 번 지각했다'는 사실에 초점을 맞출 수도 있을 것이다. 직원들은 자신이 어떤 사람인지를 바꾸기는 어렵다. 일반적으로 자신이 행동하는 방식을 바꾸기가 훨씬 쉽다.

# 21

I suspect f_____37) are a little more f_____38) "thinking" than their larger partners. Among trees, each s_____39) fights other species. Let's a_____40) the beeches native to Central Europe could emerge v_____41) in most forests there. Would this really be an advantage? What would happen if a new p_____42) came along that i_____43) most of the beeches and killed them? In that case, wouldn't it be more a_____44) if there were a certain number of other species around — oaks, maples, or firs — that would continue to grow and provide the shade needed for a new generation of young beeches to s_____45) and grow up? D_____46) provides s_____47) for ancient forests. Because f_____48) are also very d_____49) on stable conditions, they support other species underground and protect them from complete c_____50) to e_____51) that one species of tree doesn't manage to d_____52) .

나는 균류가 자신의 더 큰 상대보다 조금 더 앞서 '생각한다'고 짐작한다. 나무들 사이에서 각 종은 다른 종들과 싸운다. 중부 유럽 태생의 너도밤나무가 그곳의 숲 대부분에서 우세하게 나타날 수 있다고 가정해 보자. 이게 정말 이점일까? 만약 대부분의 너도밤나무를 감염시켜 죽게 만드는 새로운 병원균이 나타나면 어떻게 될까? 그런 경우, 주변에 참나무, 단풍나무 또는 전나무와 같은 일정한 수의 다른 종이 계속 자라서 새로운 세대의 어린 너도밤나무가 싹을 틔우고 자라는 데 필요한 그늘을 제공한다면 더 유리하지 않을까? 다양성은 오래된 숲에 안전을 제공한다. 균류도 또한 안정적인 조건에 매우 의존하기 때문에, 그들은 한 종의 나무가 우세해지지 않도록 확실히 하기 위해 땅 속에서 다른 종을 지원하고 그것들을 완전한 붕괴로부터 보호한다.

## 22

It's remarkable that p_____53) f_____54) help us r_____55) to such an extent that it shows up in p_____56) tests. If you want to u_____57) you can take some deep breaths, get a massage, or go for a walk — but you can also try simply closing your eyes and f_____58) about some future o_____59) that you might enjoy. But what about when your o_____60) is to make your wish a reality? The l_____61) thing you want to be is r_____62) . You want to be e_____63) enough to get off the couch and lose those pounds or find that job or study for that test, and you want to be m_____64) enough to stay e_____65) even when the i_____66) obstacles or c_____67) arise. The principle of "Dream it. Wish it. Do it." does not hold true, and now we know why: in dreaming it, you u_____68) the energy you need to do it. You put yourself in a t_____69) state of complete happiness, calmness — and i_____70) .

낙관적인 상상이 생리학적 검사에서 나타날 정도로 우리가 긴장을 푸는 데 도움이 된다는 것은 주목할 만하다. 만약 여러분이 긴장을 풀고 싶다면, 심호흡하거나, 마사지를 받거나, 산책을 할 수도 있지만, 단순히 눈을 감고 여러분이 누릴지도 모를 미래의 결과에 대해 상상해 볼 수도 있다. 하지만 여러분의 목표가 소망을 실현하는 것인 경우라면 어떨까? 여러분이 '가장 피해야 할' 상태는 긴장이 풀려 있는 것이다. 여러분은 소파에서 일어나 체중을 감량하거나 직업을 찾거나 시험공부를 할 수 있을 만큼 충분히 활력을 얻어야 하고, 피할 수 없는 장애물이나 문제가 발생할 때도 계속 전념할 수 있도록 충분히 동기 부여 되어야 한다. '그것을 꿈꿔라. 그것을 소망하라. 그것을 실행하라.'라는 원칙은 사실이 아니며, 우리는 이제 그 이유를 안다. 그것을 꿈꾸는 중에, 여러분은 그것을 하는 데 필요한 에너지를 약화시킨다. 여러분은 스스로를 완전한 행복, 고요, 그리고 비활동의 일시적인 상태에 빠지게 한다.

## 23

If cooking is as c_____71) to human i_____72) biology, and culture as the biological a_____73) Richard Wrangham suggests, it stands to r_____74) that the d_____75) of cooking in our time would have serious consequences for modern life, and so it has. Are they all bad? Not at all. The o_____76) of much of the work of cooking to c_____77) has relieved women of what has traditionally been their e_____78) responsibility for f_____79) the family, making it easier for them to work outside the home and have careers. It has h_____80) off many of the d_____81) c_____82) that such a large shift in g_____83) roles and family dynamics was bound to s_____84) . It has r_____85) other pressures in the household, including longer workdays and o_____86) children, and saved us time that we can now i_____87) in other pursuits. It has also allowed us to diversify our diets s_____88) making it possible even for people with no cooking skills and little money to enjoy a whole different c_____89) All that's required is a microwave.

생물인류학자인 Richard Wrangham이 말하는 것만큼 요리가 인간의 정체성, 생물학 및 문화에 중요하다면, 우리 시대의 요리 감소가 현대 생활에 심각한 결과들을 초래한다고 추론하는 것은 당연하고, 실제로 그래왔다. 그것들이 모두 나쁜가? 전혀 그렇지 않다. 요리하는 일의 많은 부분을 기업에 아웃소싱하는 것은 전통적으로 여성들에게 한정된, 가족들을 먹여야 하는 책임이었던 것에서 여성들을 벗어나게 했고, 그들이 집 밖에서 일하고 직업을 갖는 것을 더 쉽게 했다. 그것은 성 역할과 가족 역학의 그렇게 큰 변화가 촉발할 많은 가정 내 갈등을 막아냈다. 그것은 더 긴 근무일과 분주한 자녀를 포함하여 가정의 다른 곤란을 덜어주었고, 이제 우리가 다른 일에 투자할 수 있도록 시간을 절약해 주었다. 그것은 또한 우리의 식단을 상당히 다양하게 해주었고, 요리 기술이 없고 돈이 거의 없는 사람들까지도 완전히 색다른 요리를 즐길 수 있게 해주었다. 필요한 것이라곤 전자레인지뿐이다.

(.hwp) (.pdf) → www.englishjmygod.com

# 24

As you may already know, what and how you buy can be **p**_____ 90) To whom do you want to give your money? Which companies and corporations do you **v**_____ 91) and respect? Be **m**_____ 92) about every purchase by carefully researching the corporations that are taking our money to decide if they **d**_____ 93) our **s**_____ 94) Do they have a record of **p**_____ 95) the environment, or do they have fair-trade practices and an end-of-life plan for the products they make? Are they **c**_____ 96) to bringing about good in the world? For instance, my family has found a company **p**_____ 97) recycled, plastic-packaging-free toilet paper with a social **c**_____ 98) They **c**_____ 99) 50 percent of their profits to the construction of toilets around the world, and we're **g**_____ 100) happy to spend our money on this special toilet paper each month. Remember that the **c**_____ 101) world is built on consumers, so as a consumer you have the power to vote with your **w**_____ 102) and encourage companies to **e**_____ 103) healthier and more **s**_____ 104) practices with every **p**_____ 105) you choose to make.

이미 알고 있겠지만, 여러분이 무엇을 어떻게 구매하는지는 정치적일 수 있다. 여러분은 여러분의 돈을 누구에게 주고 싶은가? 여러분은 어떤 회사와 기업을 가치 있게 여기고 존중하는가? 우리의 지원을 받을 자격이 있는지를 결정하기 위해 우리의 돈을 가져가는 기업들을 면밀히 조사함으로써 모든 구매에 주의를 기울여라. 그들은 환경을 오염시킨 기록이 있는가, 아니면 그들이 만든 제품에 대한 공정 거래 관행과 제품 수명 종료 계획이 있는가? 그들은 세상에 득이 되는 것에 헌신하고 있는가? 예를 들어, 우리 가족은 사회적 양심을 가지고 재활용되고 플라스틱 포장이 없는 화장지를 생산하는 회사를 발견했다. 그들은 수익의 50%를 전 세계 화장실 건설에 기부하고 우리는 이 특별한 화장지에 매달 돈을 쓸 수 있어서 정말 기쁘다. 기업의 세계는 소비자를 기반으로 구축되므로, 소비자로서 여러분은 지갑으로 투표하고 여러분이 선택한 모든 구매를 통해 회사들이 더 건강하고 더 지속 가능한 관행을 받아들이도록 장려할 힘이 있다는 것을 기억하라.

# 26

Camille Flammarion was born at Montigny-le-Roi, France. He became interested in **a**_____ 106) at an early age, and when he was only sixteen he wrote a book on the origin of the world. The **m**_____ 107) was not published at the time, but it came to the **a**_____ 108) of Urbain Le Verrier, the director of the Paris Observatory. He became an **a**_____ 109) to Le Verrier in 1858 and worked as a **c**_____ 110) At nineteen, he wrote another book **c**_____ 111) *The Plurality of Inhabited Worlds*, in which he **p**_____ 112) claimed that life exists outside the planet Earth. His most **s**_____ 113) work, *Popular Astronomy*, was published in 1880, and **e**_____ 114) sold 130,000 copies. With his own funds, he built an **o**_____ 115) at Juvisy and spent May to November of each year there. In 1887, he **f**_____ 116) the French Astronomical Society and **s**_____ 117) as **e**_____ 118) of its monthly **p**_____ 119) .

Camille Flammarion은 프랑스 Montigny-le-Roi에서 태어났다. 그는 어린 나이에 천문학에 흥미가 생겼고, 불과 16세에 그는 세상의 기원에 관한 책을 썼다. 그 원고는 그 당시 출판되지 않았지만, Paris Observatory의 관리자인 Urbain Le Verrier의 관심을 끌게 되었다. 그는 1858년에 Le Verrier의 조수가 되었고 계산원으로 일했다. 19세에 그는 The Plurality of Inhabited Worlds라는 또 다른 책을 썼는데, 이 책에서 그는 외계에 생명체가 존재한다고 열정적으로 주장했다. 그의 가장 성공적인 저서인 Popular Astronomy는 1880년에 출판되었고, 결국 130,000부가 판매되었다. 자신의 자금으로 그는 Juvisy에 천문대를 세웠고, 매년 5월에서 11월까지 그곳에서 지냈다. 1887년에 그는 French Astronomical Society를 설립했고 그것의 월간 간행물의 편집자로 일했다.

## 29

There is little **d**_____120) that we are driven by the **s**_____121) date. Once an item is past that date it goes into the **w**_____122) stream, further **i**_____123) its **c**_____124) **f**_____125) . Remember those items have already travelled hundreds of miles to reach the **s**_____126) and once they go into waste they start a new carbon mile journey. But we all make our own **j**_____127) about sell-by dates; those **b**_____128) up during the Second World War are often **s**_____129) of the terrible waste they believe such **c**_____130) **e**_____131) . The **m**_____132) of the food has a view when making or growing something that by the time the product reaches the shelves it has already been **t**_____133) for so many days and possibly many miles. The manufacturer then decides that a product can **r**_____134) be consumed within say 90 days and 90 days minus so many days for travelling **g**_____135) the sell-by date. But whether it becomes **t**_____136) is something each individual can decide. It would seem to make sense not to buy large packs of **p**_____137) goods but non-perishable items may become **c**_____138) .

우리가 판매 유효 기한에 따라 움직인다는 것은 의심할 여지가 거의 없다. 일단 어떤 품목이 그 기한을 지나면 폐기물 흐름으로 들어가고, 이는 그것의 탄소 발자국을 더욱더 증가시킨다. 그러한 품목들이 선반에 도달하기 위해 이미 수백 마일을 이동했고 일단 그것들이 버려지게 되면 그것들은 새로운 탄소 마일 여정을 시작한다는 것을 기억하라. 그러나 우리 모두는 판매 유효 기한에 대해 자신만의 판단을 내린다. 가령, 제2차 세계 대전 중에 자란 사람들은 그들이 생각하기에 그러한 경고가 조장하는 끔찍한 낭비를 자주 경멸한다. 식품 제조업자는 무엇인가를 만들거나 재배할 때 제품이 선반에 도달할 때에는 그것은 이미 매우 오랫동안 그리고 아마도 상당한 거리를 이동해 왔다는 관점을 가지고 있다. 그래서 제조업자는 제품이 이를테면 90일 이내에는 무리 없이 소비될 수 있고 90일에서 이동에 필요한 많은 날들을 뺀 것이 판매 유효 기한이 된다고 결정한다. 그러나 그것이 유독해지는지는 각 개인이 결정할 수 있는 것이다. 큰 묶음의 상하기 쉬운 제품을 사지 않는 것이 이치에 맞는 것으로 보이겠지만, 상하지 않는 품목들의 경우에는 비용 효율이 높아질 수도 있다.

## 30

The "jolt" of caffeine does wear off. Caffeine is **r**_____139) from your system by an enzyme within your **l**_____140) which gradually **d**_____141) it over time. Based in large part on **g**_____142) some people have a more **e**_____143) version of the enzyme that **d**_____144) caffeine, allowing the liver to **r**_____145) clear it from the bloodstream. These rare individuals can drink an espresso with dinner and fall **f**_____146) asleep at **m**_____147) without a problem. Others, however, have a slower-acting version of the enzyme. It takes far longer for their system to **e**_____148) the same amount of caffeine. As a result, they are very **s**_____149) to caffeine's effects. One cup of tea or coffee in the morning will last much of the day, and **s**_____150) they have a second cup, even early in the afternoon, they will find it difficult to fall **a**_____151) in the evening. **A**_____152) also alters the speed of caffeine **c**_____153) : the older we are, the **l**_____154) it takes our brain and body to **r**_____155) caffeine, and thus the more **s**_____156) we become in later life to caffeine's **s**_____157) **i**_____158)

카페인의 '충격'은 확실히 점차 사라진다. 카페인은 여러분의 간 안에 있는 효소에 의해 여러분의 신체로부터 제거되는데, 이 효소는 시간이 지남에 따라 그것을 점진적으로 분해한다. 대체로 유전적 특징 때문에, 어떤 사람들은 카페인을 분해하는 더 효율적인 형태의 효소를 갖고 있는데, 이는 간이 그것을 혈류로부터 더 빠르게 제거할 수 있도록 한다. 이 몇 안 되는 사람들은 저녁과 함께 에스프레소를 마시고도 아무 문제 없이 한밤중에 깊이 잠들 수 있다. 그러나 다른 사람들은 더 느리게 작용하는 형태의 효소를 가지고 있다. 그들의 신체가 같은 양의 카페인을 제거하는 데 훨씬 더 오랜 시간이 걸린다. 결과적으로, 그들은 카페인의 효과에 매우 민감하다. 아침에 마시는 한 잔의 차나 커피는 그날 대부분 동안 지속될 것이고, 심지어 이른 오후라도, 두 번째 잔을 마신다면, 그들은 저녁에 잠드는 것이 어렵다는 것을 알 것이다. 노화는 또한 카페인 제거 속도를 변화시킨다. 즉, 우리가 나이가 들수록 우리의 뇌와 신체가 카페인을 제거하는 것이 더 오래 걸리고, 따라서 우리는 노후에 카페인의 수면을 방해하는 효과에 더 민감해진다.

# 31

Rebels may think they're rebels, but c_____159) marketers influence them just like the rest of us. Saying, "Everyone is doing it" may t_____160) some people off from an idea. These people will look for a_____161) which (if cleverly planned) can be exactly what a marketer or p_____162) wants you to believe. If I want you to consider an idea, and know you strongly r_____163) popular o_____164) in favor of m_____165) your i_____166) and uniqueness, I would present the m_____167) option first, which you would r_____168) in favor of my actual p_____169) We are often tricked when we try to m_____170) a position of d_____171) People use this r_____172) to make us "independently" choose an option which s_____173) their p_____174) . Some brands have taken full effect of our d_____175) towards the mainstream and positioned themselves as r_____176) ; which has created even stronger brand l_____177)

반항자들은 자신들이 반항자라고 생각할지도 모르지만, 영리한 마케터들은 나머지 우리에게 그러듯이 그들에게 영향을 준다. "모두가 그것을 하고 있다."라고 말하는 것은 일부 사람들로 하여금 어떠한 생각에 대해 흥미를 잃게 할지도 모른다. 이 사람들은 대안을 찾을 것이고, 그것은 (만약 영리하게 계획된다면) 정확히 마케터나 설득자가 여러분이 믿기를 원하는 것일 수 있다. 만약 내가 여러분이 한 아이디어를 고려하길 바라고, 여러분의 독립성과 유일성을 유지하기 위해 대중적인 의견을 강하게 거부한다는 것을 안다면, 나는 대다수가 선택하는 것을 먼저 제시할 것이고, 여러분은 내가 실제로 선호하는 것에 맞게 그것을 거부할 것이다. 우리는 반항의 입장을 유지하려고 할 때 종종 속는다. 사람들은 우리가 그들의 목적에 맞는 선택지를 '독자적으로' 택하도록 만들기 위해 이러한 반전을 사용한다. 일부 브랜드들은 주류에 대한 우리의 반항을 완전히 활용하여 스스로를 반항자로 자리매김해 왔고, 이는 훨씬 더 강력한 브랜드 충성도를 만들어 왔다.

# 32

A typical soap opera creates an a_____178) world, in which a highly complex web of relationships connects f_____179) characters that exist first only in the minds of the program's creators and are then recreated in the minds of the viewer. If you were to think about how much human p_____180) law, and even everyday physics the viewer must know in order to follow and s_____181) about the plot, you would discover it is c_____182) — at least as much as the knowledge r_____183) to follow and s_____184) about a piece of modern m_____185) and in most cases, much more. Yet viewers follow soap operas with e_____186) How are they able to cope with such a_____187) ? Because, of course, the a_____188) is built on an extremely familiar f_____189) The characters in a soap opera and the relationships between them are very much like the real people and relationships we experience every day. The a_____190) of a soap opera is only a step r_____191) from the real world. The m_____192) "training" required to follow a soap opera is provided by our everyday lives.

전형적인 드라마는 추상적인 세계를 만들어내며, 그 세계에서는 프로그램 제작자들의 마음속에만 먼저 존재하고 그리고 나서 시청자의 마음속에 재현되는 허구의 캐릭터들을 매우 복잡한 관계망이 연결한다. 만약 줄거리를 따라가고 그것에 대해 추측하기 위해 시청자가 얼마나 많은 인간 심리학, 법, 그리고 심지어 일상에서의 물리학을 알아야 하는지에 대해 생각한다면, 여러분은 그것이 상당하다는 것을, 즉 적어도 현대 수학의 한 부분을 따라가고 그것에 대해 추측하는 데 필요한 지식만큼이라는 것, 그리고 대부분의 경우 훨씬 더 많다는 것을 발견할 것이다. 하지만 시청자들은 드라마를 쉽게 따라간다. 그들은 어떻게 그런 추상에 대처할 수 있을까? 왜냐하면, 당연하게도, 그 추상은 매우 친숙한 틀 위에서 만들어졌기 때문이다. 드라마 속 인물들과 그들 사이의 관계는 우리가 매일 경험하는 실제 사람들 및 관계와 매우 흡사하다. 드라마의 추상은 현실 세계에서 불과 한 걸음 떨어져 있다. 드라마를 따라가기 위해 필요한 정신적 '훈련'은 우리의 일상에 의해 제공된다.

## 33

As always happens with natural s_____193) bats and their p_____194) have  been engaged in a life-or-death sensory arms race for millions of years. It's believed that hearing in moths a_____195) specifically in response to the t_____196) of being eaten by bats. (Not all insects can hear.) Over millions of years, moths have evolved the ability to d_____197) sounds at ever higher f_____198) and, as they have, the f_____199) of bats' v_____200) have risen, too. Some moth species have also evolved s_____201) on their wings and a fur-like coat on their bodies; both act as " a_____202) c_____203) ," by absorbing sound waves in the frequencies e_____204) by bats, thereby preventing those sound waves from bouncing back. The B-2 bomber and other "stealth" a_____205) have fuselages m_____206) of materials that do something similar with radar beams.

자연 선택에서 항상 그렇듯이, 박쥐와 그 먹잇감은 수백만 년 동안 생사를 가르는 감각 군비 경쟁에 참여해 왔다. 나방의 청력은 특히 박쥐에게 잡아먹히는 위험에 대한 반응으로 생겨난 것으로 여겨진다. (모든 곤충이 들을 수 있는 것은 아니다.) 수백만 년 동안, 나방은 계속 더 높아진 주파수의 소리를 감지하는 능력을 진화시켰고, 그것들이 그렇게 함에 따라 박쥐의 발성 주파수도 높아졌다. 일부 나방 종은 또한 날개의 비늘과 몸에 모피와 같은 외피를 진화시켰다. 둘 다 '음향 위장'의 역할을 하는데, 박쥐에 의해 방출되는 주파수의 음파를 흡수함으로써, 그것으로 음파가 되돌아가는 것을 방지한다. B-2 폭격기와 그 밖의 '스텔스' 항공기는 레이더 전파에 대해 유사한 것을 하는 재료로 만들어진 기체를 가지고 있다.

## 34

Much of human thought is designed to s_____207) out information and to sort the rest into a m_____ _208) condition. The i_____209) of data from our senses could create an o_____210) c_____211) , especially given the enormous amount of information a_____212) in culture and society. Out of all the sensory impressions and possible information, it is v_____213) to find a small amount that is most relevant to our individual needs and to organize that into a u_____214) stock of knowledge. E_____215) a_____216) some of this work, helping to s_____217) out information that is i_____218) to what is expected, and focusing our attention on clear c_____219) The processes of learning and memory are marked by a steady e_____220) of information. People notice only a part of the world around them. Then, only a f_____221) of what they notice gets p_____222) and stored into memory. And only part of what gets c_____223) to memory can be r_____224)

인간 사고의 많은 부분은 정보를 걸러내고 나머지는 처리하기 쉬운 상태로 분류하도록 설계된다. 특히 문화와 사회에서 이용할 수 있는 엄청난 양의 정보를 고려할 때, 우리의 감각에서 오는 데이터의 유입은 압도적인 혼란을 야기할 수 있다. 모든 감각적 인상과 가능한 정보 중에서, 우리의 개인적인 필요와 가장 관련이 있는 소량을 찾고 그것을 사용 가능한 지식체로 구성하는 것이 중요하다. 예상들은 이 작업의 일부를 수행하여 예상되는 것과 무관한 정보를 걸러내는 데 도움이 되고, 명확한 모순에 우리의 주의를 집중시킨다. 학습과 기억의 과정은 정보의 지속적인 제거로 특징지어진다. 사람들은 그들 주변 세계의 일부분만을 인지한다. 그런 다음, 그들이 알아차린 것의 일부만 처리되어 기억에 저장된다. 그리고 기억에 넘겨진 것의 일부만 생각해 낼 수 있다.

## 35

The irony of early d_____225) in Europe is that it t_____226) and prospered precisely because European r_____227) for a very long time were remarkably w_____228) . For more than a m_____229) after the fall of Rome, European rulers l_____230) the ability to a_____231) what their people were producing and to l_____232) substantial taxes based on this. The most striking way to i_____233) European weakness is to show how little r_____234) they collected. Europeans would eventually develop strong systems of revenue collection, but it took them an a_____235) long time to do so. In m_____236) times, and for part of the early modern era, Chinese e_____237) and Muslim caliphs were able to e_____238) much more of economic production than any European ruler with the e_____239) of small city-states.

유럽 초기 민주주의의 아이러니는 바로 유럽의 통치자들이 매우 오랫동안 현저하게 약했기 때문에 그것이 번성하고 번영했다는 것이다. 로마의 멸망 후 천 년 넘게, 유럽의 통치자들은 백성들이 생산하고 있었던 것을 평가하고 이를 바탕으로 상당한 세금을 부과할 능력이 부족했다. 유럽의 약함을 설명하는 가장 눈에 띄는 방법은 그들이 거둔 세입이 얼마나 적은지를 보여주는 것이다. 유럽인들은 결국 강력한 세입 징수 시스템을 개발했지만, 그렇게 하는 데는 엄청나게 오랜 시간이 걸렸다. 중세와 초기 근대의 일부 동안, 중국의 황제들과 이슬람 문명의 칼리프들은 작은 도시 국가들을 제외한 어떤 유럽 통치자들보다 경제적 생산물에서 훨씬 더 많은 것을 얻어낼 수 있었다.

## 36

If you drive down a busy street, you will find many c_____240) businesses, often right next to one another. For example, in most places a consumer in search of a quick meal has many choices, and more fast-food restaurants appear all the time. These competing firms a_____241) heavily. The t_____242) is to see advertising as driving up the price of a product without any b_____243) to the consumer. However, this m_____244) doesn't a_____245) for _____246) firms advertise. In markets where competitors sell slightly d_____247) products, advertising enables firms to i_____248) their customers about new products and services. Yes, costs rise, but consumers also g_____249) information to help make p_____250) decisions. Consumers also benefit from added v_____251) , and we all get a product that's pretty close to our v_____252) of a perfect good — and no other market structure d_____253) that outcome.

만약 여러분이 번화한 거리를 운전한다면, 여러분은 자주 서로의 바로 옆에서 경쟁하는 많은 업체들을 발견할 것이다. 예를 들어, 대부분의 장소에서 빠른 식사를 찾는 소비자는 많은 선택권을 가지고 있고, 더 많은 패스트푸드 식당들이 항상 나타난다. 이 경쟁하는 회사들은 광고를 많이 한다. 광고를 소비자에게 어떤 혜택도 없이 제품의 가격을 올리는 것으로 보기 쉽다. 그러나 이러한 오해는 회사들이 광고하는 이유를 설명하지 않는다. 경쟁사들이 약간 차별화된 제품들을 판매하는 시장에서, 광고는 회사들이 그들의 소비자들에게 새로운 제품과 서비스를 알릴 수 있게 해 준다. 물론 가격이 상승하기는 하지만, 소비자들은 구매 결정을 내리는 데 도움이 되는 정보도 얻는다. 소비자들은 또한 추가된 다양성으로부터 혜택을 얻고, 우리 모두는 완벽한 제품에 대한 우리의 상상에 매우 근접한 제품을 얻는데, 다른 어떤 시장 구조도 그러한 결과를 제공하지 않는다.

## 37

Architects might say a machine can never design an i_____254) or impressive building because a computer cannot be "creative." Yet consider the Elbphilharmonie, a new concert hall in Hamburg, which contains a r_____255) beautiful a_____256) c_____257) of ten thousand interlocking acoustic panels. It is the sort of space that makes one i_____258) think that only a human being — and a human with a remarkably refined creative s_____259) at that — could design something so a_____260) impressive. Yet the auditorium was, in fact, designed algorithmically, using a technique known as "parametric design." The architects gave the system a set of c_____261) and it generated a set of possible designs for the architects to choose from. Similar software has been used to design l_____262) bicycle frames and sturdier chairs, among much else. Are these systems b_____263) "creatively"? No, they are using lots of processing power to b_____264) generate varied possible designs, working in a very different way from a human being.

건축가들은 컴퓨터가 '창의적'일 수 없기 때문에 기계는 결코 혁신적이거나 인상적인 건물을 디자인할 수 없다고 말할지도 모른다. 그러나 Hamburg에 있는, 1만 개의 서로 맞물리는 음향 패널로 구성된 놀랍도록 아름다운 강당을 포함하는 새로운 콘서트 홀인 Elbphilharmonie를 생각해보라. 그것은 인간만이, 그리고 그것도 놀랍도록 세련된 창의적 감수성을 가진 인간만이, 그토록 미적으로 인상적인 것을 디자인할 수 있다고 본능적으로 생각하게 만드는 종류의 공간이다. 그러나 실제로 그 강당은 '파라메트릭 디자인'이라고 알려진 기술을 사용하여 알고리즘에 의한 방식으로 디자인되었다. 건축가들은 그 시스템에 일련의 기준을 부여했고, 그것은 그 건축가들이 선택할 수 있는 일련의 가능한 디자인을 만들어냈다. 유사한 소프트웨어가 다른 많은 것들 중에서도 경량 자전거 프레임과 더 튼튼한 의자를 디자인하는 데 사용되어 왔다. 이러한 시스템들은 '창의적으로' 작동하고 있는가? 아니다, 그것들은 인간과는 매우 다른 방식으로 작동하면서 다양한 가능한 디자인을 닥치는 대로 만들기 위해 많은 처리 능력을 사용하고 있다.

## 38

The brain is a high-energy consumer of g_____265) which is its fuel. Although the brain accounts for m_____266) 3 percent of a person's body weight, it consumes 20 percent of the a_____267) fuel. Your brain can't s_____268) fuel, however, so it has to "pay as it goes." Since your brain is incredibly a_____269) it economizes its fuel resources. Thus, during a period of high stress, it s_____270) away from the analysis of the nuances of a situation to a s_____271) and fixed focus on the stressful situation at hand. You don't sit back and speculate about the meaning of life when you are stressed. Instead, you d_____272) all your energy to trying to figure out what action to take. Sometimes, however, this shift from the higher-thinking parts of the brain to the a_____273) and r_____274) parts of the brain can lead you to do something too quickly, without thinking.

뇌는 그것의 연료인 포도당의 고에너지 소비자이다. 비록 뇌는 사람 체중의 단지 3퍼센트를 차지하지만, 사용 가능한 연료의 20퍼센트를 소비한다. 그러나 여러분의 뇌는 연료를 저장할 수 없고, 따라서 '활동하는 대로 대가를 지불'해야 한다. 여러분의 뇌는 놀라울 정도로 적응력이 뛰어나기 때문에, 그것의 연료 자원을 경제적으로 사용한다. 따라서, 극심한 스트레스를 받는 기간 동안, 뇌는 상황의 미묘한 차이의 분석에서 당면한 스트레스 상황에 대한 단일하고 고정된 초점으로 이동한다. 여러분은 스트레스를 받을 때 앉아서 삶의 의미에 대해 사색하지 않는다. 대신에, 여러분은 어떤 행동을 취해야 할지 알아내려고 노력하는 데 모든 에너지를 쏟는다. 그러나 때때로 뇌의 고차원적 사고 영역에서 자동적이고 반사적인 영역으로의 이러한 이동은 여러분이 무언가를 생각 없이 너무 빨리하도록 이끌 수 있다.

(.hwp) (.pdf) → www.englishjmygod.com

# 39

Much research has been carried out on the causes of **e**_____275) an issue that is important from both a theoretical and **p**_____276) standpoint: identifying the **d**_____277) of work engagement may enable us to **m**_____278) or influence it. The **c**_____279) of engagement fall into two major camps: situational and personal. The most **i**_____280) **s**_____281) causes are job resources, feedback and leadership, the latter, of course, being responsible for job resources and feedback. Indeed, leaders influence engagement by giving their employees honest and **c**_____282) feedback on their performance, and by providing them with the necessary resources that enable them to perform their job well. It is, however, **n**_____283) that although **e**_____284) drives job performance, job performance also drives engagement. In other words, when employees are able to do their jobs well — to the point that they match or **e**_____285) their own expectations and **a**_____286) — they will engage more, be proud of their **a**_____287) and find work more **m**_____288) This is especially **e**_____289) when people are employed in jobs that **a**_____290) with their values.

몰입의 원인에 대한 많은 연구가 수행되어왔는데, 이는 이론적 그리고 실제적 둘 다의 관점에서 중요한 문제이다. 업무 몰입의 동기를 알아내는 것은 우리가 그것을 조작하거나 그것에 영향을 주는 것을 가능하게 할지도 모른다. 몰입의 원인은 상황적인 것과 개인적인 것 두 가지 주요한 분야로 나뉜다. 가장 영향력 있는 상황적 원인은 직무 자원, 피드백, 그리고 리더십이며, 후자는 물론 직무 자원과 피드백에 대한 책임이 있다. 실제로 리더들은 직원들에게 그들의 수행에 대한 솔직하고 건설적인 피드백을 제공하고 직원들이 자신의 직무를 잘 수행할 수 있도록 필요한 자원을 제공함으로써 몰입에 영향을 미친다. 그러나 주목할 점은 몰입이 직무 수행의 동기가 되지만, 직무 수행도 몰입의 동기가 된다는 것이다. 즉, 직원들이 그들 자신의 기대와 포부에 부합하거나 그것을 능가할 정도로 그들의 직무를 잘 수행할 수 있을 때 직원들은 더 많이 몰입하고, 그들의 성과를 자랑스러워하며, 업무를 더 의미 있게 생각할 것이다. 이것은 사람들이 그들의 가치와 일치하는 직무에 종사했을 때 특히 분명하다.

# 40

In 2006, researchers **c**_____291) a study on the motivations for helping after the September 11th terrorist attacks against the United States. In the study, they found that individuals who gave money, blood, **g**_____292) or other forms of **a**_____293) because of other-focused motives (giving to reduce another's **d**_____294)) were almost four times more likely to still be giving support one year later than those whose **o**_____295) motivation was to reduce personal distress. This effect likely stems from differences in emotional **a**_____296) . The events of September 11th **e**_____297) affected people throughout the United States. Those who gave to reduce their own distress reduced their emotional **a**_____298) with their **i**_____299) gift, **d**_____300) that emotional **d**_____301) . However, those who gave to reduce others' distress did not stop empathizing with **v**_____302) who continued to **s**_____303) long after the attacks.

2006년에 연구자들은 미국을 향한 9.11 테러 공격 이후에 도움을 주려는 동기에 대한 연구를 수행했다. 그 연구에서, 그들은 타인에게 초점을 맞춘 동기(다른 사람의 곤란을 줄이기 위해 베푸는 것) 때문에 돈, 혈액, 물품, 또는 다른 형태의 도움을 주었던 사람들이 자신의 고통을 줄이는 것이 원래 동기였던 사람들보다 일 년 후에도 여전히 지원을 제공할 가능성이 거의 네 배 더 높다는 것을 발견했다. 이 결과는 감정적 자극의 차이에서 비롯된 것 같다. 9.11의 사건들은 미국 전역의 사람들에게 감정적으로 영향을 미쳤다. 자기 자신의 고통을 줄이기 위해 베푼 사람들은 초기의 베풂을 통해 그 감정적 고통을 해소하면서 감정적 자극을 줄였다. 하지만, 다른 사람들의 고통을 줄이기 위해 베푼 사람들은 공격 이후 오랫동안 계속해서 고군분투하는 피해자들에게 공감하기를 멈추지 않았다.

## 41 ~ 42

In England in the 1680s, it was **u**_____ 304) to live to the age of fifty. This was a period when knowledge was not **s**_____ 305) widely, there were few books and most people could not read. As a consequence, knowledge passed down through the **o**_____ 306) traditions of stories and shared experiences. And since older people had **a**_____ 307) more knowledge, the social **n**_____ 308) was that to be over fifty was to be wise. This social **p**_____ 309) of age began to shift with the **a**_____ 310) of new technologies such as the printing press. Over time, as more books were printed, **l**_____ 311) increased, and the oral traditions of knowledge transfer began to **f**_____ 312) With the fading of oral traditions, the wisdom of the old became less important and as a consequence being over fifty was no longer seen as **s**_____ 313) wisdom.

We are living in a **p**_____ 314) when the gap between **c**_____ 315) and biological age is changing fast and where social norms are struggling to adapt. In a video produced by the AARP (formerly the American Association of **R**_____ 316) Persons), young people were **a**_____ 317) to do **v**_____ 318) activities 'just like an old person'. When older people **j**_____ 319) them in the video, the gap between the **s**_____ 320) and the older people's actual **b**_____ 321) was **s**_____ 322) It is clear that in today's world our social norms need to be **u**_____ 323) quickly.

1680년대 영국에서는 50세까지 사는 것은 이례적인 일이었다. 이 시기는 지식이 널리 보급되지 않았고, 책이 거의 없었으며, 대부분의 사람들이 읽을 수 없었던 때였다. 결과적으로, 지식은 이야기와 공유된 경험이라는 구전 전통을 통해 전수되었다. 그리고 더 나이 든 사람들이 더 많은 지식을 축적했기 때문에 사회적 규범은 50세가 넘으면 지혜롭다는 것이었다. 나이에 대한 이런 사회적 인식은 인쇄기와 같은 새로운 기술의 출현으로 변화하기 시작했다. 시간이 지나면서 더 많은 책이 인쇄됨에 따라 문해력이 증가했고, 지식 전달의 구전 전통이 사라지기 시작했다. 구전 전통이 사라지면서 노인들의 지혜는 덜 중요해졌고, 결과적으로 50세가 넘은 것은 더 이상 지혜로움을 의미하는 것으로 여겨지지 않았다.
우리는 생활 연령과 생물학적 연령 사이의 격차가 빠르게 변하고 사회적 규범이 적응하기 위해 분투하는 시기에 살고 있다. AARP(이전의 American Association of Retired Persons)에 의해 제작된 영상에서 젊은이들은 다양한 활동을 '마치 꼭 노인처럼' 하도록 요청받았다. 영상에서 노인들이 그들에 합류했을 때, 고정관념과 노인들의 실제 행동 사이의 격차는 두드러졌다. 오늘날의 세상에서 우리의 사회적 규범은 신속하게 최신화되어야 한다는 것이 분명하다.

(.hwp) (.pdf) → www.englishjmygod.com

## 43 ~ 45

When Jack was a young man in his early twenties during the 1960s, he had tried to work in his father's i_____324) business, as was expected of him. His two older brothers fit in easily and seemed to enjoy their work. But Jack was bored with the insurance industry. "It was worse than being bored," he said. "I felt like I was dying inside." Jack felt drawn to hair styling and dreamed of owning a hair shop with a lively environment. He was sure that he would enjoy the creative and social a_____325) of it and that he'd be successful. When he was twenty-six, Jack approached his father and expressed his i_____326) of leaving the business to become a hairstylist. As Jack anticipated, his father r_____327) and accused Jack of being selfish, ungrateful, and unmanly. In the face of his father's fury, Jack felt c_____328) and fear. His resolve became weak. But then a force filled his chest and he stood firm in his decision. In following his path, Jack not only ran three f_____329) hair shops, but also helped his clients experience their inner beauty by listening and encouraging them when they faced dark times. His love for his work led to d_____330) time and talent at nursing homes, which in turn led to becoming a hospice volunteer, and eventually to starting fundraising efforts for the hospice program in his community. And all this laid a strong stepping stone for another c_____331) move in his life. When, after having two healthy children of their own, Jack and his wife, Michele, decided to bring an o_____332) child into their family, his father threatened to disown them. Jack understood that his father feared adoption, in this case especially because the child was of a different r_____333) background than their family. Jack and Michele risked rejection and went ahead with the adoption. It took years but eventually Jack's father loved the little girl and accepted his son's independent choices. Jack realized that, although he often felt fear and still does, he has always had courage. In fact, courage was the s_____334) around which he had built r_____335) into his life.

Jack은 1960년대에 20대 초반의 청년이었을 때, 그에게 기대됐던 대로 그의 아버지의 보험 회사에서 일하려고 노력했다. 그의 두 형은 쉽게 적응했고 자신들의 일을 즐기는 것처럼 보였다. 그러나 Jack은 보험 업계에 싫증이 났다. "그것은 지루한 것보다 더 나빴다."라고 그는 말했다. "나는 내면이 죽어가는 것 같았다." Jack은 미용에 매력을 느꼈고 활기찬 분위기의 미용실을 갖는 것을 꿈꿨다. 그는 자신이 그것의 창의적이고 사교적인 측면을 즐길 것이고 성공할 것이라고 확신했다. 26세가 되었을 때, Jack은 아버지에게 가서 미용사가 되기 위해 회사를 떠나겠다는 의사를 밝혔다. Jack이 예상했던 대로, 그의 아버지는 화를 내며 Jack이 이기적이고, 배은망덕하며 남자답지 못하다고 비난했다. 아버지의 분노 앞에서, Jack은 혼란과 두려움을 느꼈다. 그의 결심은 약해졌다. 그러나 그때 어떤 힘이 그의 가슴을 채웠고 그는 자신의 결정에 확고했다. 자신의 길을 가면서, Jack은 세 개의 번창하는 미용실을 운영했을 뿐만 아니라, 또한 고객들이 어두운 시기에 직면했을 때 그들의 말을 듣고 격려함으로써 그들이 가진 내면의 아름다움을 경험하도록 도왔다. 그의 일에 대한 사랑은 요양원에서 시간과 재능을 기부하는 것으로 이어졌고, 이는 결과적으로 호스피스 자원봉사자가 되고, 마침내는 그의 지역사회에서 호스피스 프로그램을 위한 기금 모금 운동을 시작하는 것으로 이어졌다. 그리고 이 모든 것은 그의 삶에서 또 다른 용기 있는 움직임을 위한 견고한 디딤돌을 놓았다. Jack과 그의 아내 Michele이 두 명의 건강한 아이를 낳은 후, 고아가 된 아이를 그들의 가정에 데려오기로 결정했을 때, 그의 아버지는 그들과 의절하겠다고 위협했다. Jack은 자신의 아버지가 입양을 두려워한다는 것을, 이 경우에는 특히 그 아이가 그들의 가족과 다른 인종적 배경을 가지고 있었기 때문임을 이해했다. Jack과 Michele은 거부의 위험을 무릅쓰고 입양을 진행했다. 몇 년이 걸렸지만, 결국 Jack의 아버지는 그 어린 여자아이를 사랑했고 자기 아들의 독립적인 선택을 받아들였다. Jack은 비록 자주 두려움을 느꼈고 여전히 그렇지만, 자신이 항상 용기가 있다는 것을 깨달았다. 사실, 용기는 그가 자신의 삶에 풍요로움을 쌓아온 발판이었다.

2023 고2 9월 모의고사 ❷ 회차 : 점 / 335점

❶ voca ❷ text ❸ [ / ] ④ _____ ❺ quiz 1 ❻ quiz 2 ❼ quiz 3 ❽ quiz 4 ❾ quiz 5

## 18

To whom it may concern,

I would like to d_____1) your a_____2) to a problem that f_____3) occurs with the No. 35 buses. There is a bus stop about h_____4) along Fenny Road, at which the No.35 buses are supposed to stop. It would appear, however, that some of your drivers are either u_____5) of this bus stop or for some reason choose to i_____6) it, driving p_____7) even though the buses are not full. I would be g_____8) if you could r_____9) your drivers that this bus stop exists and that they should be p_____10) to stop at it. I look forward to seeing an i_____11) in this service soon.

Yours f_____12) John Williams

## 19

My 10-year-old appeared, in d_____13) need of a q_____14) "A quarter? What on earth do you need a quarter for?" My tone bordered on i_____15) I didn't want to be bothered with such a t_____16) demand. "There's a g_____17) sale up the street, and there's something I just gotta have! It only costs a quarter. Please?" I p_____18) a quarter in my son's hand. Moments later, a little voice said, "Here, Mommy, this is for you." I g_____19) down at the hands of my little son and saw a four-inch cream-colored s_____20) of two small children hugging one another. I_____21) at their feet were words that read *It starts with 'L' ends with 'E' and in between are 'O' and 'V.'* As I watched him r_____22) back to the garage sale, I smiled with a heart full of happiness. That 25-cent garage sale p_____23) brought me a lot of joy.

## 20

Managers f_____24) try to play psychologist, to "figure out" why an e_____25) has acted in a certain way. E_____26) with employees in order to understand their point of view can be very h_____27) However, when d_____28) with a problem area, in p_____29) remember that it is not the person who is bad, but the actions e_____30) on the job. A_____31) making s_____32) to employees about personal t_____33) they should change; instead suggest more a_____34) ways of performing. For example, instead of focusing on a person's " u_____35) ," a manager might focus on the fact that the employee "has been late to work seven times this month." It is difficult for employees to change who they are; it is usually much easier for them to change _____36) they act.

(.hwp) (.pdf) → www.englishjmygod.com

## 21

I suspect f_____37) are a little more f_____38) "thinking" than their larger partners. Among trees, each s_____39) fights other species. Let's a_____40) the beeches native to Central Europe could emerge v_____41) in most forests there. Would this really be an advantage? What would happen if a new p_____42) came along that i_____43) most of the beeches and killed them? In that case, wouldn't it be more a_____44) if there were a certain number of other species around — oaks, maples, or firs — that would continue to grow and provide the shade needed for a new generation of young beeches to s_____45) and grow up? D_____46) provides s_____47) for ancient forests. Because f_____48) are also very d_____49) on stable conditions, they support other species underground and protect them from complete c_____50) to e_____51) that one species of tree doesn't manage to d_____52) .

## 22

It's remarkable that p_____53) f_____54) help us r_____55) to such an extent that it shows up in p_____56) tests. If you want to u_____57) you can take some deep breaths, get a massage, or go for a walk — but you can also try simply closing your eyes and f_____58) about some future o_____59) that you might enjoy. But what about when your o_____60) is to make your wish a reality? The l_____61) thing you want to be is r_____62) . You want to be e_____63) enough to get off the couch and lose those pounds or find that job or study for that test, and you want to be m_____64) enough to stay e_____65) even when the i_____66) obstacles or c_____67) arise. The principle of "Dream it. Wish it. Do it." does not hold true, and now we know why: in dreaming it, you u_____68) the energy you need to do it. You put yourself in a t_____69) state of complete happiness, calmness — and i_____70) .

## 23

If cooking is as c_____71) to human i_____72) biology, and culture as the biological a_____73) Richard Wrangham suggests, it stands to r_____74) that the d_____75) of cooking in our time would have serious consequences for modern life, and so it has. Are they all bad? Not at all. The o_____76) of much of the work of cooking to c_____77) has relieved women of what has traditionally been their e_____78) responsibility for f_____79) the family, making it easier for them to work outside the home and have careers. It has h_____80) off many of the d_____81) c_____82) that such a large shift in g_____83) roles and family dynamics was bound to s_____84) . It has r_____85) other pressures in the household, including longer workdays and o_____86) children, and saved us time that we can now i_____87) in other pursuits. It has also allowed us to diversify our diets s_____88) making it possible even for people with no cooking skills and little money to enjoy a whole different c_____89) All that's required is a microwave.

## 24

As you may already know, what and how you buy can be **p**_____90) To whom do you want to give your money? Which companies and corporations do you **v**_____91) and respect? Be **m**_____92) about every purchase by carefully researching the corporations that are taking our money to decide if they **d**_____93) our **s**_____94) Do they have a record of **p**_____95) the environment, or do they have fair-trade practices and an end-of-life plan for the products they make? Are they **c**_____96) to bringing about good in the world? For instance, my family has found a company **p**_____97) recycled, plastic-packaging-free toilet paper with a social **c**_____98) They **c**_____99) 50 percent of their profits to the construction of toilets around the world, and we're **g**_____100) happy to spend our money on this special toilet paper each month. Remember that the **c**_____101) world is built on consumers, so as a consumer you have the power to vote with your **w**_____102) and encourage companies to **e**_____103) healthier and more **s**_____104) practices with every **p**_____105) you choose to make.

## 26

Camille Flammarion was born at Montigny-le-Roi, France. He became interested in **a**_____106) at an early age, and when he was only sixteen he wrote a book on the origin of the world. The **m**_____107) was not published at the time, but it came to the **a**_____108) of Urbain Le Verrier, the director of the Paris Observatory. He became an **a**_____109) to Le Verrier in 1858 and worked as a **c**_____110) At nineteen, he wrote another book **c**_____111) *The Plurality of Inhabited Worlds*, in which he **p**_____112) claimed that life exists outside the planet Earth. His most **s**_____113) work, *Popular Astronomy*, was published in 1880, and **e**_____114) sold 130,000 copies. With his own funds, he built an **o**_____115) at Juvisy and spent May to November of each year there. In 1887, he **f**_____116) the French Astronomical Society and **s**_____117) as **e**_____118) of its monthly **p**_____119) .

## 29

There is little **d**_____120) that we are driven by the **s**_____121) date. Once an item is past that date it goes into the **w**_____122) stream, further **i**_____123) its **c**_____124) **f**_____125) . Remember those items have already travelled hundreds of miles to reach the **s**_____126) and once they go into waste they start a new carbon mile journey. But we all make our own **j**_____127) about sell-by dates; those **b**_____128) up during the Second World War are often **s**_____129) of the terrible waste they believe such **c**_____130) **e**_____131) . The **m**_____132) of the food has a view when making or growing something that by the time the product reaches the shelves it has already been **t**_____133) for so many days and possibly many miles. The manufacturer then decides that a product can **r**_____134) be consumed within say 90 days and 90 days minus so many days for travelling **g**_____135) the sell-by date. But whether it becomes **t**_____136) is something each individual can decide. It would seem to make sense not to buy large packs of **p**_____137) goods but non-perishable items may become **c**_____138) .

# 30

The "jolt" of caffeine does wear off. Caffeine is **r**_____139) from your system by an enzyme within your **l**_____140) which gradually **d**_____141) it over time. Based in large part on **g**_____142) some people have a more **e**_____143) version of the enzyme that **d**_____144) caffeine, allowing the liver to **r**_____145) clear it from the bloodstream. These rare individuals can drink an espresso with dinner and fall **f**_____146) asleep at **m**_____147) without a problem. Others, however, have a slower-acting version of the enzyme. It takes far longer for their system to **e**_____148) the same amount of caffeine. As a result, they are very **s**_____149) to caffeine's effects. One cup of tea or coffee in the morning will last much of the day, and **s**_____150) they have a second cup, even early in the afternoon, they will find it difficult to fall **a**_____ **_151)** in the evening. **A**_____152) also alters the speed of caffeine **c**_____153) : the older we are, the **l**_____154) it takes our brain and body to **r**_____155) caffeine, and thus the more **s**_____156) we become in later life to caffeine's **s**_____157) **i**_____158)

# 31

Rebels may think they're rebels, but **c**_____159) marketers influence them just like the rest of us. Saying, "Everyone is doing it" may **t**_____160) some people off from an idea. These people will look for **a**_____ **_161)** which (if cleverly planned) can be exactly what a marketer or **p**_____162) wants you to believe. If I want you to consider an idea, and know you strongly **r**_____163) popular **o**_____164) in favor of **m**_____165) your **i**_____166) and uniqueness, I would present the **m**_____167) option first, which you would **r**_____168) in favor of my actual **p**_____169) We are often tricked when we try to **m**_____170) a position of **d**_____171) People use this **r**_____172) to make us "independently" choose an option which **s**_____173) their **p**_____174) . Some brands have taken full effect of our **d**_____175) towards the mainstream and positioned themselves as **r**_____176) ; which has created even stronger brand **l**_____177)

# 32

A typical soap opera creates an **a**_____178) world, in which a highly complex web of relationships connects **f**_____179) characters that exist first only in the minds of the program's creators and are then recreated in the minds of the viewer. If you were to think about how much human **p**_____180) law, and even everyday physics the viewer must know in order to follow and **s**_____181) about the plot, you would discover it is **c**_____ **_182)** — at least as much as the knowledge **r**_____183) to follow and **s**_____184) about a piece of modern **m**_____185) and in most cases, much more. Yet viewers follow soap operas with **e**_____186) How are they able to cope with such **a**_____187) ? Because, of course, the **a**_____188) is built on an extremely familiar **f**_____189) The characters in a soap opera and the relationships between them are very much like the real people and relationships we experience every day. The **a**_____190) of a soap opera is only a step **r**_____191) from the real world. The **m**_____192) "training" required to follow a soap opera is provided by our everyday lives.

## 33

As always happens with natural **s**_____193) bats and their **p**_____194) have been engaged in a life-or-death sensory arms race for millions of years. It's believed that hearing in moths **a**_____195) specifically in response to the **t**_____196) of being eaten by bats. (Not all insects can hear.) Over millions of years, moths have evolved the ability to **d**_____197) sounds at ever higher **f**_____198) and, as they have, the **f**_____199) of bats' **v**_____200) have risen, too. Some moth species have also evolved **s**_____201) on their wings and a fur-like coat on their bodies; both act as " **a**_____202) **c**_____203) ," by absorbing sound waves in the frequencies **e**_____204) by bats, thereby preventing those sound waves from bouncing back. The B-2 bomber and other "stealth" **a**_____205) have fuselages **m**_____206) of materials that do something similar with radar beams.

## 34

Much of human thought is designed to **s**_____207) out information and to sort the rest into a **m**_____208) condition. The **i**_____209) of data from our senses could create an **o**_____210) **c**_____211) , especially given the enormous amount of information **a**_____212) in culture and society. Out of all the sensory impressions and possible information, it is **v**_____213) to find a small amount that is most relevant to our individual needs and to organize that into a **u**_____214) stock of knowledge. **E**_____215) **a**_____216) some of this work, helping to **s**_____217) out information that is **i**_____218) to what is expected, and focusing our attention on clear **c**_____219) The processes of learning and memory are marked by a steady **e**_____220) of information. People notice only a part of the world around them. Then, only a **f**_____221) of what they notice gets **p**_____222) and stored into memory. And only part of what gets **c**_____223) to memory can be **r**_____224)

## 35

The irony of early **d**_____225) in Europe is that it **t**_____226) and prospered precisely because European **r**_____227) for a very long time were remarkably **w**_____228) . For more than a **m**_____229) after the fall of Rome, European rulers **l**_____230) the ability to **a**_____231) what their people were producing and to **l**_____232) substantial taxes based on this. The most striking way to **i**_____233) European weakness is to show how little **r**_____234) they collected. Europeans would eventually develop strong systems of revenue collection, but it took them an **a**_____235) long time to do so. In **m**_____236) times, and for part of the early modern era, Chinese **e**_____237) and Muslim caliphs were able to **e**_____238) much more of economic production than any European ruler with the **e**_____239) of small city-states.

## 36

If you drive down a busy street, you will find many **c**_____ 240) businesses, often right next to one another. For example, in most places a consumer in search of a quick meal has many choices, and more fast-food restaurants appear all the time. These competing firms **a**_____ 241) heavily. The **t**_____ 242) is to see advertising as driving up the price of a product without any **b**_____ 243) to the consumer. However, this **m**_____ 244) doesn't **a**_____ 245) for _____ 246) firms advertise. In markets where competitors sell slightly **d**_____ 247) products, advertising enables firms to **i**_____ 248) their customers about new products and services. Yes, costs rise, but consumers also **g**_____ 249) information to help make **p**_____ 250) decisions. Consumers also benefit from added **v**_____ 251) , and we all get a product that's pretty close to our **v**_____ 252) of a perfect good — and no other market structure **d**_____ 253) that outcome.

## 37

Architects might say a machine can never design an **i**_____ 254) or impressive building because a computer cannot be "creative." Yet consider the Elbphilharmonie, a new concert hall in Hamburg, which contains a **r**_____ 255) beautiful **a**_____ 256) **c**_____ 257) of ten thousand interlocking acoustic panels. It is the sort of space that makes one **i**_____ 258) think that only a human being — and a human with a remarkably refined creative **s**_____ 259) at that — could design something so **a**_____ 260) impressive. Yet the auditorium was, in fact, designed algorithmically, using a technique known as "parametric design." The architects gave the system a set of **c**_____ 261) and it generated a set of possible designs for the architects to choose from. Similar software has been used to design **l**_____ 262) bicycle frames and sturdier chairs, among much else. Are these systems **b**_____ 263) "creatively"? No, they are using lots of processing power to **b**_____ 264) generate varied possible designs, working in a very different way from a human being.

## 38

The brain is a high-energy consumer of **g**_____ 265) which is its fuel. Although the brain accounts for **m**_____ 266) 3 percent of a person's body weight, it consumes 20 percent of the **a**_____ 267) fuel. Your brain can't **s**_____ 268) fuel, however, so it has to "pay as it goes." Since your brain is incredibly **a**_____ 269) it economizes its fuel resources. Thus, during a period of high stress, it **s**_____ 270) away from the analysis of the nuances of a situation to a **s**_____ 271) and fixed focus on the stressful situation at hand. You don't sit back and speculate about the meaning of life when you are stressed. Instead, you **d**_____ 272) all your energy to trying to figure out what action to take. Sometimes, however, this shift from the higher-thinking parts of the brain to the **a**_____ 273) and **r**_____ 274) parts of the brain can lead you to do something too quickly, without thinking.

## 39

Much research has been carried out on the causes of **e**_____275) an issue that is important from both a theoretical and **p**_____276) standpoint: identifying the **d**_____277) of work engagement may enable us to **m**_____278) or influence it. The **c**_____279) of engagement fall into two major camps: situational and personal. The most **i**_____280) **s**_____281) causes are job resources, feedback and leadership, the latter, of course, being responsible for job resources and feedback. Indeed, leaders influence engagement by giving their employees honest and **c**_____282) feedback on their performance, and by providing them with the necessary resources that enable them to perform their job well. It is, however, **n**_____283) that although **e**_____284) drives job performance, job performance also drives engagement. In other words, when employees are able to do their jobs well — to the point that they match or **e**_____285) their own expectations and **a**_____286) — they will engage more, be proud of their **a**_____287) and find work more **m**_____288) This is especially **e**_____289) when people are employed in jobs that **a**_____290) with their values.

## 40

In 2006, researchers **c**_____291) a study on the motivations for helping after the September 11th terrorist attacks against the United States. In the study, they found that individuals who gave money, blood, **g**_____292) or other forms of **a**_____293) because of other-focused motives (giving to reduce another's **d**_____294)) were almost four times more likely to still be giving support one year later than those whose **o**_____295) motivation was to reduce personal distress. This effect likely stems from differences in emotional **a**_____296) . The events of September 11th **e**_____297) affected people throughout the United States. Those who gave to reduce their own distress reduced their emotional **a**_____298) with their **i**_____299) gift, **d**_____300) that emotional **d**_____301) . However, those who gave to reduce others' distress did not stop empathizing with **v**_____302) who continued to **s**_____303) long after the attacks.

# 41 ~ 42

In England in the 1680s, it was **u**_____304) to live to the age of fifty. This was a period when knowledge was not **s**_____305) widely, there were few books and most people could not read. As a consequence, knowledge passed down through the **o**_____306) traditions of stories and shared experiences. And since older people had **a**_____307) more knowledge, the social **n**_____308) was that to be over fifty was to be wise. This social **p**_____309) of age began to shift with the **a**_____310) of new technologies such as the printing press. Over time, as more books were printed, **l**_____311) increased, and the oral traditions of knowledge transfer began to **f**_____312) With the fading of oral traditions, the wisdom of the old became less important and as a consequence being over fifty was no longer seen as **s**_____313) wisdom.

   We are living in a **p**_____314) when the gap between **c**_____315) and biological age is changing fast and where social norms are struggling to adapt. In a video produced by the AARP (formerly the American Association of **R**_____316) Persons), young people were **a**_____317) to do **v**_____318) activities 'just like an old person'. When older people **j**_____319) them in the video, the gap between the **s**_____320) and the older people's actual **b**_____321) was **s**_____322) It is clear that in today's world our social norms need to be **u**_____323) quickly.

1680년대 영국에서는 50세까지 사는 것은 이례적인 일이었다. 이 시기는 지식이 널리 보급되지 않았고, 책이 거의 없었으며, 대부분의 사람들이 읽을 수 없었던 때였다. 결과적으로, 지식은 이야기와 공유된 경험이라는 구전 전통을 통해 전수되었다. 그리고 더 나이 든 사람들이 더 많은 지식을 축적했기 때문에 사회적 규범은 50세가 넘으면 지혜롭다는 것이었다. 나이에 대한 이런 사회적 인식은 인쇄기와 같은 새로운 기술의 출현으로 변화하기 시작했다. 시간이 지나면서 더 많은 책이 인쇄됨에 따라 문해력이 증가했고, 지식 전달의 구전 전통이 사라지기 시작했다. 구전 전통이 사라지면서 노인들의 지혜는 덜 중요해졌고, 결과적으로 50세가 넘은 것은 더 이상 지혜로움을 의미하는 것으로 여겨지지 않았다.
   우리는 생활 연령과 생물학적 연령 사이의 격차가 빠르게 변하고 사회적 규범이 적응하기 위해 분투하는 시기에 살고 있다. AARP(이전의 American Association of Retired Persons)에 의해 제작된 영상에서 젊은이들은 다양한 활동을 '마치 꼭 노인처럼' 하도록 요청받았다. 영상에서 노인들이 그들에 합류했을 때, 고정관념과 노인들의 실제 행동 사이의 격차는 두드러졌다. 오늘날의 세상에서 우리의 사회적 규범은 신속하게 최신화되어야 한다는 것이 분명하다.

# 43 ~ 45

When Jack was a young man in his early twenties during the 1960s, he had tried to work in his father's i_____ 324) business, as was expected of him. His two older brothers fit in easily and seemed to enjoy their work. But Jack was bored with the insurance industry. "It was worse than being bored," he said. "I felt like I was dying inside." Jack felt drawn to hair styling and dreamed of owning a hair shop with a lively environment. He was sure that he would enjoy the creative and social a_____ 325) of it and that he'd be successful. When he was twenty-six, Jack approached his father and expressed his i_____ 326) of leaving the business to become a hairstylist. As Jack anticipated, his father r_____ 327) and accused Jack of being selfish, ungrateful, and unmanly. In the face of his father's fury, Jack felt c_____ 328) and fear. His resolve became weak. But then a force filled his chest and he stood firm in his decision. In following his path, Jack not only ran three f_____ 329) hair shops, but also helped his clients experience their inner beauty by listening and encouraging them when they faced dark times. His love for his work led to d_____ 330) time and talent at nursing homes, which in turn led to becoming a hospice volunteer, and eventually to starting fundraising efforts for the hospice program in his community. And all this laid a strong stepping stone for another c_____ 331) move in his life. When, after having two healthy children of their own, Jack and his wife, Michele, decided to bring an o_____ 332) child into their family, his father threatened to disown them. Jack understood that his father feared adoption, in this case especially because the child was of a different r_____ 333) background than their family. Jack and Michele risked rejection and went ahead with the adoption. It took years but eventually Jack's father loved the little girl and accepted his son's independent choices. Jack realized that, although he often felt fear and still does, he has always had courage. In fact, courage was the s_____ 334) around which he had built r_____ 335) into his life.

Jack은 1960년대에 20대 초반의 청년이었을 때, 그에게 기대됐던 대로 그의 아버지의 보험 회사에서 일하려고 노력했다. 그의 두 형은 쉽게 적응했고 자신들의 일을 즐기는 것처럼 보였다. 그러나 Jack은 보험 업계에 싫증이 났다. "그것은 지루한 것보다 더 나빴다."라고 그는 말했다. "나는 내면이 죽어가는 것 같았다." Jack은 미용에 매력을 느꼈고 활기찬 분위기의 미용실을 갖는 것을 꿈꿨다. 그는 자신이 그것의 창의적이고 사교적인 측면을 즐길 것이고 성공할 것이라고 확신했다. 26세가 되었을 때, Jack은 아버지에게 가서 미용사가 되기 위해 회사를 떠나겠다는 의사를 밝혔다. Jack이 예상했던 대로, 그의 아버지는 화를 내며 Jack이 이기적이고, 배은망덕하며 남자답지 못하다고 비난했다. 아버지의 분노 앞에서, Jack은 혼란과 두려움을 느꼈다. 그의 결심은 약해졌다. 그러나 그때 어떤 힘이 그의 가슴을 채웠고 그는 자신의 결정에 확고했다. 자신의 길을 가면서, Jack은 세 개의 번창하는 미용실을 운영했을 뿐만 아니라, 또한 고객들이 어두운 시기에 직면했을 때 그들의 말을 듣고 격려함으로써 그들이 가진 내면의 아름다움을 경험하도록 도왔다. 그의 일에 대한 사랑은 요양원에서 시간과 재능을 기부하는 것으로 이어졌고, 이는 결과적으로 호스피스 자원봉사자가 되고, 마침내는 그의 지역사회에서 호스피스 프로그램을 위한 기금 모금 운동을 시작하는 것으로 이어졌다. 그리고 이 모든 것은 그의 삶에서 또 다른 용기 있는 움직임을 위한 견고한 디딤돌을 놓았다. Jack과 그의 아내 Michele이 두 명의 건강한 아이를 낳은 후, 고아가 된 아이를 그들의 가정에 데려오기로 결정했을 때, 그의 아버지는 그들과 의절하겠다고 위협했다. Jack은 자신의 아버지가 입양을 두려워한다는 것을, 이 경우에는 특히 그 아이가 그들의 가족과 다른 인종적 배경을 가지고 있었기 때문임을 이해했다. Jack과 Michele은 거부의 위험을 무릅쓰고 입양을 진행했다. 몇 년이 걸렸지만, 결국 Jack의 아버지는 그 어린 여자아이를 사랑했고 자기 아들의 독립적인 선택을 받아들였다. Jack은 비록 자주 두려움을 느꼈고 여전히 그렇지만, 자신이 항상 용기가 있다는 것을 깨달았다. 사실, 용기는 그가 자신의 삶에 풍요로움을 쌓아온 발판이었다.

(.hwp) (.pdf) → www.englishjmygod.com

# 2023 고2 9월 모의고사

❶ voca  ❷ text  ❸ [ / ]  ❹ ____  ❺ quiz 1  ❻ quiz 2  ❼ quiz 3  ❽ quiz 4  ❾ quiz 5

☑ 다음 글을 읽고 물음에 답하시오. (18)

It would appear, however, that some of your drivers are either unaware of this bus stop or for some reason choose to ignore it, driving past even though the buses are not full.

To whom it may concern, I would like to draw your attention to a problem that frequently occurs with the No. 35 buses.( ① )  There is a bus stop about halfway along Fenny Road, at which the No.35 buses are supposed to stop.( ② )  I would be grateful if you could remind your drivers that this bus stop exists and that they should be prepared to stop at it.( ③ )  I look forward to seeing an improvement in this service soon.( ④ )  Yours faithfully, John Williams.( ⑤ )

1. 1)글의 흐름으로 보아, 주어진 문장이 들어가기에 가장 적절한 곳은?

☑ 다음 글을 읽고 물음에 답하시오. (19)

Moments later, a little voice said, "Here, Mommy, this is for you".

My 10-year-old appeared, in desperate need of a quarter. "A quarter? What on earth do you need a quarter for"? My tone bordered on irritation.( ① )  I didn't want to be bothered with such a trivial demand.( ② )  "There's a garage sale up the street, and there's something I just gotta have! It only costs a quarter. Please"? I placed a quarter in my son's hand.( ③ )  I glanced down at the hands of my little son and saw a four-inch cream-colored statue of two small children hugging one another.( ④ )  Inscribed at their feet were words that read It starts with 'L' ends with 'E' and in between are 'O' and 'V'. As I watched him race back to the garage sale, I smiled with a heart full of happiness.( ⑤ )  That 25-cent garage sale purchase brought me a lot of joy.

1. 2)글의 흐름으로 보아, 주어진 문장이 들어가기에 가장 적절한 곳은?

☑ 다음 글을 읽고 물음에 답하시오. (20)

However, when dealing with a problem area, in particular, remember that it is not the person who is bad, but the actions exhibited on the job.

Managers frequently try to play psychologist, to "figure out" why an employee has acted in a certain way.( ① )  Empathizing with employees in order to understand their point of view can be very helpful.( ② )  Avoid making suggestions to employees about personal traits they should change;( ③ )  instead suggest more acceptable ways of performing.( ④ )  For example, instead of focusing on a person's "unreliability", a manager might focus on the fact that the employee "has been late to work seven times this month".( ⑤ )  It is difficult for employees to change who they are; it is usually much easier for them to change how they act.

2. 3)글의 흐름으로 보아, 주어진 문장이 들어가기에 가장 적절한 곳은?

☑ 다음 글을 읽고 물음에 답하시오. (21)

In that case, wouldn't it be more advantageous if there were a certain number of other species around — oaks, maples, or firs — that would continue to grow and provide the shade needed for a new generation of young beeches to sprout and grow up?

I suspect fungi are a little more forward "thinking" than their larger partners.( ① )　Among trees, each species fights other species.( ② )　Let's assume the beeches native to Central Europe could emerge victorious in most forests there.( ③ )　Would this really be an advantage? What would happen if a new pathogen came along that infected most of the beeches and killed them?( ④ )　Diversity provides security for ancient forests.( ⑤ )　Because fungi are also very dependent on stable conditions, they support other species underground and protect them from complete collapse to ensure that one species of tree doesn't manage to dominate.

3. 4)글의 흐름으로 보아, 주어진 문장이 들어가기에 가장 적절한 곳은?

☑ 다음 글을 읽고 물음에 답하시오. (22)

The principle of "Dream it. Wish it. Do it". does not hold true, and now we know why: in dreaming it, you undercut the energy you need to do it.

It's remarkable that positive fantasies help us relax to such an extent that it shows up in physiological tests.( ① )　If you want to unwind, you can take some deep breaths, get a massage, or go for a walk — but you can also try simply closing your eyes and fantasizing about some future outcome that you might enjoy.( ② ) But what about when your objective is to make your wish a reality?( ③ )　The last thing you want to be is relaxed.( ④ )　You want to be energized enough to get off the couch and lose those pounds or find that job or study for that test, and you want to be motivated enough to stay engaged even when the inevitable obstacles or challenges arise.( ⑤ )　You put yourself in a temporary state of complete happiness, calmness — and inactivity.

4. 5)글의 흐름으로 보아, 주어진 문장이 들어가기에 가장 적절한 곳은?

☑ 다음 글을 읽고 물음에 답하시오. (23)

It has headed off many of the domestic conflicts that such a large shift in gender roles and family dynamics was bound to spark.

If cooking is as central to human identity, biology, and culture as the biological anthropologist Richard Wrangham suggests, it stands to reason that the decline of cooking in our time would have serious consequences for modern life, and so it has. Are they all bad?( ① )　Not at all. The outsourcing of much of the work of cooking to corporations has relieved women of what has traditionally been their exclusive responsibility for feeding the family, making it easier for them to work outside the home and have careers.( ② ) It has relieved other pressures in the household, including longer workdays and overscheduled children, and saved us time that we can now invest in other pursuits.( ③ )　It has also allowed us to diversify our diets substantially, making it possible even for people with no cooking skills and little money to enjoy a whole different cuisine.( ④ )　All that's required is a microwave.( ⑤ )

5. 6)글의 흐름으로 보아, 주어진 문장이 들어가기에 가장 적절한 곳은?

(.hwp) (.pdf) → www.englishjmygod.com

☑ **다음 글을 읽고 물음에 답하시오.** (24)

> For instance, my family has found a company producing recycled, plastic-packaging-free toilet paper with a social conscience.

As you may already know, what and how you buy can be political.( ① ) To whom do you want to give your money? Which companies and corporations do you value and respect?( ② ) Be mindful about every purchase by carefully researching the corporations that are taking our money to decide if they deserve our support.( ③ ) Do they have a record of polluting the environment, or do they have fair-trade practices and an end-of-life plan for the products they make? Are they committed to bringing about good in the world?( ④ ) They contribute 50 percent of their profits to the construction of toilets around the world, and we're genuinely happy to spend our money on this special toilet paper each month.( ⑤ ) Remember that the corporate world is built on consumers, so as a consumer you have the power to vote with your wallet and encourage companies to embrace healthier and more sustainable practices with every purchase you choose to make.

6. 7)글의 흐름으로 보아, 주어진 문장이 들어가기에 가장 적절한 곳은?

☑ **다음 글을 읽고 물음에 답하시오.** (26)

> At nineteen, he wrote another book called The Plurality of Inhabited Worlds, in which he passionately claimed that life exists outside the planet Earth.

Camille Flammarion was born at Montigny-le-Roi, France.( ① ) He became interested in astronomy at an early age, and when he was only sixteen he wrote a book on the origin of the world.( ② ) The manuscript was not published at the time, but it came to the attention of Urbain Le Verrier, the director of the Paris

Observatory.( ③ ) He became an assistant to Le Verrier in 1858 and worked as a calculator.( ④ ) His most successful work, Popular Astronomy, was published in 1880, and eventually sold 130,000 copies.( ⑤ ) With his own funds, he built an observatory at Juvisy and spent May to November of each year there. In 1887, he founded the French Astronomical Society and served as editor of its monthly publication.

7. 8)글의 흐름으로 보아, 주어진 문장이 들어가기에 가장 적절한 곳은?

☑ **다음 글을 읽고 물음에 답하시오.** (29)

> But whether it becomes toxic is something each individual can decide.

There is little doubt that we are driven by the sell-by date. Once an item is past that date it goes into the waste stream, further increasing its carbon footprint.( ① ) Remember those items have already travelled hundreds of miles to reach the shelves and once they go into waste they start a new carbon mile journey.( ② ) But we all make our own judgement about sell-by dates; those brought up during the Second World War are often scornful of the terrible waste they believe such caution encourages.( ③ ) The manufacturer of the food has a view when making or growing something that by the time the product reaches the shelves it has already been travelling for so many days and possibly many miles.( ④ ) The manufacturer then decides that a product can reasonably be consumed within say 90 days and 90 days minus so many days for travelling gives the sell-by date.( ⑤ ) It would seem to make sense not to buy large packs of perishable goods but non-perishable items may become cost-effective.

8. 9)글의 흐름으로 보아, 주어진 문장이 들어가기에 가장 적절한 곳은?

☑ **다음 글을 읽고 물음에 답하시오.** (30)

> Others, however, have a slower-acting version of the enzyme. It takes far longer for their system to eliminate the same amount of caffeine.

The "jolt" of caffeine does wear off. Caffeine is removed from your system by an enzyme within your liver, which gradually degrades it over time.( ① )   Based in large part on genetics, some people have a more efficient version of the enzyme that degrades caffeine, allowing the liver to rapidly clear it from the bloodstream.( ② )   These rare individuals can drink an espresso with dinner and fall fast asleep at midnight without a problem.( ③ )   As a result, they are very sensitive to caffeine's effects.( ④ )   One cup of tea or coffee in the morning will last much of the day, and should they have a second cup, even early in the afternoon, they will find it difficult to fall asleep in the evening.( ⑤ )   Aging also alters the speed of caffeine clearance: the older we are, the longer it takes our brain and body to remove caffeine, and thus the more sensitive we become in later life to caffeine's sleep-disrupting influence.

9. 10)글의 흐름으로 보아, 주어진 문장이 들어가기에 <u>가장 적절한</u> 곳은?

☑ **다음 글을 읽고 물음에 답하시오.** (31)

> These people will look for alternatives, which (if cleverly planned) can be exactly what a marketer or persuader wants you to believe.

Rebels may think they're rebels, but clever marketers influence them just like the rest of us.( ① )   Saying, "Everyone is doing it" may turn some people off from an idea.( ② )   If I want you to consider an idea, and know you strongly reject popular opinion in favor of maintaining your independence and uniqueness, I would present the majority option first, which you would reject in favor of my actual preference.( ③ )   We are often tricked when we try to maintain a position of defiance.( ④ )   People use this reversal to make us "independently" choose an option which suits their purposes.( ⑤ )   Some brands have taken full effect of our defiance towards the mainstream and positioned themselves as rebels; which has created even stronger brand loyalty.

10. 11)글의 흐름으로 보아, 주어진 문장이 들어가기에 <u>가장 적절한</u> 곳은?

☑ **다음 글을 읽고 물음에 답하시오.** (32)

> Yet viewers follow soap operas with ease. How are they able to cope with such abstraction?

A typical soap opera creates an abstract world, in which a highly complex web of relationships connects fictional characters that exist first only in the minds of the program's creators and are then recreated in the minds of the viewer.( ① )   If you were to think about how much human psychology, law, and even everyday physics the viewer must know in order to follow and speculate about the plot, you would discover it is considerable — at least as much as the knowledge required to follow and speculate about a piece of modern mathematics, and in most cases, much more.( ② )   Because, of course, the abstraction is built on an extremely familiar framework.( ③ )   The characters in a soap opera and the relationships between them are very much like the real people and relationships we experience every day.( ④ )   The abstraction of a soap opera is only a step removed from the real world.( ⑤ )   The mental "training" required to follow a soap opera is provided by our everyday lives.

11. 12)글의 흐름으로 보아, 주어진 문장이 들어가기에 <u>가장 적절한</u> 곳은?

## ☑ 다음 글을 읽고 물음에 답하시오. (33)

Over millions of years, moths have evolved the ability to detect sounds at ever higher frequencies, and, as they have, the frequencies of bats' vocalizations have risen, too.

As always happens with natural selection, bats and their prey have been engaged in a life-or-death sensory arms race for millions of years.( ① )  It's believed that hearing in moths arose specifically in response to the threat of being eaten by bats.( ② )  Not all insects can hear.( ③ )  Some moth species have also evolved scales on their wings and a fur-like coat on their bodies;( ④ ) both act as "acoustic camouflage", by absorbing sound waves in the frequencies emitted by bats, thereby preventing those sound waves from bouncing back.( ⑤ ) The B-2 bomber and other "stealth" aircraft have fuselages made of materials that do something similar with radar beams.

12. 13)글의 흐름으로 보아, 주어진 문장이 들어가기에 가장 적절한 곳은?

## ☑ 다음 글을 읽고 물음에 답하시오. (34)

The processes of learning and memory are marked by a steady elimination of information. People notice only a part of the world around them.

Much of human thought is designed to screen out information and to sort the rest into a manageable condition.( ① )  The inflow of data from our senses could create an overwhelming chaos, especially given the enormous amount of information available in culture and society.( ② )  Out of all the sensory impressions and possible information, it is vital to find a small amount that is most relevant to our individual needs and to organize that into a usable stock of knowledge.( ③ )  Expectancies accomplish some of this work, helping to screen out information that is irrelevant to what is expected, and focusing our attention on clear contradictions.( ④ )  Then, only a fraction of what they notice gets processed and stored into memory.( ⑤ ) And only part of what gets committed to memory can be retrieved.

13. 14)글의 흐름으로 보아, 주어진 문장이 들어가기에 가장 적절한 곳은?

## ☑ 다음 글을 읽고 물음에 답하시오. (35)

And also, they lacked the ability to levy substantial taxes based on this.

The irony of early democracy in Europe is that it thrived and prospered precisely because European rulers for a very long time were remarkably weak.( ① )  For more than a millennium after the fall of Rome, European rulers lacked the ability to assess what their people were producing.( ② )  The most striking way to illustrate European weakness is to show how little revenue they collected.( ③ )  Europeans would eventually develop strong systems of revenue collection, but it took them an awfully long time to do so.( ④ )  In medieval times, and for part of the early modern era, Chinese emperors and Muslim caliphs were able to extract much more of economic production than any European ruler with the exception of small city-states.( ⑤ )

14. 15)글의 흐름으로 보아, 주어진 문장이 들어가기에 가장 적절한 곳은?

☑ **다음 글을 읽고 물음에 답하시오.** (36)

> However, this misconception doesn't account for why firms advertise.

If you drive down a busy street, you will find many competing businesses, often right next to one another.( ① )  For example, in most places a consumer in search of a quick meal has many choices, and more fast-food restaurants appear all the time. These competing firms advertise heavily.( ② )  The temptation is to see advertising as driving up the price of a product without any benefit to the consumer.( ③ )  In markets where competitors sell slightly differentiated products, advertising enables firms to inform their customers about new products and services.( ④ )  Yes, costs rise, but consumers also gain information to help make purchasing decisions.( ⑤ )  Consumers also benefit from added variety, and we all get a product that's pretty close to our vision of a perfect good — and no other market structure delivers that outcome.

15. 16)글의 흐름으로 보아, 주어진 문장이 들어가기에 <u>가장 적절한</u> 곳은?

☑ **다음 글을 읽고 물음에 답하시오.** (37)

> Yet the auditorium was, in fact, designed algorithmically, using a technique known as "parametric design".

Architects might say a machine can never design an innovative or impressive building because a computer cannot be "creative".( ① )  Yet consider the Elbphilharmonie, a new concert hall in Hamburg, which contains a remarkably beautiful auditorium composed of ten thousand interlocking acoustic panels.( ② )  It is the sort of space that makes one instinctively think that only a human being — and a human with a remarkably refined creative sensibility, at that — could design something so aesthetically impressive.( ③ )  The architects gave the system a set of criteria, and it generated a set of possible designs for the architects to choose from.( ④ )  Similar software has been used to design lightweight bicycle frames and sturdier chairs, among much else.( ⑤ )  Are these systems behaving "creatively"? No, they are using lots of processing power to blindly generate varied possible designs, working in a very different way from a human being.

16. 17)글의 흐름으로 보아, 주어진 문장이 들어가기에 <u>가장 적절한</u> 곳은?

☑ **다음 글을 읽고 물음에 답하시오.** (38)

> Instead, you devote all your energy to trying to figure out what action to take.

The brain is a high-energy consumer of glucose, which is its fuel. Although the brain accounts for merely 3 percent of a person's body weight, it consumes 20 percent of the available fuel.( ① )  Your brain can't store fuel, however, so it has to "pay as it goes".( ② )  Since your brain is incredibly adaptive, it economizes its fuel resources.( ③ )  Thus, during a period of high stress, it shifts away from the analysis of the nuances of a situation to a singular and fixed focus on the stressful situation at hand.( ④ )  You don't sit back and speculate about the meaning of life when you are stressed.( ⑤ )  Sometimes, however, this shift from the higher-thinking parts of the brain to the automatic and reflexive parts of the brain can lead you to do something too quickly, without thinking.

17. 18)글의 흐름으로 보아, 주어진 문장이 들어가기에 <u>가장 적절한</u> 곳은?

(.hwp) (.pdf) → www.englishjmygod.com

☑ **다음 글을 읽고 물음에 답하시오.** (39.)

> It is, however, noteworthy that although engagement drives job performance, job performance also drives engagement.

Much research has been carried out on the causes of engagement, an issue that is important from both a theoretical and practical standpoint: identifying the drivers of work engagement may enable us to manipulate or influence it.( ① ) The causes of engagement fall into two major camps: situational and personal.( ② ) The most influential situational causes are job resources, feedback and leadership, the latter, of course, being responsible for job resources and feedback.( ③ ) Indeed, leaders influence engagement by giving their employees honest and constructive feedback on their performance, and by providing them with the necessary resources that enable them to perform their job well.( ④ ) In other words, when employees are able to do their jobs well — to the point that they match or exceed their own expectations and ambitions — they will engage more, be proud of their achievements, and find work more meaningful.( ⑤ ) This is especially evident when people are employed in jobs that align with their values.

18. 19)글의 흐름으로 보아, 주어진 문장이 들어가기에 <u>가장</u> <u>적절한</u> 곳은?

☑ **다음 글을 읽고 물음에 답하시오.** (40.)

> This effect likely stems from differences in emotional arousal.

In 2006, researchers conducted a study on the motivations for helping after the September 11th terrorist attacks against the United States.( ① ) In the study, they found that individuals who gave money, blood, goods, or other forms of assistance because of other-focused motives (giving to reduce another's discomfort) were almost four times more likely to still be giving support one year later than those whose original motivation was to reduce personal distress.( ② ) The events of September 11th emotionally affected people throughout the United States.( ③ ) Those who gave to reduce their own distress reduced their emotional arousal.( ④ ) They reduced themselves with their initial gift, discharging that emotional distress.( ⑤ ) However, those who gave to reduce others' distress did not stop empathizing with victims who continued to struggle long after the attacks.

19. 20)글의 흐름으로 보아, 주어진 문장이 들어가기에 <u>가장</u> <u>적절한</u> 곳은?

☑ **다음 글을 읽고 물음에 답하시오.** (41, 42)

> This social perception of age began to shift with the advent of new technologies such as the printing press.

In England in the 1680s, it was unusual to live to the age of fifty. This was a period when knowledge was not spread widely, there were few books and most people could not read.( ① ) As a consequence, knowledge passed down through the oral traditions of stories and shared experiences. And since older people had accumulated more knowledge, the social norm was that to be over fifty was to be wise.( ② ) Over time, as more books were printed, literacy increased, and the oral traditions of knowledge transfer began to fade.( ③ ) With the fading of oral traditions, the wisdom of the old became less important and as a consequence being over fifty was no longer seen as signifying wisdom. We are living in a period when the gap between chronological and biological age is changing fast and where social norms are struggling to adapt.( ④ ) In a video produced by the AARP (formerly the American Association of Retired Persons), young people were asked to do various activities 'just like an old person'.( ⑤ ) When older people joined them in the video, the gap between the stereotype and the older people's actual behaviour was striking. It is clear that in today's world our social norms need to be updated quickly.

20. 21)글의 흐름으로 보아, 주어진 문장이 들어가기에 <u>가장</u> <u>적절한</u> 곳은?

☑ **다음 글을 읽고 물음에 답하시오.** (41, 42)

> Over time, as more books were printed, literacy increased, and the oral traditions of knowledge transfer began to fade.

In England in the 1680s, it was unusual to live to the age of fifty. This was a period when knowledge was not spread widely, there were few books and most people could not read. As a consequence, knowledge passed down through the oral traditions of stories and shared experiences.( ① )　And since older people had accumulated more knowledge, the social norm was that to be over fifty was to be wise. This social perception of age began to shift with the advent of new technologies such as the printing press.( ② )　With the fading of oral traditions, the wisdom of the old became less important and as a consequence being over fifty was no longer seen as signifying wisdom.( ③ )　We are living in a period when the gap between chronological and biological age is changing fast and where social norms are struggling to adapt.( ④ )　In a video produced by the AARP (formerly the American Association of Retired Persons), young people were asked to do various activities 'just like an old person'. When older people joined them in the video, the gap between the stereotype and the older people's actual behaviour was striking.( ⑤ )　It is clear that in today's world our social norms need to be updated quickly.

21. 22)글의 흐름으로 보아, 주어진 문장이 들어가기에 <u>가장 적절한</u> 곳은?

☑ **다음 글을 읽고 물음에 답하시오.** (43, 44, 45)

> When he was twenty-six, Jack approached his father and expressed his intentions of leaving the business to become a hairstylist. As Jack anticipated, his father raged and accused Jack of being selfish, ungrateful, and unmanly.

When Jack was a young man in his early twenties during the 1960s, he had tried to work in his father's insurance business, as was expected of him. His two older brothers fit in easily and seemed to enjoy their work.( ① )　But Jack was bored with the insurance industry. "It was worse than being bored", he said. "I felt like I was dying inside". Jack felt drawn to hair styling and dreamed of owning a hair shop with a lively environment. He was sure that he would enjoy the creative and social aspects of it and that he'd be successful.( ② )　In the face of his father's fury, Jack felt confusion and fear. His resolve became weak. But then a force filled his chest and he stood firm in his decision.( ③ )　In following his path, Jack not only ran three flourishing hair shops, but also helped his clients experience their inner beauty by listening and encouraging them when they faced dark times.( ④ )　His love for his work led to donating time and talent at nursing homes, which in turn led to becoming a hospice volunteer, and eventually to starting fundraising efforts for the hospice program in his community. And all this laid a strong stepping stone for another courageous move in his life. ( ⑤ ) When, after having two healthy children of their own, Jack and his wife, Michele, decided to bring an orphaned child into their family, his father threatened to disown them. Jack understood that his father feared adoption, in this case especially because the child was of a different racial background than their family. Jack and Michele risked rejection and went ahead with the adoption. It took years but eventually Jack's father loved the little girl and accepted his son's independent choices. Jack realized that, although he often felt fear and still does, he has always had courage. In fact, courage was the scaffolding around which he had built richness into his life.

22. 23)글의 흐름으로 보아, 주어진 문장이 들어가기에 <u>가장 적절한</u> 곳은?

(.hwp) (.pdf) → www.englishjmygod.com

☑ **다음 글을 읽고 물음에 답하시오.** (43, 44, 45)

In following his path, Jack not only ran three flourishing hair shops, but also helped his clients experience their inner beauty by listening and encouraging them when they faced dark times.

When Jack was a young man in his early twenties during the 1960s, he had tried to work in his father's insurance business, as was expected of him. His two older brothers fit in easily and seemed to enjoy their work. But Jack was bored with the insurance industry. "It was worse than being bored", he said. "I felt like I was dying inside". Jack felt drawn to hair styling and dreamed of owning a hair shop with a lively environment.( ① ) He was sure that he would enjoy the creative and social aspects of it and that he'd be successful. When he was twenty-six, Jack approached his father and expressed his intentions of leaving the business to become a hairstylist. As Jack anticipated, his father raged and accused Jack of being selfish, ungrateful, and unmanly.( ② ) In the face of his father's fury, Jack felt confusion and fear. His resolve became weak. But then a force filled his chest and he stood firm in his decision.( ③ ) His love for his work led to donating time and talent at nursing homes, which in turn led to becoming a hospice volunteer, and eventually to starting fundraising efforts for the hospice program in his community. And all this laid a strong stepping stone for another courageous move in his life. When, after having two healthy children of their own, Jack and his wife, Michele, decided to bring an orphaned child into their family, his father threatened to disown them.( ④ ) Jack understood that his father feared adoption, in this case especially because the child was of a different racial background than their family. Jack and Michele risked rejection and went ahead with the adoption.( ⑤ ) It took years but eventually Jack's father loved the little girl and accepted his son's independent choices. Jack realized that, although he often felt fear and still does, he has always had courage. In fact, courage was the scaffolding around which he had built richness into his life.

23. 24)글의 흐름으로 보아, 주어진 문장이 들어가기에 <u>가장 적절한 곳은?</u>

**1. 25)** [18]

To whom it may concern, I would like to draw your attention to a problem that frequently occurs with the No. 35 buses.

(A) Yours faithfully, John Williams.

(B) I look forward to seeing an improvement in this service soon.

(C) It would appear, however, that some of your drivers are either unaware of this bus stop or for some reason choose to ignore it, driving past even though the buses are not full.

(D) There is a bus stop about halfway along Fenny Road, at which the No.35 buses are supposed to stop.

(E) I would be grateful if you could remind your drivers that this bus stop exists and that they should be prepared to stop at it.

**1. 26)** [19]

My 10-year-old appeared, in desperate need of a quarter.

(A) "A quarter? What on earth do you need a quarter for?" My tone bordered on irritation. I didn't want to be bothered with such a trivial demand. "There's a garage sale up the street, and there's something I just gotta have!

(B) I glanced down at the hands of my little son and saw a four-inch cream-colored statue of two small children hugging one another. Inscribed at their feet were words that read It starts with 'L' ends with 'E' and in between are 'O' and 'V'. As I watched him race back to the garage sale, I smiled with a heart full of happiness. That 25-cent garage sale purchase brought me a lot of joy.

(C) It only costs a quarter. Please?" I placed a quarter in my son's hand. Moments later, a little voice said, "Here, Mommy, this is for you."

**2. 27)** [20]

Managers frequently try to play psychologist, to "figure out" why an employee has acted in a certain way.

(A) Empathizing with employees in order to understand their point of view can be very helpful.

(B) Avoid making suggestions to employees about personal traits they should change; instead suggest more acceptable ways of performing.

(C) However, when dealing with a problem area, in particular, remember that it is not the person who is bad, but the actions exhibited on the job.

(D) It is difficult for employees to change who they are; it is usually much easier for them to change how they act.

(E) For example, instead of focusing on a person's "unreliability," a manager might focus on the fact that the employee "has been late to work seven times this month."

**3. 28)** [21]

I suspect fungi are a little more forward "thinking" than their larger partners.

(A) In that case, wouldn't it be more advantageous if there were a certain number of other species around — oaks, maples, or firs — that would continue to grow and provide the shade needed for a new generation of young beeches to sprout and grow up? Diversity provides security for ancient forests.

(B) Among trees, each species fights other species. Let's assume the beeches native to Central Europe could emerge victorious in most forests there.

(C) Because fungi are also very dependent on stable conditions, they support other species underground and protect them from complete collapse to ensure that one species of tree doesn't manage to dominate.

(D) Would this really be an advantage? What would happen if a new pathogen came along that infected most of the beeches and killed them?

(.hwp) (.pdf) → www.englishjmygod.com

4. 29) [22]

It's remarkable that positive fantasies help us relax to such an extent that it shows up in physiological tests.

(A) The last thing you want to be is relaxed. You want to be energized enough to get off the couch and lose those pounds or find that job or study for that test, and you want to be motivated enough to stay engaged even when the inevitable obstacles or challenges arise.

(B) If you want to unwind, you can take some deep breaths, get a massage, or go for a walk — but you can also try simply closing your eyes and fantasizing about some future outcome that you might enjoy. But what about when your objective is to make your wish a reality?

(C) The principle of "Dream it. Wish it.

(D) Do it." does not hold true, and now we know why: in dreaming it, you undercut the energy you need to do it. You put yourself in a temporary state of complete happiness, calmness — and inactivity.

5. 30) [23]

If cooking is as central to human identity, biology, and culture as the biological anthropologist Richard Wrangham suggests, it stands to reason that the decline of cooking in our time would have serious consequences for modern life, and so it has.

(A) It has also allowed us to diversify our diets substantially, making it possible even for people with no cooking skills and little money to enjoy a whole different cuisine.

(B) The outsourcing of much of the work of cooking to corporations has relieved women of what has traditionally been their exclusive responsibility for feeding the family, making it easier for them to work outside the home and have careers. It has headed off many of the domestic conflicts that such a large shift in gender roles and family dynamics was bound to spark.

(C) All that's required is a microwave.

(D) It has relieved other pressures in the household, including longer workdays and overscheduled children, and saved us time that we can now invest in other pursuits.

(E) Are they all bad? Not at all.

6. 31) [24]

As you may already know, what and how you buy can be political.

(A) They contribute 50 percent of their profits to the construction of toilets around the world, and we're genuinely happy to spend our money on this special toilet paper each month. Remember that the corporate world is built on consumers, so as a consumer you have the power to vote with your wallet and encourage companies to embrace healthier and more sustainable practices with every purchase you choose to make.

(B) Be mindful about every purchase by carefully researching the corporations that are taking our money to decide if they deserve our support. Do they have a record of polluting the environment, or do they have fair-trade practices and an end-of-life plan for the products they make?

(C) To whom do you want to give your money? Which companies and corporations do you value and respect?

(D) Are they committed to bringing about good in the world? For instance, my family has found a company producing recycled, plastic-packaging-free toilet paper with a social conscience.

7. 32) 26

Camille Flammarion was born at Montigny-le-Roi, France.

(A) At nineteen, he wrote another book called The Plurality of Inhabited Worlds, in which he passionately claimed that life exists outside the planet Earth. His most successful work, Popular Astronomy, was published in 1880, and eventually sold 130,000 copies.

(B) He became interested in astronomy at an early age, and when he was only sixteen he wrote a book on the origin of the world. The manuscript was not published at the time, but it came to the attention of Urbain Le Verrier, the director of the Paris Observatory. He became an assistant to Le Verrier in 1858 and worked as a calculator.

(C) With his own funds, he built an observatory at Juvisy and spent May to November of each year there. In 1887, he founded the French Astronomical Society and served as editor of its monthly publication.

8. 33) 29

There is little doubt that we are driven by the sell-by date.

(A) The manufacturer then decides that a product can reasonably be consumed within say 90 days and 90 days minus so many days for travelling gives the sell-by date. But whether it becomes toxic is something each individual can decide.

(B) Once an item is past that date it goes into the waste stream, further increasing its carbon footprint. Remember those items have already travelled hundreds of miles to reach the shelves and once they go into waste they start a new carbon mile journey.

(C) But we all make our own judgement about sell-by dates; those brought up during the Second World War are often scornful of the terrible waste they believe such caution encourages. The manufacturer of the food has a view when making or growing something that by the time the product reaches the shelves it has already been travelling for so many days and possibly many miles.

(D) It would seem to make sense not to buy large packs of perishable goods but non-perishable items may become cost-effective.

9. 34) 30

The "jolt" of caffeine does wear off.

(A) It takes far longer for their system to eliminate the same amount of caffeine. As a result, they are very sensitive to caffeine's effects.

(B) Caffeine is removed from your system by an enzyme within your liver, which gradually degrades it over time. Based in large part on genetics, some people have a more efficient version of the enzyme that degrades caffeine, allowing the liver to rapidly clear it from the bloodstream.

(C) One cup of tea or coffee in the morning will last much of the day, and should they have a second cup, even early in the afternoon, they will find it difficult to fall asleep in the evening.

(D) Aging also alters the speed of caffeine clearance: the older we are, the longer it takes our brain and body to remove caffeine, and thus the more sensitive we become in later life to caffeine's sleep-disrupting influence.

(E) These rare individuals can drink an espresso with dinner and fall fast asleep at midnight without a problem. Others, however, have a slower-acting version of the enzyme.

10. 35) 31

Rebels may think they're rebels, but clever marketers influence them just like the rest of us.

(A) We are often tricked when we try to maintain a position of defiance.

(B) Saying, "Everyone is doing it" may turn some people off from an idea. These people will look for alternatives, which (if cleverly planned) can be exactly what a marketer or persuader wants you to believe.

(C) Some brands have taken full effect of our defiance towards the mainstream and positioned themselves as rebels; which has created even stronger brand loyalty.

(D) People use this reversal to make us "independently" choose an option which suits their purposes.

(E) If I want you to consider an idea, and know you strongly reject popular opinion in favor of maintaining your independence and uniqueness, I would present the majority option first, which you would reject in favor of my actual preference.

11. 36) 32

A typical soap opera creates an abstract world, in which a highly complex web of relationships connects fictional characters that exist first only in the minds of the program's creators and are then recreated in the minds of the viewer.

(A) The characters in a soap opera and the relationships between them are very much like the real people and relationships we experience every day.

(B) If you were to think about how much human psychology, law, and even everyday physics the viewer must know in order to follow and speculate about the plot, you would discover it is considerable — at least as much as the knowledge required to follow and speculate about a piece of modern mathematics, and in most cases, much more. Yet viewers follow soap operas with ease.

(C) The mental "training" required to follow a soap opera is provided by our everyday lives.

(D) The abstraction of a soap opera is only a step removed from the real world.

(E) How are they able to cope with such abstraction? Because, of course, the abstraction is built on an extremely familiar framework.

12. 37) 33

As always happens with natural selection, bats and their prey have been engaged in a life-or-death sensory arms race for millions of years.

(A) The B-2 bomber and other "stealth" aircraft have fuselages made of materials that do something similar with radar beams.

(B) It's believed that hearing in moths arose specifically in response to the threat of being eaten by bats.

(C) Some moth species have also evolved scales on their wings and a fur-like coat on their bodies; both act as "acoustic camouflage," by absorbing sound waves in the frequencies emitted by bats, thereby preventing those sound waves from bouncing back.

(D) (Not all insects can hear.) Over millions of years, moths have evolved the ability to detect sounds at ever higher frequencies, and, as they have, the frequencies of bats' vocalizations have risen, too.

13. 38) 34

Much of human thought is designed to screen out information and to sort the rest into a manageable condition.

(A) The inflow of data from our senses could create an overwhelming chaos, especially given the enormous amount of information available in culture and society. Out of all the sensory impressions and possible information, it is vital to find a small amount that is most relevant to our individual needs and to organize that into a usable stock of knowledge. Expectancies accomplish some of this work, helping to screen out information that is irrelevant to what is expected, and focusing our attention on clear contradictions.

(B) Then, only a fraction of what they notice gets processed and stored into memory. And only part of what gets committed to memory can be retrieved.

(C) The processes of learning and memory are marked by a steady elimination of information. People notice only a part of the world around them.

14. 39) 35

The irony of early democracy in Europe is that it thrived and prospered precisely because European rulers for a very long time were remarkably weak.

(A) The most striking way to illustrate European weakness is to show how little revenue they collected.

(B) For more than a millennium after the fall of Rome, European rulers lacked the ability to assess what their people were producing and to levy substantial taxes based on this.

(C) Europeans would eventually develop strong systems of revenue collection, but it took them an awfully long time to do so.

(D) In medieval times, and for part of the early modern era, Chinese emperors and Muslim caliphs were able to extract much more of economic production than any European ruler with the exception of small city-states.

15. 40) 36

If you drive down a busy street, you will find many competing businesses, often right next to one another.

(A) Consumers also benefit from added variety, and we all get a product that's pretty close to our vision of a perfect good — and no other market structure delivers that outcome.

(B) Yes, costs rise, but consumers also gain information to help make purchasing decisions.

(C) In markets where competitors sell slightly differentiated products, advertising enables firms to inform their customers about new products and services.

(D) For example, in most places a consumer in search of a quick meal has many choices, and more fast-food restaurants appear all the time. These competing firms advertise heavily.

(E) The temptation is to see advertising as driving up the price of a product without any benefit to the consumer. However, this misconception doesn't account for why firms advertise.

16. 41) 37

Architects might say a machine can never design an innovative or impressive building because a computer cannot be "creative."

(A) The architects gave the system a set of criteria, and it generated a set of possible designs for the architects to choose from. Similar software has been used to design lightweight bicycle frames and sturdier chairs, among much else.

(B) Yet consider the Elbphilharmonie, a new concert hall in Hamburg, which contains a remarkably beautiful auditorium composed of ten thousand interlocking acoustic panels. It is the sort of space that makes one instinctively think that only a human being — and a human with a remarkably refined creative sensibility, at that — could design something so aesthetically impressive. Yet the auditorium was, in fact, designed algorithmically, using a technique known as "parametric design."

(C) Are these systems behaving "creatively"? No, they are using lots of processing power to blindly generate varied possible designs, working in a very different way from a human being.

17. 42) 38

The brain is a high-energy consumer of glucose, which is its fuel.

(A) Although the brain accounts for merely 3 percent of a person's body weight, it consumes 20 percent of the available fuel. Your brain can't store fuel, however, so it has to "pay as it goes."

(B) Sometimes, however, this shift from the higher-thinking parts of the brain to the automatic and reflexive parts of the brain can lead you to do something too quickly, without thinking.

(C) Since your brain is incredibly adaptive, it economizes its fuel resources. Thus, during a period of high stress, it shifts away from the analysis of the nuances of a situation to a singular and fixed focus on the stressful situation at hand.

(D) You don't sit back and speculate about the meaning of life when you are stressed. Instead, you devote all your energy to trying to figure out what action to take.

18. 43) 39.

Much research has been carried out on the causes of engagement, an issue that is important from both a theoretical and practical standpoint: identifying the drivers of work engagement may enable us to manipulate or influence it.

(A) In other words, when employees are able to do their jobs well — to the point that they match or exceed their own expectations and ambitions — they will engage more, be proud of their achievements, and find work more meaningful. This is especially evident when people are employed in jobs that align with their values.

(B) Indeed, leaders influence engagement by giving their employees honest and constructive feedback on their performance, and by providing them with the necessary resources that enable them to perform their job well. It is, however, noteworthy that although engagement drives job performance, job performance also drives engagement.

(C) The causes of engagement fall into two major camps: situational and personal. The most influential situational causes are job resources, feedback and leadership, the latter, of course, being responsible for job resources and feedback.

19. 44) 40.

In 2006, researchers conducted a study on the motivations for helping after the September 11th terrorist attacks against the United States.

(A) The events of September 11th emotionally affected people throughout the United States.

(B) Those who gave to reduce their own distress reduced their emotional arousal with their initial gift, discharging that emotional distress.

(C) However, those who gave to reduce others' distress did not stop empathizing with victims who continued to struggle long after the attacks.

(D) In the study, they found that individuals who gave money, blood, goods, or other forms of assistance because of other-focused motives (giving to reduce another's discomfort) were almost four times more likely to still be giving support one year later than those whose original motivation was to reduce personal distress. This effect likely stems from differences in emotional arousal.

20. 45) 41, 42

In England in the 1680s, it was unusual to live to the age of fifty.

(A) In a video produced by the AARP (formerly the American Association of Retired Persons), young people were asked to do various activities 'just like an old person'. When older people joined them in the video, the gap between the stereotype and the older people's actual behaviour was striking. It is clear that in today's world our social norms need to be updated quickly.

(B) Over time, as more books were printed, literacy increased, and the oral traditions of knowledge transfer began to fade. With the fading of oral traditions, the wisdom of the old became less important and as a consequence being over fifty was no longer seen as signifying wisdom. We are living in a period when the gap between chronological and biological age is changing fast and where social norms are struggling to adapt.

(C) This was a period when knowledge was not spread widely, there were few books and most people could not read. As a consequence, knowledge passed down through the oral traditions of stories and shared experiences. And since older people had accumulated more knowledge, the social norm was that to be over fifty was to be wise. This social perception of age began to shift with the advent of new technologies such as the printing press.

21. 46) 43, 44, 45

When Jack was a young man in his early twenties during the 1960s, he had tried to work in his father's insurance business, as was expected of him.

(A) Jack understood that his father feared adoption, in this case especially because the child was of a different racial background than their family. Jack and Michele risked rejection and went ahead with the adoption. It took years but eventually Jack's father loved the little girl and accepted his son's independent choices. Jack realized that, although he often felt fear and still does, he has always had courage. In fact, courage was the scaffolding around which he had built richness into his life.

(B) His two older brothers fit in easily and seemed to enjoy their work. But Jack was bored with the insurance industry. "It was worse than being bored," he said. "I felt like I was dying inside." Jack felt drawn to hair styling and dreamed of owning a hair shop with a lively environment.

(C) He was sure that he would enjoy the creative and social aspects of it and that he'd be successful. When he was twenty-six, Jack approached his father and expressed his intentions of leaving the business to become a hairstylist. As Jack anticipated, his father raged and accused Jack of being selfish, ungrateful, and unmanly. In the face of his father's fury, Jack felt confusion and fear. His resolve became weak.

(D) But then a force filled his chest and he stood firm in his decision. In following his path, Jack not only ran three flourishing hair shops, but also helped his clients experience their inner beauty by listening and encouraging them when they faced dark times. His love for his work led to donating time and talent at nursing homes, which in turn led to becoming a hospice volunteer, and eventually to starting fundraising efforts for the hospice program in his community. And all this laid a strong stepping stone for another courageous move in his life. When, after having two healthy children of their own, Jack and his wife, Michele, decided to bring an orphaned child into their family, his father threatened to disown them.

# 2023 고2 9월 모의고사

❶ voca    ❷ text    ❸ [ / ]    ❹ ____    ❺ quiz 1    ❻ quiz 2    ❼ quiz 3    ❽ quiz 4    ❾ quiz 5

**1.** ¹⁾밑줄 친 ⓐ~ⓗ 중 어법, 혹은 문맥상 어휘의 사용이 어색한 것끼리 짝지어진 것을 고르시오. ¹⁸

To whom it may concern, I would like to draw your attention ⓐ **to** a problem that frequently ⓑ **occurs** with the No. 35 buses. There is a bus stop about halfway along Fenny Road, at ⓒ **which** the No.35 buses are supposed to stop. It would ⓓ **be appeared**, however, ⓔ **which** some of your drivers are either unaware of this bus stop or for some reason choose to ignore it, ⓕ **driving** past even though the buses are not full. I would be grateful if you could remind your drivers ⓖ **that** this bus stop exists and that they should be prepared to stop at it. I look forward to ⓗ **seeing** an improvement in this service soon.

Yours faithfully, John Williams

① ⓐ, ⓔ        ② ⓓ, ⓔ        ③ ⓓ, ⓕ
④ ⓓ, ⓗ        ⑤ ⓐ, ⓓ, ⓖ, ⓗ

**2.** ²⁾밑줄 친 ⓐ~ⓖ 중 어법, 혹은 문맥상 어휘의 사용이 어색한 것끼리 짝지어진 것을 고르시오. ¹⁹

My 10-year-old ⓐ **was appeared**, in desperate need of a quarter. "A quarter? What on earth do you need a quarter ⓑ **x**"? My tone bordered on irritation. I didn't want to ⓒ **be bothered** with such a trivial demand. "There's a garage sale up the street, and there's something I just gotta have! It only costs a quarter. Please"? I placed a quarter in my son's hand. Moments later, a little voice said, "Here, Mommy, this is for you". I glanced down at the hands of my little son and saw a four-inch cream-colored statue of two small children ⓓ **hugging** one another. ⓔ **Described** at their feet ⓕ **were** words that read It starts with 'L' ends with 'E' and in between are 'O' and 'V'. As I watched him ⓖ **to race** back to the garage sale, I smiled with a heart full of happiness. That 25-cent garage sale purchase brought me a lot of joy.

**3.** ³⁾밑줄 친 ⓐ~ⓛ 중 어법, 혹은 문맥상 어휘의 사용이 어색한 것끼리 짝지어진 것을 고르시오. ²⁰

Managers frequently try to play psychologist, to "figure out" why an employee has ⓐ **been acted** in a certain way. ⓑ **Empathizing** with employees in order to understand their point of view can be very helpful. ⓒ **However**, when ⓓ **dealing** with a problem area, in particular, ⓔ **remember** ⓕ **that** it is not the person who is bad, but the actions exhibited on the job. Avoid ⓖ **making** suggestions to employees about personal traits they should change; instead ⓗ **suggest** more acceptable ways of performing. For example, instead of focusing on a person's "unreliability", a manager might focus on the fact ⓘ **which** the employee "has been ⓙ **late** to work seven times this month". It is difficult ⓚ **for** employees to change who they are; it is usually ⓛ **much** easier for them to change how they act.

① ⓐ, ⓑ        ② ⓐ, ⓖ        ③ ⓐ, ⓘ
④ ⓐ, ⓚ        ⑤ ⓕ, ⓖ

(.hwp) (.pdf) → www.englishjmygod.com

## 4. ⁴⁾밑줄 친 ⓐ~ⓘ 중 어법, 혹은 문맥상 어휘의 사용이 어색한 것끼리 짝지어진 것을 고르시오. ²¹

I suspect fungi ⓐ **is** a little more forward "thinking" than ⓑ **their** larger partners. Among trees, each species ⓒ **fights** other species. Let's assume the beeches native to Central Europe could emerge victorious in most forests there. Would this really be an advantage? What would happen if a new pathogen ⓓ **came** along that infected most of the beeches and killed them? In that case, wouldn't it be more advantageous if there were ⓔ **a** certain number of other species around — oaks, maples, or firs — ⓕ **which** would continue to grow and provide the shade needed for a new generation of young beeches to sprout and grow up? Diversity provides security for ancient forests. Because fungi ⓖ **are** also very ⓗ **dependent** on stable conditions, they support other species underground and protect ⓘ **it** from complete collapse to ensure that one species of tree doesn't manage to dominate.

① ⓐ, ⓕ, ⓖ      ② ⓐ, ⓕ, ⓘ      ③ ⓑ, ⓕ, ⓘ
④ ⓐ, ⓑ, ⓓ, ⓗ      ⑤ ⓑ, ⓒ, ⓕ, ⓖ

## 5. ⁵⁾밑줄 친 ⓐ~ⓚ 중 어법, 혹은 문맥상 어휘의 사용이 어색한 것끼리 짝지어진 것을 고르시오. ²²

It's remarkable that positive fantasies help us ⓐ **relaxing** to such an extent ⓑ **that** it shows up in physiological tests. If you want to unwind, you can take some deep breaths, ⓒ **get** a massage, or go for a walk — but you can also try simply closing your eyes and ⓓ **fantasizing** about some future outcome that you might enjoy. But what about when your ⓔ **subjective** is to make your wish a reality? The last thing you want to be is ⓕ **relaxed**. You want to be ⓖ **energized enough** to get off

the couch and lose those pounds or find that job or study for that test, and you want to be motivated enough to stay ⓗ **engaging** even when the inevitable obstacles or challenges ⓘ **arise**. The ⓙ **principal** of "Dream it. Wish it. Do it". does not hold true, and now we know why: in dreaming it, you undercut the energy you need to do it. You put yourself in a ⓚ **temporary** state of complete happiness, calmness — and inactivity.

① ⓓ, ⓖ      ② ⓑ, ⓔ, ⓘ      ③ ⓒ, ⓓ, ⓔ
④ ⓐ, ⓔ, ⓗ, ⓙ      ⑤ ⓔ, ⓕ, ⓗ, ⓙ

## 6. ⁶⁾밑줄 친 ⓐ~ⓚ 중 어법, 혹은 문맥상 어휘의 사용이 어색한 것끼리 짝지어진 것을 고르시오. ²³

If cooking is as central to human identity, biology, and culture as the biological anthropologist Richard Wrangham suggests, ⓐ **it** stands to reason that the decline of cooking in our time would have serious consequences for modern life, and so it ⓑ **is**. Are they all bad? Not at all. The outsourcing of much of the work of cooking to ⓒ **cooperations** has ⓓ **relieved** women of what has traditionally been their ⓔ **exclusive** responsibility for feeding the family, ⓕ **making** ⓖ **that** easier for them to work outside the home and have careers. It has headed off many of the domestic conflicts that such a large shift in gender roles and family dynamics was bound to spark. It has relieved other pressures in the household, including longer workdays and overscheduled children, and ⓗ **saved** us time that we can now invest in other pursuits. It has also ⓘ **allowed** us to diversify our diets substantially, ⓙ **making** it possible even for people with no cooking skills and little money to enjoy a whole different cuisine. All that's ⓚ **required** is a microwave.

① ⓖ, ⓘ      ② ⓑ, ⓒ, ⓖ      ③ ⓑ, ⓕ, ⓗ
④ ⓕ, ⓖ, ⓘ      ⑤ ⓕ, ⓖ, ⓚ

**7.** 7)밑줄 친 ⓐ~ⓚ 중 어법, 혹은 문맥상 어휘의 사용이 어색한 것끼리 짝지어진 것을 고르시오. 24

As you may already know, what and how you buy can be political. To ⓐ **whom** do you want to give your money? Which companies and ⓑ **cooperations** do you value and respect? Be mindful about every purchase by carefully researching the corporations that are ⓒ **taking** our money to decide ⓓ **if** they deserve our support. Do they have a record of polluting the environment, or do they have fair-trade practices and an end-of-life plan for the products they make? Are they ⓔ **committed** to ⓕ **bring** about good in the world? For instance, my family has ⓖ **found** a company producing recycled, plastic-packaging-free toilet paper with a social conscience. They ⓗ **contribute** 50 percent of their profits to the ⓘ **construction** of toilets around the world, and we're genuinely happy to spend our money on this special toilet paper each month. Remember ⓙ **that** the corporate world is built on consumers, so as a consumer you have the power to vote with your wallet and encourage companies ⓚ **to embrace** healthier and more sustainable practices with every purchase you choose to make.

① ⓑ, ⓕ    ② ⓑ, ⓙ    ③ ⓓ, ⓕ
④ ⓕ, ⓘ    ⑤ ⓐ, ⓔ, ⓕ, ⓖ

**8.** 8)밑줄 친 ⓐ~ⓖ 중 어법, 혹은 문맥상 어휘의 사용이 어색한 것끼리 짝지어진 것을 고르시오. 26

Camille Flammarion was born at Montigny-le-Roi, France. He became interested in ⓐ **astrology** at an early age, and when he was only sixteen he wrote a book on the origin of the world. The manuscript was not published at the time, but it came to the attention of Urbain Le Verrier, the director of the Paris Observatory. He became an assistant to Le Verrier in 1858 and worked as a calculator. ⓑ **At** nineteen, he wrote another

book ⓒ **called** The Plurality of Inhabited Worlds, in ⓓ **what** he passionately claimed ⓔ **which** life exists outside the planet Earth. His most successful work, Popular Astronomy, was published in 1880, and eventually sold 130,000 copies. With his own funds, he built an ⓕ **observant** at Juvisy and spent May to November of each year there. In 1887, he ⓖ **founded** the French Astronomical Society and served as editor of its monthly publication.

① ⓒ, ⓕ    ② ⓓ, ⓕ, ⓖ    ③ ⓐ, ⓑ, ⓓ, ⓕ
④ ⓐ, ⓓ, ⓔ, ⓕ    ⑤ ⓐ, ⓓ, ⓔ, ⓖ

**9.** 9)밑줄 친 ⓐ~ⓚ 중 어법, 혹은 문맥상 어휘의 사용이 어색한 것끼리 짝지어진 것을 고르시오. 29

There is ⓐ **a little** doubt that we are driven by the sell-by date. Once an item is past that date it goes into the waste stream, ⓑ **further** increasing its carbon footprint. ⓒ **Remembering** those items have already travelled hundreds of miles to ⓓ **reach** the shelves and once they go into waste they start a new carbon mile journey. But we all make our own judgement about sell-by dates; those brought up ⓔ **during** the Second World War are often scornful of the terrible waste they believe such caution ⓕ **encourages**. The manufacturer of the food has a view when ⓖ **making** or ⓗ **grow** something that by the time the product ⓘ **reaches** the shelves it has already been travelling for so many days and possibly many miles. The manufacturer then decides that a product can reasonably be consumed within say 90 days and 90 days minus so many days for travelling ⓙ **gives** the sell-by date. But ⓚ **whether** it becomes toxic is something each individual can decide. It would seem to make sense not to buy large packs of perishable goods but non-perishable items may become cost-effective.

① ⓒ, ⓓ    ② ⓒ, ⓔ    ③ ⓐ, ⓒ, ⓗ
④ ⓒ, ⓓ, ⓔ    ⑤ ⓐ, ⓓ, ⓖ, ⓗ

(.hwp) (.pdf) → www.englishjmygod.com

## 10. 10)밑줄 친 ⓐ~ⓙ 중 어법, 혹은 문맥상 어휘의 사용이 어색한 것끼리 짝지어진 것을 고르시오. 30

The "jolt" of caffeine does wear off. Caffeine ⓐ **is removed** from your system by an enzyme within your liver, ⓑ **which** gradually degrades it over time. Based in large part on genetics, some people have a more ⓒ **efficient** version of the enzyme that degrades caffeine, ⓓ **allowing** the liver to rapidly clear it from the bloodstream. These rare individuals can drink an espresso with dinner and fall fast asleep at midnight without a problem. Others, ⓔ **however**, have a slower-acting version of the enzyme. It takes far longer for their system to ⓕ **illuminate** the same amount of caffeine. As a result, they are very ⓖ **sensitive** to caffeine's effects. One cup of tea or coffee in the morning will ⓗ **last** much of the day, and should they have a second cup, even early in the afternoon, they will find ⓘ **that** difficult to fall asleep in the evening. Aging also alters the speed of caffeine clearance: the older we are, the longer it takes our brain and body to remove caffeine, and thus the more sensitive we become in later life to caffeine's sleep-ⓙ **disrupting** influence.

① ⓐ, ⓕ      ② ⓒ, ⓕ      ③ ⓒ, ⓘ
④ ⓓ, ⓕ      ⑤ ⓕ, ⓘ

## 11. 11)밑줄 친 ⓐ~ⓗ 중 어법, 혹은 문맥상 어휘의 사용이 어색한 것끼리 짝지어진 것을 고르시오. 31

Rebels may think they're rebels, but clever marketers ⓐ **influence on** them just like the rest of us. Saying, "Everyone is doing it" may turn some people off from an idea. These people will look ⓑ **after** alternatives, ⓒ **which** (if cleverly planned) can be exactly what a marketer or persuader wants you to believe. If I want you to consider an idea, and know you strongly reject popular opinion in favor of ⓓ **maintaining** your independence and uniqueness, I would present the majority option first, which you would reject in favor of my actual preference. We are often tricked when we try to maintain a position of defiance. People use this reversal to make us "independently" choose an option ⓔ **which** suits their purposes. Some brands have ⓕ **taken** full effect of our ⓖ **defiance** towards the mainstream and positioned ⓗ **themselves** as rebels; which has created even stronger brand loyalty.

① ⓐ, ⓑ      ② ⓑ, ⓕ      ③ ⓑ, ⓗ
④ ⓔ, ⓕ, ⓖ      ⑤ ⓐ, ⓒ, ⓓ, ⓖ

## 12. 12)밑줄 친 ⓐ~ⓗ 중 어법, 혹은 문맥상 어휘의 사용이 어색한 것끼리 짝지어진 것을 고르시오. 32

A typical soap opera creates an abstract world, in ⓐ **which** a highly complex web of relationships connects fictional characters that ⓑ **are existed** first only in the minds of the program's creators and are then recreated in the minds of the viewer. If you were to think about how ⓒ **much** human psychology, law, and even everyday physics the viewer must know in order to follow and speculate about the plot, you would discover it is ⓓ **considerate** — at least as much as the knowledge required to follow and speculate about a piece of modern mathematics, and in most cases, much more. Yet viewers follow soap operas with ease. How are they able to cope with such abstraction? Because, of course, the ⓔ **abstraction** is built on an extremely familiar framework. The characters in a soap opera and the relationships between ⓕ **themselves** are very much like the real people and relationships we experience every day. The abstraction of a soap opera is only a step ⓖ **removed** from the real world. The mental "training" ⓗ **is required** to follow a soap opera is provided by our everyday lives.

① ⓐ, ⓒ      ② ⓐ, ⓒ, ⓓ      ③ ⓐ, ⓑ, ⓒ, ⓔ
④ ⓑ, ⓒ, ⓕ, ⓗ      ⑤ ⓑ, ⓓ, ⓕ, ⓗ

**13.** 13)**밑줄 친 ⓐ~ⓖ 중 어법, 혹은 문맥상 어휘의 사용이 어색한 것끼리 짝지어진 것을 고르시오.** 33

As always happens with natural selection, bats and their prey have ⓐ **engaged** in a life-or-death sensory arms race for millions of years. It's believed that hearing in moths ⓑ **arose** specifically in response to the threat of ⓒ **eating** by bats. (Not all insects can hear.) Over millions of years, moths have evolved the ability to detect sounds at ever higher frequencies, and, as they have, the frequencies of bats' vocalizations have ⓓ **risen**, too. Some moth species have also evolved scales on their wings and a fur-like coat on their bodies; both act as "acoustic camouflage", by absorbing sound waves in the frequencies ⓔ **emitted** by bats, thereby preventing those sound waves from bouncing back. The B-2 bomber and other "stealth" aircraft have fuselages ⓕ **made** of materials that do ⓖ **something similar** with radar beams.

① ⓐ, ⓒ      ② ⓐ, ⓕ      ③ ⓐ, ⓖ
④ ⓒ, ⓓ      ⑤ ⓔ, ⓕ

**14.** 14)**밑줄 친 ⓐ~ⓗ 중 어법, 혹은 문맥상 어휘의 사용이 어색한 것끼리 짝지어진 것을 고르시오.** 34

Much of human thought is designed to screen out information and to sort the rest into a manageable condition. The inflow of data from our senses could create an ⓐ **overwhelming** chaos, especially ⓑ **giving** the enormous amount of information available in culture and society. Out of all the sensory impressions and possible information, ⓒ **which** is vital to find a small amount that is most ⓓ **relevant** to our individual needs and to organize that into a usable stock of knowledge. Expectancies accomplish some of this work, ⓔ **helping** to screen out information that is irrelevant to what is expected, and ⓕ **focusing** our attention on clear contradictions. The processes of learning and memory are marked by a steady elimination of information. People notice only a part of the world around ⓖ **them**. Then, only a fraction of what they notice gets ⓗ **processing** and stored into memory. And only part of what gets committed to memory can be retrieved.

① ⓑ, ⓕ      ② ⓐ, ⓒ, ⓕ      ③ ⓑ, ⓒ, ⓗ
④ ⓑ, ⓔ, ⓕ      ⑤ ⓒ, ⓓ, ⓗ

**15.** 15)**밑줄 친 ⓐ~ⓙ 중 어법, 혹은 문맥상 어휘의 사용이 어색한 것끼리 짝지어진 것을 고르시오.** 35

The irony of early democracy in Europe is ⓐ **that** it thrived and ⓑ **prospered** precisely because European rulers for a very long time ⓒ **were** remarkably weak. For more than a millennium after the fall of Rome, European rulers lacked the ability to ⓓ **access** ⓔ **what** their people were producing and ⓕ **to levy** substantial taxes based on this. The most striking way to ⓖ **illuminate** European weakness is to show how ⓗ **little** revenue they collected. Europeans would eventually develop strong systems of revenue collection, but it took them an awfully long time to do so. In medieval times, and for part of the early modern era, Chinese emperors and Muslim caliphs were able to ⓘ **contract** much more of economic production than any European ruler with the ⓙ **expectations** of small city-states.

① ⓒ, ⓓ, ⓗ      ② ⓐ, ⓒ, ⓖ, ⓗ      ③ ⓒ, ⓔ, ⓕ, ⓖ
④ ⓓ, ⓔ, ⓖ, ⓙ      ⑤ ⓓ, ⓖ, ⓘ, ⓙ

## 16. 16)밑줄 친 ⓐ~ⓖ 중 어법, 혹은 문맥상 어휘의 사용이 어색한 것끼리 짝지어진 것을 고르시오. 36

If you drive down a busy street, you will find many competing businesses, often right next to one another. For example, in most places a consumer in search of a quick meal has many choices, and more fast-food restaurants ⓐ **appear** all the time. These ⓑ **competitive** firms advertise heavily. The temptation is to see advertising as driving up the price of a product without any benefit to the consumer. ⓒ **However**, this misconception doesn't account for why firms advertise. In markets where competitors sell slightly ⓓ **differentiated** products, advertising enables firms ⓔ **informing** their customers about new products and services. Yes, costs ⓕ **rise**, but consumers also gain information to help make purchasing decisions. Consumers also benefit from added variety, and we all get a product that's pretty close to our vision of a perfect good — and no other market structure delivers that ⓖ **income**.

① ⓐ, ⓒ, ⓓ  　　② ⓐ, ⓒ, ⓖ  　　③ ⓐ, ⓓ, ⓖ
④ ⓑ, ⓔ, ⓖ  　　⑤ ⓒ, ⓓ, ⓕ, ⓖ

## 17. 17)밑줄 친 ⓐ~ⓘ 중 어법, 혹은 문맥상 어휘의 사용이 어색한 것끼리 짝지어진 것을 고르시오. 37

Architects might say a machine can never design an innovative or impressive building because a computer cannot be "creative". Yet ⓐ **consider** the Elbphilharmonie, a new concert hall in Hamburg, ⓑ **which** contains a remarkably beautiful auditorium ⓒ **consisted** of ten thousand interlocking acoustic panels. It is the sort of space that makes one instinctively think that only a human being — and a human with a remarkably ⓓ **confined** creative sensibility, at that — could design something so aesthetically impressive. Yet the auditorium was, in fact, ⓔ **designed** algorithmically, using a technique known as "parametric design". The architects gave the system a set of criteria, and ⓕ **which** generated a set of possible designs for the architects to choose from. ⓖ **Similar** software has been used to ⓗ **design** lightweight bicycle frames and sturdier chairs, among much else. Are these systems behaving "creatively"? No, they are using lots of processing power to blindly generate varied possible designs, ⓘ **worked** in a very different way from a human being.

① ⓑ, ⓓ, ⓗ  　　② ⓓ, ⓔ, ⓕ  　　③ ⓓ, ⓔ, ⓖ
④ ⓑ, ⓓ, ⓔ, ⓕ  　　⑤ ⓒ, ⓓ, ⓕ, ⓘ

## 18. 18)밑줄 친 ⓐ~ⓗ 중 어법, 혹은 문맥상 어휘의 사용이 어색한 것끼리 짝지어진 것을 고르시오. 38

The brain is a high-energy consumer of glucose, which is its fuel. Although the brain ⓐ **accounts** for merely 3 percent of a person's body weight, it ⓑ **consumes** 20 percent of the available fuel. Your brain can't store fuel, ⓒ **therefore**, so it has to "pay as it goes".  Since your brain is incredibly ⓓ **adaptive**, it economizes its fuel resources. Thus, ⓔ **during** a period of high stress, it shifts away from the analysis of the nuances of a situation to a singular and fixed focus on the stressful situation at hand. You don't sit back and speculate about the meaning of life when you are stressed. Instead, you devote all your energy to ⓕ **try** to figure out what action to take. Sometimes, however, this shift from the higher-thinking parts of the brain to the ⓖ **automatic** and ⓗ **reflective** parts of the brain can lead you to do something too quickly, without thinking.

① ⓔ, ⓗ  　　② ⓐ, ⓒ, ⓓ  　　③ ⓑ, ⓓ, ⓗ
④ ⓒ, ⓕ, ⓗ  　　⑤ ⓒ, ⓖ, ⓗ

19. 19)밑줄 친 ⓐ~ⓙ 중 어법, 혹은 문맥상 어휘의 사용이 어색한 것끼리 짝지어진 것을 고르시오. 39.

Much research has ⓐ **been carried** out on the causes of engagement, an issue that is important from both a theoretical and practical standpoint: ⓑ **identifying** the drivers of work engagement may enable us to manipulate or influence ⓒ **it**. The causes of engagement fall into two major camps: situational and personal. The most ⓓ **influenced** situational causes are job resources, feedback and leadership, the ⓔ **latter**, of course, being responsible for job resources and feedback. Indeed, leaders influence engagement by giving their employees honest and ⓕ **constructive** feedback on their performance, and by providing ⓖ **them** with the necessary resources that enable them to perform their job well. It is, however, noteworthy that although engagement drives job performance, job performance also drives engagement. In other words, when employees are able to do their jobs well — to the point that they match or ⓗ **proceed** their own expectations and ambitions — they will engage more, be proud of their achievements, and find work more ⓘ **meaningful**. This is especially evident when people are employed in jobs that ⓙ **align** with their values.

① ⓒ, ⓓ    ② ⓓ, ⓗ    ③ ⓓ, ⓘ

④ ⓖ, ⓘ    ⑤ ⓗ, ⓙ

20. 20)밑줄 친 ⓐ~ⓕ 중 어법, 혹은 문맥상 어휘의 사용이 어색한 것끼리 짝지어진 것을 고르시오. 40.

In 2006, researchers ⓐ **conducting** a study on the motivations for helping after the September 11th terrorist attacks against the United States. In the study, they found ⓑ **that** individuals who gave money, blood, goods, or other forms of assistance because of other-focused motives (giving to reduce another's discomfort) were almost four times more likely to still be giving support one year later than those ⓒ **whose** original motivation was to reduce personal distress. This effect likely stems from differences in emotional arousal. The events of September 11th emotionally ⓓ **affected** people throughout the United States. Those who gave to reduce their own distress reduced their emotional arousal with their initial gift, ⓔ **discharged** that emotional distress. However, those who gave to reduce others' distress did not stop ⓕ **to empathize** with victims who continued to struggle long after the attacks.

① ⓐ, ⓒ    ② ⓐ, ⓔ, ⓕ    ③ ⓒ, ⓔ, ⓕ

④ ⓑ, ⓒ, ⓓ, ⓕ    ⑤ ⓑ, ⓒ, ⓔ, ⓕ

**21.** 21)**밑줄 친 ⓐ~ⓙ 중 어법, 혹은 문맥상 어휘의 사용이 어색한 것끼리 짝지어진 것을 고르시오.** 41~42

In England in the 1680s, it was unusual to live to the age of fifty. This was a period when knowledge was not spread widely, there were ⓐ **a few** books and most people could not read. As a consequence, knowledge passed down through the oral traditions of stories and shared experiences. And since older people had ⓑ **accumulated** more knowledge, the social norm was that to be over fifty was to be wise. This social perception of age began to shift with the ⓒ **advertent** of new technologies such as the printing press. Over time, as more books were printed, ⓓ **literacy** increased, and the oral traditions of knowledge transfer began to fade. With the fading of oral traditions, the wisdom of the old became ⓔ **less** important and as a consequence being over fifty was no longer seen as ⓕ **signifying** wisdom.

We are living in a period when the gap between chronological and biological age is ⓖ **changed** fast and where social norms are struggling to ⓗ **adapt**. In a video produced by the AARP (formerly the American Association of Retired Persons), young people ⓘ **were asked** to do various activities 'just like an old person'. When older people joined ⓙ **them** in the video, the gap between the stereotype and the older people's actual behaviour was striking. It is clear that in today's world our social norms need to be updated quickly.

① ⓐ, ⓑ     ② ⓔ, ⓖ     ③ ⓐ, ⓒ, ⓖ
④ ⓑ, ⓕ, ⓖ     ⑤ ⓖ, ⓗ, ⓘ

**22.** 22)**밑줄 친 ⓐ~ⓜ 중 어법, 혹은 문맥상 어휘의 사용이 어색한 것끼리 짝지어진 것을 고르시오.** 43~45

When Jack was a young man in his early twenties ⓐ **during** the 1960s, he had tried to work in his father's insurance business, as was expected of him. His two older brothers fit in easily and seemed to enjoy their work. But Jack was ⓑ **bored** with the insurance industry. "It was worse than ⓒ **being bored**", he said. "I felt like I was dying inside". Jack felt drawn to hair styling and dreamed of owning a hair shop with a lively environment. He was sure ⓓ **that** he would enjoy the creative and social aspects of it and that he'd be successful. When he was twenty-six, Jack ⓔ **approached** his father and expressed his intentions of leaving the business to become a hairstylist. As Jack anticipated, his father raged and accused Jack of being selfish, ungrateful, and unmanly. In the face of his father's fury, Jack felt confusion and fear. His resolve became weak. But then a force filled his chest and he stood firm in his decision. In ⓕ **following** his path, Jack not only ran three flourishing hair shops, but also helped his clients ⓖ **experiencing** their inner beauty by listening and encouraging ⓗ **it** when they faced dark times. His love for his work led to ⓘ **donating** time and talent at nursing homes, which in turn led to becoming a hospice volunteer, and eventually to starting fundraising efforts for the hospice program in his community. And all this ⓙ **laid** a strong stepping stone for another courageous move in his life. When, after having two healthy children of their own, Jack and his wife, Michele, decided to bring an orphaned child into their family, his father threatened to disown them. Jack understood that his father feared ⓚ **adoption**, in this case especially because the child was of a different racial background than their family. Jack and Michele risked rejection and went ahead with the adoption. It took years but eventually Jack's father loved the little girl and accepted his son's independent choices. Jack realized that, although he often felt fear and still ⓛ **does**, he has always had courage. In fact, courage was the scaffolding around ⓜ **which** he had built richness into his life.

① ⓑ, ⓖ     ② ⓓ, ⓖ     ③ ⓓ, ⓛ
④ ⓖ, ⓗ     ⑤ ⓖ, ⓙ, ⓛ

## 2023 고2 9월 모의고사

❶ voca    ❷ text    ❸ [ / ]    ❹ ＿＿    ❺ quiz 1    ❻ quiz 2    ❼ quiz 3    ❽ quiz 4    ❾ quiz 5

**1.** 1)글의 밑줄 친 부분 중 어법, 혹은 문맥상 어휘의 쓰임이 어색한 것을 모두 고르시오. 18

To whom it may concern, I would like to draw your attention ① **x** a problem that frequently ② **is occurred** with the No. 35 buses. There is a bus stop about halfway along Fenny Road, at which the No.35 buses are supposed to stop. It would ③ **be appeared**, however, ④ **that** some of your drivers are either unaware of this bus stop or for some reason choose to ignore it, ⑤ **drive** past even though the buses are not full. I would be grateful if you could remind your drivers that this bus stop exists and that they should be prepared to stop at it. I look forward to seeing an improvement in this service soon.

Yours faithfully, John Williams

**2.** 2)글의 밑줄 친 부분 중 어법, 혹은 문맥상 어휘의 쓰임이 어색한 것을 모두 고르시오. 19

My 10-year-old appeared, in desperate need of a quarter. "A quarter? What on earth do you need a quarter ① **for**"? My tone bordered on irritation. I didn't want to ② **be bothered** with such a trivial demand. "There's a garage sale up the street, and there's something I just gotta have! It only costs a quarter. Please"? I placed a quarter in my son's hand. Moments later, a little voice said, "Here, Mommy, this is for you". I glanced down at the hands of my little son and saw a four-inch cream-colored statue of two small children hugging one another. ③ **Described** at their feet ④ **were** words that read It starts with 'L' ends with 'E' and in between are 'O' and 'V'. As I watched him ⑤ **race** back to the garage sale, I smiled with a heart full of happiness. That 25-cent garage sale purchase brought me a lot of joy.

**3.** 3)글의 밑줄 친 부분 중 어법, 혹은 문맥상 어휘의 쓰임이 어색한 것을 모두 고르시오. 20

Managers frequently try to play psychologist, to "figure out" why an employee has acted in a certain way. ① **Empathizing** with employees in order to understand their point of view can be very helpful. However, when ② **dealing** with a problem area, in particular, ③ **remembering** that it is not the person who is bad, but the actions exhibited on the job. Avoid making suggestions to employees about personal traits they should change; instead suggest more acceptable ways of performing. For example, instead of focusing on a person's "unreliability", a manager might focus on the fact ④ **which** the employee "has been late to work seven times this month". It is difficult ⑤ **for** employees to change who they are; it is usually much easier for them to change how they act.

**4.** 4)글의 밑줄 친 부분 중 어법, 혹은 문맥상 어휘의 쓰임이 어색한 것을 모두 고르시오. 21

I suspect fungi are a little more forward "thinking" than ① **is** larger partners. Among trees, each species fights other species. Let's assume the beeches native to Central Europe could emerge victorious in most forests there. Would this really be an advantage? What would happen if a new pathogen ② **came** along that infected most of the beeches and killed them? In that case, wouldn't it be more advantageous if there were ③ **a** certain number of other species around — oaks, maples, or firs — ④ **which** would continue to grow and provide the shade needed for a new generation of young beeches to sprout and grow up? Diversity provides security for ancient forests. Because fungi are also very ⑤ **independent** on stable conditions, they support other species underground and protect them from complete collapse to ensure that one species of tree doesn't manage to dominate.

## 5. 5)글의 밑줄 친 부분 중 어법, 혹은 문맥상 어휘의 쓰임이 어색한 것을 모두 고르시오. 22

It's remarkable that positive fantasies help us relax to such an extent that it shows up in physiological tests. If you want to unwind, you can take some deep breaths, ① **getting** a massage, or go for a walk — but you can also try simply closing your eyes and fantasizing about some future outcome that you might enjoy. But what about when your ② **subjective** is to make your wish a reality? The last thing you want to be is relaxed. You want to be ③ **enough energized** to get off the couch and lose those pounds or find that job or study for that test, and you want to be motivated enough to stay ④ **engaging** even when the inevitable obstacles or challenges arise. The principle of "Dream it. Wish it. Do it". does not hold true, and now we know why: in dreaming it, you undercut the energy you need to do it. You put yourself in a ⑤ **temporary** state of complete happiness, calmness — and inactivity.

## 6. 6)글의 밑줄 친 부분 중 어법, 혹은 문맥상 어휘의 쓰임이 어색한 것을 모두 고르시오. 23

If cooking is as central to human identity, biology, and culture as the biological anthropologist Richard Wrangham suggests, it stands to reason that the decline of cooking in our time would have serious consequences for modern life, and so it ① **is**. Are they all bad? Not at all. The outsourcing of much of the work of cooking to corporations has ② **relieved** women of what has traditionally been their exclusive responsibility for feeding the family, ③ **makes** it easier for them to work outside the home and have careers. It has headed off many of the domestic conflicts that such a large shift in gender roles and family dynamics was bound to spark. It has relieved other pressures in the household, including longer workdays and overscheduled children, and ④ **saved** us time that we can now invest in other pursuits. It has also ⑤ **been allowed** us to diversify our diets substantially, making it possible even for people with no cooking skills and little money to enjoy a whole different cuisine. All that's required is a microwave.

## 7. 7)글의 밑줄 친 부분 중 어법, 혹은 문맥상 어휘의 쓰임이 어색한 것을 모두 고르시오. 24

As you may already know, what and how you buy can be political. To whom do you want to give your money? Which companies and corporations do you value and respect? Be mindful about every purchase by carefully researching the corporations that are ① **taken** our money to decide if they deserve our support. Do they have a record of polluting the environment, or do they have fair-trade practices and an end-of-life plan for the products they make? Are they committed to ② **bringing** about good in the world? For instance, my family has ③ **been found** a company producing recycled, plastic-packaging-free toilet paper with a social conscience. They ④ **contribute** 50 percent of their profits to the construction of toilets around the world, and we're genuinely happy to spend our money on this special toilet paper each month. Remember ⑤ **that** the corporate world is built on consumers, so as a consumer you have the power to vote with your wallet and encourage companies to embrace healthier and more sustainable practices with every purchase you choose to make.

## 8. 8)글의 밑줄 친 부분 중 어법, 혹은 문맥상 어휘의 쓰임이 어색한 것을 모두 고르시오. 26

Camille Flammarion was born at Montigny-le-Roi, France. He became interested in ① **astronomy** at an early age, and when he was only sixteen he wrote a book on the origin of the world. The manuscript was not published at the time, but it came to the attention of Urbain Le Verrier, the director of the Paris Observatory. He became an assistant to Le Verrier in 1858 and worked as a calculator. ② **At** nineteen, he wrote another book called The Plurality of Inhabited Worlds, in ③ **what** he passionately claimed that life exists outside the planet Earth. His most successful work, Popular Astronomy, was published in 1880, and eventually sold 130,000 copies. With his own funds, he built an ④ **observant** at Juvisy and spent May to November of each year there. In 1887, he ⑤ **found** the French Astronomical Society and served as editor of its monthly publication.

## 9. 9)글의 밑줄 친 부분 중 어법, 혹은 문맥상 어휘의 쓰임이 어색한 것을 모두 고르시오. 29

There is ① **little** doubt that we are driven by the sell-by date. Once an item is past that date it goes into the waste stream, further increasing its carbon footprint. Remember those items have already travelled hundreds of miles to ② **reach at** the shelves and once they go into waste they start a new carbon mile journey. But we all make our own judgement about sell-by dates; those brought up ③ **while** the Second World War are often scornful of the terrible waste they believe such caution encourages. The manufacturer of the food has a view when making or ④ **growing** something that by the time the product reaches the shelves it has already been travelling for so many days and possibly many miles. The manufacturer then decides that a product can reasonably be consumed within say 90 days and 90 days minus so many days for travelling gives the sell-by date. But ⑤ **whether** it becomes toxic is something each individual can decide. It would seem to make sense not to buy large packs of perishable goods but non-perishable items may become cost-effective.

## 10. 10)글의 밑줄 친 부분 중 어법, 혹은 문맥상 어휘의 쓰임이 어색한 것을 모두 고르시오. 30

The "jolt" of caffeine does wear off. Caffeine ① **removes** from your system by an enzyme within your liver, which gradually degrades it over time. Based in large part on genetics, some people have a more efficient version of the enzyme that degrades caffeine, ② **allowed** the liver to rapidly clear it from the bloodstream. These rare individuals can drink an espresso with dinner and fall fast asleep at midnight without a problem. Others, however, have a slower-acting version of the enzyme. It takes far longer for their system to ③ **illuminate** the same amount of caffeine. As a result, they are very sensitive to caffeine's effects. One cup of tea or coffee in the morning will ④ **be lasted** much of the day, and should they have a second cup, even early in the afternoon, they will find it difficult to fall asleep in the evening. Aging also alters the speed of caffeine clearance: the older we are, the longer it takes our brain and body to remove caffeine, and thus the more sensitive we become in later life to caffeine's sleep-⑤ **disrupted** influence.

## 11. 11)글의 밑줄 친 부분 중 어법, 혹은 문맥상 어휘의 쓰임이 어색한 것을 모두 고르시오. 31

Rebels may think they're rebels, but clever marketers influence them just like the rest of us. Saying, "Everyone is doing it" may turn some people off from an idea. These people will look ① **after** alternatives, which (if cleverly planned) can be exactly what a marketer or persuader wants you to believe. If I want you to consider an idea, and know you strongly reject popular opinion in favor of ② **containing** your independence and uniqueness, I would present the majority option first, which you would reject in favor of my actual preference. We are often tricked when we try to maintain a position of defiance. People use this reversal to make us "independently" choose an option which suits their purposes. Some brands have ③ **taken** full effect of our ④ **definition** towards the mainstream and positioned ⑤ **them** as rebels; which has created even stronger brand loyalty.

## 12. 12)글의 밑줄 친 부분 중 어법, 혹은 문맥상 어휘의 쓰임이 어색한 것을 모두 고르시오. 32

A typical soap opera creates an abstract world, in ① **what** a highly complex web of relationships connects fictional characters that ② **exist** first only in the minds of the program's creators and are then recreated in the minds of the viewer. If you were to think about how ③ **much** human psychology, law, and even everyday physics the viewer must know in order to follow and speculate about the plot, you would discover it is considerable — at least as much as the knowledge required to follow and speculate about a piece of modern mathematics, and in most cases, much more. Yet viewers follow soap operas with ease. How are they able to cope with such abstraction? Because, of course, the ④ **contraction** is built on an extremely familiar framework. The characters in a soap opera and the relationships between them are very much like the real people and relationships we experience every day. The abstraction of a soap opera is only a step removed from the real world. The mental "training" ⑤ **required** to follow a soap opera is provided by our everyday lives.

(.hwp) (.pdf) → www.englishjmygod.com

**13.** 13)글의 밑줄 친 부분 중 어법, 혹은 문맥상 어휘의 쓰임이 어색한 것을 모두 고르시오. 33

As always happens with natural selection, bats and their prey have been engaged in a life-or-death sensory arms race for millions of years. It's believed that hearing in moths ① **arose** specifically in response to the threat of ② **being eaten** by bats. (Not all insects can hear.) Over millions of years, moths have evolved the ability to detect sounds at ever higher frequencies, and, as they have, the frequencies of bats' vocalizations have risen, too. Some moth species have also evolved scales on their wings and a fur-like coat on their bodies; both act as "acoustic camouflage", by absorbing sound waves in the frequencies ③ **emitted** by bats, thereby preventing those sound waves from bouncing back. The B-2 bomber and other "stealth" aircraft have fuselages ④ **making** of materials that do ⑤ **something similar** with radar beams.

**14.** 14)글의 밑줄 친 부분 중 어법, 혹은 문맥상 어휘의 쓰임이 어색한 것을 모두 고르시오. 34

Much of human thought is designed to screen out information and to sort the rest into a manageable condition. The inflow of data from our senses could create an overwhelming chaos, especially ① **given** the enormous amount of information available in culture and society. Out of all the sensory impressions and possible information, ② **which** is vital to find a small amount that is most relevant to our individual needs and to organize that into a usable stock of knowledge. Expectancies accomplish some of this work, ③ **help** to screen out information that is irrelevant to what is expected, and ④ **focusing** our attention on clear contradictions. The processes of learning and memory are marked by a steady elimination of information. People notice only a part of the world around ⑤ **them**. Then, only a fraction of what they notice gets processed and stored into memory. And only part of what gets committed to memory can be retrieved.

**15.** 15)글의 밑줄 친 부분 중 어법, 혹은 문맥상 어휘의 쓰임이 어색한 것을 모두 고르시오. 35

The irony of early democracy in Europe is ① **what** it thrived and ② **prospered** precisely because European rulers for a very long time were remarkably weak. For more than a millennium after the fall of Rome, European rulers lacked the ability to assess ③ **that** their people were producing and to levy substantial taxes based on this. The most striking way to illustrate European weakness is to show how ④ **a little** revenue they collected. Europeans would eventually develop strong systems of revenue collection, but it took them an awfully long time to do so. In medieval times, and for part of the early modern era, Chinese emperors and Muslim caliphs were able to ⑤ **contract** much more of economic production than any European ruler with the exception of small city-states.

**16.** 16)글의 밑줄 친 부분 중 어법, 혹은 문맥상 어휘의 쓰임이 어색한 것을 모두 고르시오. 36

If you drive down a busy street, you will find many competing businesses, often right next to one another. For example, in most places a consumer in search of a quick meal has many choices, and more fast-food restaurants ① **are appeared** all the time. These ② **competing** firms advertise heavily. The temptation is to see advertising as driving up the price of a product without any benefit to the consumer. ③ **However**, this misconception doesn't account for why firms advertise. In markets where competitors sell slightly differentiated products, advertising enables firms to inform their customers about new products and services. Yes, costs ④ **raise**, but consumers also gain information to help make purchasing decisions. Consumers also benefit from added variety, and we all get a product that's pretty close to our vision of a perfect good — and no other market structure delivers that ⑤ **outcome**.

**17.** 17)글의 밑줄 친 부분 중 어법, 혹은 문맥상 어휘의 쓰임이 어색한 것을 모두 고르시오. 37

Architects might say a machine can never design an innovative or impressive building because a computer cannot be "creative". Yet ① **consider** the Elbphilharmonie, a new concert hall in Hamburg, ② **which** contains a remarkably beautiful auditorium ③ **composed** of ten thousand interlocking acoustic panels. It is the sort of space that makes one instinctively think that only a human being — and a human with a remarkably refined creative sensibility, at that — could design something so aesthetically impressive. Yet the auditorium was, in fact, ④ **designed** algorithmically, using a technique known as "parametric design". The architects gave the system a set of criteria, and it generated a set of possible designs for the architects to choose from. Similar software has been used to design lightweight bicycle frames and sturdier chairs, among much else. Are these systems behaving "creatively"? No, they are using lots of processing power to blindly generate varied possible designs, ⑤ **working** in a very different way from a human being.

**18.** 18)글의 밑줄 친 부분 중 어법, 혹은 문맥상 어휘의 쓰임이 어색한 것을 모두 고르시오. 38

The brain is a high-energy consumer of glucose, which is its fuel. Although the brain accounts for merely 3 percent of a person's body weight, it ① **consumes** 20 percent of the available fuel. Your brain can't store fuel, ② **therefore**, so it has to "pay as it goes". Since your brain is incredibly ③ **adoptive**, it economizes its fuel resources. Thus, ④ **during** a period of high stress, it shifts away from the analysis of the nuances of a situation to a singular and fixed focus on the stressful situation at hand. You don't sit back and speculate about the meaning of life when you are stressed. Instead, you devote all your energy to trying to figure out what action to take. Sometimes, however, this shift from the higher-thinking parts of the brain to the automatic and ⑤ **reflexive** parts of the brain can lead you to do something too quickly, without thinking.

**19.** 19)글의 밑줄 친 부분 중 어법, 혹은 문맥상 어휘의 쓰임이 어색한 것을 모두 고르시오. 39.

Much research has been carried out on the causes of engagement, an issue that is important from both a theoretical and practical standpoint: ① **identified** the drivers of work engagement may enable us to manipulate or influence it. The causes of engagement fall into two major camps: situational and personal. The most influential situational causes are job resources, feedback and leadership, the latter, of course, being responsible for job resources and feedback. Indeed, leaders influence engagement by giving their employees honest and constructive feedback on their performance, and by providing ② **it** with the necessary resources that enable them to perform their job well. It is, however, noteworthy that although engagement drives job performance, job performance also drives engagement. In other words, when employees are able to do their jobs well — to the point that they match or ③ **proceed** their own expectations and ambitions — they will engage more, be proud of their achievements, and find work more ④ **meaningfully**. This is especially evident when people are employed in jobs that ⑤ **alien** with their values.

**20.** 20)글의 밑줄 친 부분 중 어법, 혹은 문맥상 어휘의 쓰임이 어색한 것을 모두 고르시오. 40.

In 2006, researchers conducted a study on the motivations for helping after the September 11th terrorist attacks against the United States. In the study, they found ① **what** individuals who gave money, blood, goods, or other forms of assistance because of other-focused motives (giving to reduce another's discomfort) were almost four times more likely to still be giving support one year later than those ② **who** original motivation was to reduce personal distress. This effect likely stems from differences in emotional arousal. The events of September 11th emotionally ③ **affected** people throughout the United States. Those who gave to reduce their own distress reduced their emotional arousal with their initial gift, ④ **discharging** that emotional distress. However, those who gave to reduce others' distress did not stop ⑤ **to empathize** with victims who continued to struggle long after the attacks.

**21.** 21)글의 밑줄 친 부분 중 어법, 혹은 문맥상 어휘의 쓰임이 어색한 것을 모두 고르시오. 41~42

In England in the 1680s, it was unusual to live to the age of fifty. This was a period when knowledge was not spread widely, there were ① **a few** books and most people could not read. As a consequence, knowledge passed down through the oral traditions of stories and shared experiences. And since older people had ② **been accumulated** more knowledge, the social norm was that to be over fifty was to be wise. This social perception of age began to shift with the ③ **advent** of new technologies such as the printing press. Over time, as more books were printed, literacy increased, and the oral traditions of knowledge transfer began to fade. With the fading of oral traditions, the wisdom of the old became ④ **more** important and as a consequence being over fifty was no longer seen as signifying wisdom.

We are living in a period when the gap between chronological and biological age is ⑤ **changing** fast and where social norms are struggling to adapt. In a video produced by the AARP (formerly the American Association of Retired Persons), young people were asked to do various activities 'just like an old person'. When older people joined them in the video, the gap between the stereotype and the older people's actual behaviour was striking. It is clear that in today's world our social norms need to be updated quickly.

**22.** 22)글의 밑줄 친 부분 중 어법, 혹은 문맥상 어휘의 쓰임이 어색한 것을 모두 고르시오. 43~45

When Jack was a young man in his early twenties during the 1960s, he had tried to work in his father's insurance business, as was expected of him. His two older brothers fit in easily and seemed to enjoy their work. But Jack was ① **boring** with the insurance industry. "It was worse than ② **being bored**", he said. "I felt like I was dying inside". Jack felt drawn to hair styling and dreamed of owning a hair shop with a lively environment. He was sure that he would enjoy the creative and social aspects of it and that he'd be successful. When he was twenty-six, Jack approached his father and expressed his intentions of leaving the business to become a hairstylist. As Jack anticipated, his father raged and accused Jack of being selfish, ungrateful, and unmanly. In the face of his father's fury, Jack felt confusion and fear. His resolve became weak. But then a force filled his chest and he stood firm in his decision. In ③ **following** his path, Jack not only ran three flourishing hair shops, but also helped his clients ④ **experience** their inner beauty by listening and encouraging them when they faced dark times. His love for his work led to donating time and talent at nursing homes, which in turn led to becoming a hospice volunteer, and eventually to starting fundraising efforts for the hospice program in his community. And all this laid a strong stepping stone for another courageous move in his life. When, after having two healthy children of their own, Jack and his wife, Michele, decided to bring an orphaned child into their family, his father threatened to disown them. Jack understood that his father feared adoption, in this case especially because the child was of a different racial background than their family. Jack and Michele risked rejection and went ahead with the adoption. It took years but eventually Jack's father loved the little girl and accepted his son's independent choices. Jack realized that, although he often felt fear and still ⑤ **is**, he has always had courage. In fact, courage was the scaffolding around which he had built richness into his life.

## 2023 고2 9월 모의고사

❶ voca  ❷ text  ❸ [ / ]  ❹ ____  ❺ quiz 1  ❻ quiz 2  ❼ quiz 3  ⑧ quiz 4  ❾ quiz 5

**23. 1)밑줄 부분 중 어법, 혹은 문맥상 어휘의 쓰임이 어색한 것을 올바르게 고쳐 쓰시오. (2개)** [18]

To whom it may concern, I would like to draw your attention ① **to** a problem that frequently ② **occurs** with the No. 35 buses. There is a bus stop about halfway along Fenny Road, at ③ **that** the No.35 buses are supposed to stop. It would ④ **appear**, however, ⑤ **which** some of your drivers are either unaware of this bus stop or for some reason choose to ignore it, ⑥ **driving** past even though the buses are not full. I would be grateful if you could remind your drivers ⑦ **that** this bus stop exists and that they should be prepared to stop at it. I look forward to ⑧ **seeing** an improvement in this service soon.

Yours faithfully, John Williams

| 기호 | 어색한 표현 | | 올바른 표현 |
|---|---|---|---|
| ( ) | _____ | ⇨ | _____ |
| ( ) | _____ | ⇨ | _____ |

**24. 2)밑줄 부분 중 어법, 혹은 문맥상 어휘의 쓰임이 어색한 것을 올바르게 고쳐 쓰시오. (6개)** [19]

My 10-year-old ① **was appeared**, in desperate need of a quarter. "A quarter? What on earth do you need a quarter ② **x**"? My tone bordered on irritation. I didn't want to ③ **bother** with such a trivial demand. "There's a garage sale up the street, and there's something I just gotta have! It only costs a quarter. Please"? I placed a quarter in my son's hand. Moments later, a little voice said, "Here, Mommy, this is for you". I glanced down at the hands of my little son and saw a four-inch cream-colored statue of two small children ④ **to hug** one another. ⑤ **Inscribed** at their feet ⑥ **was** words that read It starts with 'L' ends with 'E' and in between are 'O' and 'V'. As I watched him ⑦ **to race** back to the garage sale, I smiled with a heart full of happiness. That 25-cent garage sale purchase brought me a lot of joy.

| 기호 | 어색한 표현 | | 올바른 표현 |
|---|---|---|---|
| ( ) | _____ | ⇨ | _____ |
| ( ) | _____ | ⇨ | _____ |
| ( ) | _____ | ⇨ | _____ |
| ( ) | _____ | ⇨ | _____ |
| ( ) | _____ | ⇨ | _____ |
| ( ) | _____ | ⇨ | _____ |

(.hwp) (.pdf) → www.englishjmygod.com

**25.** 3)**밑줄 부분 중 어법, 혹은 문맥상 어휘의 쓰임이 어색한 것을 올바르게 고쳐 쓰시오. (5개)** [20]

Managers frequently try to play psychologist, to "figure out" why an employee has ① **been acted** in a certain way. ② **Empathized** with employees in order to understand their point of view can be very helpful. ③ **However**, when ④ **to deal** with a problem area, in particular, ⑤ **remember** ⑥ **what** it is not the person who is bad, but the actions exhibited on the job. Avoid ⑦ **to make** suggestions to employees about personal traits they should change; instead ⑧ **suggest** more acceptable ways of performing. For example, instead of focusing on a person's "unreliability", a manager might focus on the fact ⑨ **that** the employee "has been ⑩ **late** to work seven times this month". It is difficult ⑪ **for** employees to change who they are; it is usually ⑫ **much** easier for them to change how they act.

| 기호 | 어색한 표현 | | 올바른 표현 |
|---|---|---|---|
| (　) | ＿＿＿＿＿＿＿＿ | ⇨ | ＿＿＿＿＿＿＿＿ |
| (　) | ＿＿＿＿＿＿＿＿ | ⇨ | ＿＿＿＿＿＿＿＿ |
| (　) | ＿＿＿＿＿＿＿＿ | ⇨ | ＿＿＿＿＿＿＿＿ |
| (　) | ＿＿＿＿＿＿＿＿ | ⇨ | ＿＿＿＿＿＿＿＿ |
| (　) | ＿＿＿＿＿＿＿＿ | ⇨ | ＿＿＿＿＿＿＿＿ |

**26.** 4)**밑줄 부분 중 어법, 혹은 문맥상 어휘의 쓰임이 어색한 것을 올바르게 고쳐 쓰시오. (4개)** [21]

I suspect fungi ① **is** a little more forward "thinking" than ② **is** larger partners. Among trees, each species ③ **fight** other species. Let's assume the beeches native to Central Europe could emerge victorious in most forests there. Would this really be an advantage? What would happen if a new pathogen ④ **came** along that infected most of the beeches and killed them? In that case, wouldn't it be more advantageous if there were ⑤ **the** certain number of other species around — oaks, maples, or firs — ⑥ **that** would continue to grow and provide the shade needed for a new generation of young beeches to sprout and grow up? Diversity provides security for ancient forests. Because fungi ⑦ **are** also very ⑧ **dependent** on stable conditions, they support other species underground and protect ⑨ **them** from complete collapse to ensure that one species of tree doesn't manage to dominate.

| 기호 | 어색한 표현 | | 올바른 표현 |
|---|---|---|---|
| (　) | ＿＿＿＿＿＿＿＿ | ⇨ | ＿＿＿＿＿＿＿＿ |
| (　) | ＿＿＿＿＿＿＿＿ | ⇨ | ＿＿＿＿＿＿＿＿ |
| (　) | ＿＿＿＿＿＿＿＿ | ⇨ | ＿＿＿＿＿＿＿＿ |
| (　) | ＿＿＿＿＿＿＿＿ | ⇨ | ＿＿＿＿＿＿＿＿ |

**27.** 5)밑줄 부분 중 어법, 혹은 문맥상 어휘의 쓰임이 어색한 것을 올바르게 고쳐 쓰시오. (11개) 22

It's remarkable that positive fantasies help us ① **relaxing** to such an extent ② **when** it shows up in physiological tests. If you want to unwind, you can take some deep breaths, ③ **getting** a massage, or go for a walk — but you can also try simply closing your eyes and ④ **to fantasize** about some future outcome that you might enjoy. But what about when your ⑤ **subjective** is to make your wish a reality? The last thing you want to be is ⑥ **relaxing**. You want to be ⑦ **enough energized** to get off the couch and lose those pounds or find that job or study for that test, and you want to be motivated enough to stay ⑧ **engaging** even when the inevitable obstacles or challenges ⑨ **arouse**. The ⑩ **principal** of "Dream it. Wish it. Do it". does not hold true, and now we know why: in dreaming it, you undercut the energy you need to do it. You put yourself in a ⑪ **temporal** state of complete happiness, calmness — and inactivity.

기호          어색한 표현                                          올바른 표현

(      ) _____ ⇨ _____

(      ) _____ ⇨ _____

(      ) _____ ⇨ _____

(      ) _____ ⇨ _____

(      ) _____ ⇨ _____

(      ) _____ ⇨ _____

(      ) _____ ⇨ _____

(      ) _____ ⇨ _____

(      ) _____ ⇨ _____

(      ) _____ ⇨ _____

(      ) _____ ⇨ _____

**28.** 6)밑줄 부분 중 어법, 혹은 문맥상 어휘의 쓰임이 어색한 것을 올바르게 고쳐 쓰시오. (6개) 23

If cooking is as central to human identity, biology, and culture as the biological anthropologist Richard Wrangham suggests, ① **they** stands to reason that the decline of cooking in our time would have serious consequences for modern life, and so it ② **has**. Are they all bad? Not at all. The outsourcing of much of the work of cooking to ③ **cooperations** has ④ **relieved** women of what has traditionally been their ⑤ **inclusive** responsibility for feeding the family, ⑥ **makes** ⑦ **it** easier for them to work outside the home and have careers. It has headed off many of the domestic conflicts that such a large shift in gender roles and family dynamics was bound to spark. It has relieved other pressures in the household, including longer workdays and overscheduled children, and ⑧ **saved** us time that we can now invest in other pursuits. It has also ⑨ **allowed** us to diversify our diets substantially, ⑩ **makes** it possible even for people with no cooking skills and little money to enjoy a whole different cuisine. All that's ⑪ **requiring** is a microwave.

기호          어색한 표현                                          올바른 표현

(      ) _____ ⇨ _____

(      ) _____ ⇨ _____

(      ) _____ ⇨ _____

(      ) _____ ⇨ _____

(      ) _____ ⇨ _____

(      ) _____ ⇨ _____

(.hwp) (.pdf) → www.englishjmygod.com

## 29. 7)밑줄 부분 중 어법, 혹은 문맥상 어휘의 쓰임이 어색한 것을 올바르게 고쳐 쓰시오. (8개) <sup>24</sup>

As you may already know, what and how you buy can be political. To ① **who** do you want to give your money? Which companies and ② **cooperations** do you value and respect? Be mindful about every purchase by carefully researching the corporations that are ③ **taking** our money to decide ④ **that** they deserve our support. Do they have a record of polluting the environment, or do they have fair-trade practices and an end-of-life plan for the products they make? Are they ⑤ **committing** to ⑥ **bring** about good in the world? For instance, my family has ⑦ **found** a company producing recycled, plastic-packaging-free toilet paper with a social conscience. They ⑧ **constitute** 50 percent of their profits to the ⑨ **construction** of toilets around the world, and we're genuinely happy to spend our money on this special toilet paper each month. Remember ⑩ **what** the corporate world is built on consumers, so as a consumer you have the power to vote with your wallet and encourage companies ⑪ **embracing** healthier and more sustainable practices with every purchase you choose to make.

| 기호 | 어색한 표현 | | 올바른 표현 |
|---|---|---|---|
| ( ) | _____ | ⇨ | _____ |
| ( ) | _____ | ⇨ | _____ |
| ( ) | _____ | ⇨ | _____ |
| ( ) | _____ | ⇨ | _____ |
| ( ) | _____ | ⇨ | _____ |
| ( ) | _____ | ⇨ | _____ |
| ( ) | _____ | ⇨ | _____ |
| ( ) | _____ | ⇨ | _____ |

## 30. 8)밑줄 부분 중 어법, 혹은 문맥상 어휘의 쓰임이 어색한 것을 올바르게 고쳐 쓰시오. (3개) <sup>26</sup>

Camille Flammarion was born at Montigny-le-Roi, France. He became interested in ① **astronomy** at an early age, and when he was only sixteen he wrote a book on the origin of the world. The manuscript was not published at the time, but it came to the attention of Urbain Le Verrier, the director of the Paris Observatory. He became an assistant to Le Verrier in 1858 and worked as a calculator. ② **At** nineteen, he wrote another book ③ **was called** The Plurality of Inhabited Worlds, in ④ **what** he passionately claimed ⑤ **which** life exists outside the planet Earth. His most successful work, Popular Astronomy, was published in 1880, and eventually sold 130,000 copies. With his own funds, he built an ⑥ **observatory** at Juvisy and spent May to November of each year there. In 1887, he ⑦ **founded** the French Astronomical Society and served as editor of its monthly publication.

| 기호 | 어색한 표현 | | 올바른 표현 |
|---|---|---|---|
| ( ) | _____ | ⇨ | _____ |
| ( ) | _____ | ⇨ | _____ |
| ( ) | _____ | ⇨ | _____ |

**31. 9)밑줄 부분 중 어법, 혹은 문맥상 어휘의 쓰임이 어색한 것을 올바르게 고쳐 쓰시오. (11개)** [29]

There is ① **a little** doubt that we are driven by the sell-by date. Once an item is past that date it goes into the waste stream, ② **farther** increasing its carbon footprint. ③ **Remembering** those items have already travelled hundreds of miles to ④ **reach at** the shelves and once they go into waste they start a new carbon mile journey. But we all make our own judgement about sell-by dates; those brought up ⑤ **while** the Second World War are often scornful of the terrible waste they believe such caution ⑥ **discourages**. The manufacturer of the food has a view when ⑦ **to make** or ⑧ **grow** something that by the time the product ⑨ **reaches out** the shelves it has already been travelling for so many days and possibly many miles. The manufacturer then decides that a product can reasonably be consumed within say 90 days and 90 days minus so many days for travelling ⑩ **giving** the sell-by date. But ⑪ **that** it becomes toxic is something each individual can decide. It would seem to make sense not to buy large packs of perishable goods but non-perishable items may become cost-effective.

| 기호 | 어색한 표현 | | 올바른 표현 |
|---|---|---|---|
| ( ) | _____ | ⇨ | _____ |
| ( ) | _____ | ⇨ | _____ |
| ( ) | _____ | ⇨ | _____ |
| ( ) | _____ | ⇨ | _____ |
| ( ) | _____ | ⇨ | _____ |
| ( ) | _____ | ⇨ | _____ |
| ( ) | _____ | ⇨ | _____ |
| ( ) | _____ | ⇨ | _____ |
| ( ) | _____ | ⇨ | _____ |
| ( ) | _____ | ⇨ | _____ |
| ( ) | _____ | ⇨ | _____ |

**32. 10)밑줄 부분 중 어법, 혹은 문맥상 어휘의 쓰임이 어색한 것을 올바르게 고쳐 쓰시오. (6개)** [30]

The "jolt" of caffeine does wear off. Caffeine ① **is removed** from your system by an enzyme within your liver, ② **which** gradually degrades it over time. Based in large part on genetics, some people have a more ③ **affectionate** version of the enzyme that degrades caffeine, ④ **allowed** the liver to rapidly clear it from the bloodstream. These rare individuals can drink an espresso with dinner and fall fast asleep at midnight without a problem. Others, ⑤ **therefore**, have a slower-acting version of the enzyme. It takes far longer for their system to ⑥ **eliminate** the same amount of caffeine. As a result, they are very ⑦ **sensible** to caffeine's effects. One cup of tea or coffee in the morning will ⑧ **be lasted** much of the day, and should they have a second cup, even early in the afternoon, they will find ⑨ **it** difficult to fall asleep in the evening. Aging also alters the speed of caffeine clearance: the older we are, the longer it takes our brain and body to remove caffeine, and thus the more sensitive we become in later life to caffeine's sleep-⑩ **disrupted** influence.

| 기호 | 어색한 표현 | | 올바른 표현 |
|---|---|---|---|
| ( ) | _____ | ⇨ | _____ |
| ( ) | _____ | ⇨ | _____ |
| ( ) | _____ | ⇨ | _____ |
| ( ) | _____ | ⇨ | _____ |
| ( ) | _____ | ⇨ | _____ |
| ( ) | _____ | ⇨ | _____ |

### 33. 11)밑줄 부분 중 어법, 혹은 문맥상 어휘의 쓰임이 어색한 것을 올바르게 고쳐 쓰시오. (5개) 31

Rebels may think they're rebels, but clever marketers ① **influence on** them just like the rest of us. Saying, "Everyone is doing it" may turn some people off from an idea. These people will look ② **for** alternatives, ③ **that** (if cleverly planned) can be exactly what a marketer or persuader wants you to believe. If I want you to consider an idea, and know you strongly reject popular opinion in favor of ④ **maintaining** your independence and uniqueness, I would present the majority option first, which you would reject in favor of my actual preference. We are often tricked when we try to maintain a position of defiance. People use this reversal to make us "independently" choose an option ⑤ **what** suits their purposes. Some brands have ⑥ **been taken** full effect of our ⑦ **definition** towards the mainstream and positioned ⑧ **themselves** as rebels; which has created even stronger brand loyalty.

| 기호 | 어색한 표현 | | 올바른 표현 |
|---|---|---|---|
| ( ) | _____ | ⇨ | _____ |
| ( ) | _____ | ⇨ | _____ |
| ( ) | _____ | ⇨ | _____ |
| ( ) | _____ | ⇨ | _____ |
| ( ) | _____ | ⇨ | _____ |

### 34. 12)밑줄 부분 중 어법, 혹은 문맥상 어휘의 쓰임이 어색한 것을 올바르게 고쳐 쓰시오. (4개) 32

A typical soap opera creates an abstract world, in ① **what** a highly complex web of relationships connects fictional characters that ② **exist** first only in the minds of the program's creators and are then recreated in the minds of the viewer. If you were to think about how ③ **much** human psychology, law, and even everyday physics the viewer must know in order to follow and speculate about the plot, you would discover it is ④ **considerate** — at least as much as the knowledge required to follow and speculate about a piece of modern mathematics, and in most cases, much more. Yet viewers follow soap operas with ease. How are they able to cope with such abstraction? Because, of course, the ⑤ **contraction** is built on an extremely familiar framework. The characters in a soap opera and the relationships between ⑥ **them** are very much like the real people and relationships we experience every day. The abstraction of a soap opera is only a step ⑦ **removed** from the real world. The mental "training" ⑧ **is required** to follow a soap opera is provided by our everyday lives.

| 기호 | 어색한 표현 | | 올바른 표현 |
|---|---|---|---|
| ( ) | _____ | ⇨ | _____ |
| ( ) | _____ | ⇨ | _____ |
| ( ) | _____ | ⇨ | _____ |
| ( ) | _____ | ⇨ | _____ |

**35.** 13)**밑줄 부분 중 어법, 혹은 문맥상 어휘의 쓰임이 어색한 것을 올바르게 고쳐 쓰시오. (7개)** 33

As always happens with natural selection, bats and their prey have ① **engaged** in a life-or-death sensory arms race for millions of years. It's believed that hearing in moths ② **arouse** specifically in response to the threat of ③ **eating** by bats. (Not all insects can hear.) Over millions of years, moths have evolved the ability to detect sounds at ever higher frequencies, and, as they have, the frequencies of bats' vocalizations have ④ **been risen**, too. Some moth species have also evolved scales on their wings and a fur-like coat on their bodies; both act as "acoustic camouflage", by absorbing sound waves in the frequencies ⑤ **omitted** by bats, thereby preventing those sound waves from bouncing back. The B-2 bomber and other "stealth" aircraft have fuselages ⑥ **making** of materials that do ⑦ **similar something** with radar beams.

| 기호 | 어색한 표현 | | 올바른 표현 |
|---|---|---|---|
| (　　) | ＿＿＿＿＿＿＿＿ | ⇨ | ＿＿＿＿＿＿＿＿ |
| (　　) | ＿＿＿＿＿＿＿＿ | ⇨ | ＿＿＿＿＿＿＿＿ |
| (　　) | ＿＿＿＿＿＿＿＿ | ⇨ | ＿＿＿＿＿＿＿＿ |
| (　　) | ＿＿＿＿＿＿＿＿ | ⇨ | ＿＿＿＿＿＿＿＿ |
| (　　) | ＿＿＿＿＿＿＿＿ | ⇨ | ＿＿＿＿＿＿＿＿ |
| (　　) | ＿＿＿＿＿＿＿＿ | ⇨ | ＿＿＿＿＿＿＿＿ |
| (　　) | ＿＿＿＿＿＿＿＿ | ⇨ | ＿＿＿＿＿＿＿＿ |

**36.** 14)**밑줄 부분 중 어법, 혹은 문맥상 어휘의 쓰임이 어색한 것을 올바르게 고쳐 쓰시오. (2개)** 34

Much of human thought is designed to screen out information and to sort the rest into a manageable condition. The inflow of data from our senses could create an ① **overwhelmed** chaos, especially ② **given** the enormous amount of information available in culture and society. Out of all the sensory impressions and possible information, ③ **it** is vital to find a small amount that is most ④ **relevant** to our individual needs and to organize that into a usable stock of knowledge. Expectancies accomplish some of this work, ⑤ **helping** to screen out information that is irrelevant to what is expected, and ⑥ **focus** our attention on clear contradictions. The processes of learning and memory are marked by a steady elimination of information. People notice only a part of the world around ⑦ **them**. Then, only a fraction of what they notice gets ⑧ **processed** and stored into memory. And only part of what gets committed to memory can be retrieved.

| 기호 | 어색한 표현 | | 올바른 표현 |
|---|---|---|---|
| (　　) | ＿＿＿＿＿＿＿＿ | ⇨ | ＿＿＿＿＿＿＿＿ |
| (　　) | ＿＿＿＿＿＿＿＿ | ⇨ | ＿＿＿＿＿＿＿＿ |

(.hwp) (.pdf) → www.englishjmygod.com

**37.** <sup>15)</sup>**밑줄 부분 중 어법, 혹은 문맥상 어휘의 쓰임이 어색한 것을 올바르게 고쳐 쓰시오. (7개)** <sup>35</sup>

The irony of early democracy in Europe is ① **what** it thrived and ② **processed** precisely because European rulers for a very long time ③ **were** remarkably weak. For more than a millennium after the fall of Rome, European rulers lacked the ability to ④ **access** ⑤ **that** their people were producing and ⑥ **leving** substantial taxes based on this. The most striking way to ⑦ **illuminate** European weakness is to show how ⑧ **little** revenue they collected. Europeans would eventually develop strong systems of revenue collection, but it took them an awfully long time to do so. In medieval times, and for part of the early modern era, Chinese emperors and Muslim caliphs were able to ⑨ **contract** much more of economic production than any European ruler with the ⑩ **exception** of small city-states.

| 기호 | 어색한 표현 | | 올바른 표현 |
|---|---|---|---|
| ( ) | _____ | ⇨ | _____ |
| ( ) | _____ | ⇨ | _____ |
| ( ) | _____ | ⇨ | _____ |
| ( ) | _____ | ⇨ | _____ |
| ( ) | _____ | ⇨ | _____ |
| ( ) | _____ | ⇨ | _____ |
| ( ) | _____ | ⇨ | _____ |

**38.** <sup>16)</sup>**밑줄 부분 중 어법, 혹은 문맥상 어휘의 쓰임이 어색한 것을 올바르게 고쳐 쓰시오. (6개)** <sup>36</sup>

If you drive down a busy street, you will find many competing businesses, often right next to one another. For example, in most places a consumer in search of a quick meal has many choices, and more fast-food restaurants ① **are appeared** all the time. These ② **competitive** firms advertise heavily. The temptation is to see advertising as driving up the price of a product without any benefit to the consumer. ③ **Therefore**, this misconception doesn't account for why firms advertise. In markets where competitors sell slightly ④ **identical** products, advertising enables firms ⑤ **to inform** their customers about new products and services. Yes, costs ⑥ **raise**, but consumers also gain information to help make purchasing decisions. Consumers also benefit from added variety, and we all get a product that's pretty close to our vision of a perfect good — and no other market structure delivers that ⑦ **income**.

| 기호 | 어색한 표현 | | 올바른 표현 |
|---|---|---|---|
| ( ) | _____ | ⇨ | _____ |
| ( ) | _____ | ⇨ | _____ |
| ( ) | _____ | ⇨ | _____ |
| ( ) | _____ | ⇨ | _____ |
| ( ) | _____ | ⇨ | _____ |
| ( ) | _____ | ⇨ | _____ |

**39.** 17)**밑줄 부분 중 어법, 혹은 문맥상 어휘의 쓰임이 어색한 것을 올바르게 고쳐 쓰시오. (9개)** [37]

Architects might say a machine can never design an innovative or impressive building because a computer cannot be "creative". Yet ① **considering** the Elbphilharmonie, a new concert hall in Hamburg, ② **that** contains a remarkably beautiful auditorium ③ **consisted** of ten thousand interlocking acoustic panels. It is the sort of space that makes one instinctively think that only a human being — and a human with a remarkably ④ **confined** creative sensibility, at that — could design something so aesthetically impressive. Yet the auditorium was, in fact, ⑤ **desinging** algorithmically, using a technique known as "parametric design". The architects gave the system a set of criteria, and ⑥ **which** generated a set of possible designs for the architects to choose from. ⑦ **Dissimilar** software has been used to ⑧ **designing** lightweight bicycle frames and sturdier chairs, among much else. Are these systems behaving "creatively"? No, they are using lots of processing power to blindly generate varied possible designs, ⑨ **worked** in a very different way from a human being.

| 기호 | 어색한 표현 | | 올바른 표현 |
|---|---|---|---|
| ( ) | _____ | ⇨ | _____ |
| ( ) | _____ | ⇨ | _____ |
| ( ) | _____ | ⇨ | _____ |
| ( ) | _____ | ⇨ | _____ |
| ( ) | _____ | ⇨ | _____ |
| ( ) | _____ | ⇨ | _____ |
| ( ) | _____ | ⇨ | _____ |
| ( ) | _____ | ⇨ | _____ |
| ( ) | _____ | ⇨ | _____ |

**40.** 18)**밑줄 부분 중 어법, 혹은 문맥상 어휘의 쓰임이 어색한 것을 올바르게 고쳐 쓰시오. (6개)** [38]

The brain is a high-energy consumer of glucose, which is its fuel. Although the brain ① **is accounted** for merely 3 percent of a person's body weight, it ② **presumes** 20 percent of the available fuel. Your brain can't store fuel, ③ **therefore**, so it has to "pay as it goes".  Since your brain is incredibly ④ **adaptive**, it economizes its fuel resources. Thus, ⑤ **during** a period of high stress, it shifts away from the analysis of the nuances of a situation to a singular and fixed focus on the stressful situation at hand. You don't sit back and speculate about the meaning of life when you are stressed. Instead, you devote all your energy to ⑥ **try** to figure out what action to take. Sometimes, however, this shift from the higher-thinking parts of the brain to the ⑦ **anatomic** and ⑧ **reflective** parts of the brain can lead you to do something too quickly, without thinking.

| 기호 | 어색한 표현 | | 올바른 표현 |
|---|---|---|---|
| ( ) | _____ | ⇨ | _____ |
| ( ) | _____ | ⇨ | _____ |
| ( ) | _____ | ⇨ | _____ |
| ( ) | _____ | ⇨ | _____ |
| ( ) | _____ | ⇨ | _____ |
| ( ) | _____ | ⇨ | _____ |

(.hwp) (.pdf) → www.englishjmygod.com

**41.** [19]**밑줄 부분 중 어법, 혹은 문맥상 어휘의 쓰임이 어색한 것을 올바르게 고쳐 쓰시오. (2개)** [39.]

Much research has ① **carried** out on the causes of engagement, an issue that is important from both a theoretical and practical standpoint: ② **identifying** the drivers of work engagement may enable us to manipulate or influence ③ **it**. The causes of engagement fall into two major camps: situational and personal. The most ④ **influential** situational causes are job resources, feedback and leadership, the ⑤ **later**, of course, being responsible for job resources and feedback. Indeed, leaders influence engagement by giving their employees honest and ⑥ **constructive** feedback on their performance, and by providing ⑦ **them** with the necessary resources that enable them to perform their job well. It is, however, noteworthy that although engagement drives job performance, job performance also drives engagement. In other words, when employees are able to do their jobs well — to the point that they match or ⑧ **exceed** their own expectations and ambitions — they will engage more, be proud of their achievements, and find work more ⑨ **meaningful**. This is especially evident when people are employed in jobs that ⑩ **align** with their values.

기호       어색한 표현             올바른 표현

(    ) _____ ⇨ _____

(    ) _____ ⇨ _____


**42.** [20]**밑줄 부분 중 어법, 혹은 문맥상 어휘의 쓰임이 어색한 것을 올바르게 고쳐 쓰시오. (4개)** [40.]

In 2006, researchers ① **conducting** a study on the motivations for helping after the September 11th terrorist attacks against the United States. In the study, they found ② **what** individuals who gave money, blood, goods, or other forms of assistance because of other-focused motives (giving to reduce another's discomfort) were almost four times more likely to still be giving support one year later than those ③ **whose** original motivation was to reduce personal distress. This effect likely stems from differences in emotional arousal. The events of September 11th emotionally ④ **affected on** people throughout the United States. Those who gave to reduce their own distress reduced their emotional arousal with their initial gift, ⑤ **discharging** that emotional distress. However, those who gave to reduce others' distress did not stop ⑥ **to empathize** with victims who continued to struggle long after the attacks.

기호       어색한 표현             올바른 표현

(    ) _____ ⇨ _____

(    ) _____ ⇨ _____

(    ) _____ ⇨ _____

(    ) _____ ⇨ _____

**43.** 21)**밑줄 부분 중 어법, 혹은 문맥상 어휘의 쓰임이 어색한 것을 올바르게 고쳐 쓰시오. (1개)** 41~42

In England in the 1680s, it was unusual to live to the age of fifty. This was a period when knowledge was not spread widely, there were ① **few** books and most people could not read. As a consequence, knowledge passed down through the oral traditions of stories and shared experiences. And since older people had ② **accumulated** more knowledge, the social norm was that to be over fifty was to be wise. This social perception of age began to shift with the ③ **advent** of new technologies such as the printing press. Over time, as more books were printed, ④ **literacy** increased, and the oral traditions of knowledge transfer began to fade. With the fading of oral traditions, the wisdom of the old became ⑤ **more** important and as a consequence being over fifty was no longer seen as ⑥ **signifying** wisdom.

We are living in a period when the gap between chronological and biological age is ⑦ **changing** fast and where social norms are struggling to ⑧ **adapt**. In a video produced by the AARP (formerly the American Association of Retired Persons), young people ⑨ **were asked** to do various activities 'just like an old person'. When older people joined ⑩ **them** in the video, the gap between the stereotype and the older people's actual behaviour was striking. It is clear that in today's world our social norms need to be updated quickly.

| 기호 | 어색한 표현 | | 올바른 표현 |
|---|---|---|---|
| (   ) | _____ | ⇨ | _____ |

**44.** 22)**밑줄 부분 중 어법, 혹은 문맥상 어휘의 쓰임이 어색한 것을 올바르게 고쳐 쓰시오. (3개)** 43~45

When Jack was a young man in his early twenties ① **for** the 1960s, he had tried to work in his father's insurance business, as was expected of him. His two older brothers fit in easily and seemed to enjoy their work. But Jack was ② **boring** with the insurance industry. "It was worse than ③ **being bored**", he said. "I felt like I was dying inside". Jack felt drawn to hair styling and dreamed of owning a hair shop with a lively environment. He was sure ④ **that** he would enjoy the creative and social aspects of it and that he'd be successful. When he was twenty-six, Jack ⑤ **approached** his father and expressed his intentions of leaving the business to become a hairstylist. As Jack anticipated, his father raged and accused Jack of being selfish, ungrateful, and unmanly. In the face of his father's fury, Jack felt confusion and fear. His resolve became weak. But then a force filled his chest and he stood firm in his decision. In ⑥ **following** his path, Jack not only ran three flourishing hair shops, but also helped his clients ⑦ **experience** their inner beauty by listening and encouraging ⑧ **them** when they faced dark times. His love for his work led to ⑨ **donating** time and talent at nursing homes, which in turn led to becoming a hospice volunteer, and eventually to starting fundraising efforts for the hospice program in his community. And all this ⑩ **laid** a strong stepping stone for another courageous move in his life. When, after having two healthy children of their own, Jack and his wife, Michele, decided to bring an orphaned child into their family, his father threatened to disown them. Jack understood that his father feared ⑪ **adoption**, in this case especially because the child was of a different racial background than their family. Jack and Michele risked rejection and went ahead with the adoption. It took years but eventually Jack's father loved the little girl and accepted his son's independent choices. Jack realized that, although he often felt fear and still ⑫ **does**, he has always had courage. In fact, courage was the scaffolding around ⑬ **when** he had built richness into his life.

| 기호 | 어색한 표현 | | 올바른 표현 |
|---|---|---|---|
| (   ) | _____ | ⇨ | _____ |
| (   ) | _____ | ⇨ | _____ |
| (   ) | _____ | ⇨ | _____ |

(.hwp) (.pdf) → www.englishjmygod.com

# 2023 고2 9월 모의고사

❶ voca    ❷ text    ❸ [ / ]    ❹ _____    ❺ quiz 1    ❻ quiz 2    ❼ quiz 3    ❽ quiz 4    ❾ quiz 5

☑ **다음 글을 읽고 물음에 답하시오.** (2023_고2_09_18번)

ⓐ To who it may concern,I would like drawing your attention to a problem that frequently occur with the No. 35 buses. There is a bus stop about halfway along Fenny Road, at where the No.35 buses are supposed to stop. It would <sup>나타나다,보이다</sup> _____, however, that some of your drivers are either unaware of this bus stop or for some reason choose to <sup>무시하다</sup> _____ it, driving past even though the buses are not full. I would be <sup>감사하다</sup> _____ if you could <sup>상기시키다</sup> _____ your drivers that this bus stop exists and that they should be prepared to stop at it. I look forward to seeing an <sup>개선점</sup> _____ in this service soon.  Yours faithfully, John Williams

1. ¹⁾힌트를 참고하여 각 빈칸에 알맞은 단어를 쓰시오.

2. ²⁾밑줄 친 ⓐ에서, 어법 혹은 문맥상 어색한 부분을 찾아 올바르게 고쳐 쓰시오.

ⓐ        잘못된 표현                바른 표현

  (            ) ⇨ (            )
  (            ) ⇨ (            )
  (            ) ⇨ (            )
  (            ) ⇨ (            )

☑ **다음 글을 읽고 물음에 답하시오.** (2023_고2_09_19번)

My 10-year-old appeared, in <sup>절실하다</sup> _____ need of a quarter. "A quarter? What on earth do you need a quarter for"? My tone bordered on <sup>짜증</sup> _____. I didn't want to be bothered with such a <sup>사소한</sup> _____ demand. "There's a garage sale up the street, and there's something I just gotta have! It only costs a quarter. Please"? I <sup>쥐어주다</sup> _____ a quarter in my son's hand. Moments later, a little voice said, "Here, Mommy, this is for you". I glanced down at the hands of my little son and saw a four-inch cream-colored statue of two small children hugging one another. Inscribed at their feet were words that read It starts with 'L' ends with 'E' and in between are 'O' and 'V'. (가) 아이가 중고 물품 판매 행사로 서둘러 돌아가는 모습을 바라보며 나는 행복이 가득한 마음으로 미소를 지었다. That 25-cent garage sale <sup>구매</sup> _____ brought me a lot of joy.

3. ³⁾힌트를 참고하여 각 빈칸에 알맞은 단어를 쓰시오.

4. ⁴⁾위 글에 주어진 (가)의 한글과 같은 의미를 가지도록, 각각의 주어진 단어들을 알맞게 배열하시오.

(가) full / race / I / of / a heart / with / I / watched / him / the garage / happiness. / smiled / As / sale, / back / to

☑ **다음 글을 읽고 물음에 답하시오.** (2023_고2_09_20번)

Managers frequently try to play <sup>심리학자</sup> _____, to "figure out" why an employee has acted in a certain way. <sup>공감하다</sup> _____ with employees in order to understand their point of view can be very helpful. ⓐ <u>However, which dealing with a problem area, in particular, remembering that it is not the person which is bad, but the actions exhibit on the job.</u> Avoid making suggestions to employees about personal <sup>특성</sup> _____ they should change; instead suggest more acceptable ways of <sup>수행</sup> _____. For example, instead of focusing on a person's "unreliability", a manager might focus on the fact that the employee "has been late to work seven times this month". (가) <u>직원들은 자신이 어떤 사람인지를 바꾸기는 어렵다.</u>; it is usually much easier for them to change how they act.

5. 5)힌트를 참고하여 각 <u>빈칸에 알맞은</u> 단어를 쓰시오.

6. 6)밑줄 친 ⓐ에서, 어법 혹은 문맥상 어색한 부분을 찾아 올바르게 고쳐 쓰시오.

| ⓐ 잘못된 표현 | | 바른 표현 |
|---|---|---|
| ( ) | ⇨ | ( ) |
| ( ) | ⇨ | ( ) |
| ( ) | ⇨ | ( ) |
| ( ) | ⇨ | ( ) |

7. 7)위 글에 주어진 (가)의 한글과 같은 의미를 가지도록, 각각의 주어진 단어들을 알맞게 배열하시오.

(가) for / they / to / difficult / change / who / employees / are / It / is

☑ **다음 글을 읽고 물음에 답하시오.** (2023_고2_09_21번)

I suspect <sup>균류</sup> _____ are a little more forward "thinking" than their larger partners. (가) <u>나무들 사이에서 각 종은 다른 종들과 싸운다.</u> Let's assume the beeches native to Central Europe could emerge <sup>우세하다</sup> _____ in most forests there. Would this really be an <sup>이점</sup> _____? ⓐ <u>What would happen if a new pathogen came along that infected most of the beeches and killed them?</u> In that case, wouldn't it be more advantageous if there were a certain number of other species around — oaks, maples, or firs — that would continue to grow and provide the shade needed for a new generation of young beeches to sprout and grow up? Diversity provides <sup>안전</sup> _____ for ancient forests. Because fungi are also very dependent on stable conditions, they support other species underground and protect them from complete <sup>무너지다,붕괴하다</sup> _____ to <sup>확실히 하다</sup> _____ that one species of tree doesn't manage to <sup>우세하다</sup> _____.

8. 8)힌트를 참고하여 각 <u>빈칸에 알맞은</u> 단어를 쓰시오.

9. 9)밑줄 친 ⓐ에서, 어법 혹은 문맥상 어색한 부분을 찾아 올바르게 고쳐 쓰시오.

| ⓐ 잘못된 표현 | | 바른 표현 |
|---|---|---|
| ( ) | ⇨ | ( ) |

10. 10)위 글에 주어진 (가)의 한글과 같은 의미를 가지도록, 각각의 주어진 단어들을 알맞게 배열하시오.

(가) trees, / other / each / Among / species. / fights / species

## ☑ 다음 글을 읽고 물음에 답하시오. (2023_고2_09_22번)

It's <sup>주목할 만 한</sup> _____ that positive fantasies help us relax to such an <sup>범위</sup> _____ that it shows up in <sup>생리학적</sup> _____ tests. ⓐ <u>If you want to unwind, you can take some deep breaths, getting a massage, or going for a walk — but you can also try simply close your eyes and fantasize about some future outcome that you might enjoying.</u> But what about when your <sup>목적</sup> _____ is to make your wish a reality? The last thing you want to be is relaxed. You want to be <sup>활력을 얻다</sup> _____ enough to get off the couch and lose those pounds or find that job or study for that test, and you want to be motivated enough to stay engaged even when the <sup>피할수 없는</sup> _____ <sup>장애물</sup> _____ or challenges arise. The principle of "Dream it. Wish it. Do it". does not hold true, and now we know why: in dreaming it, you undercut the energy you need to do it. You put yourself in a <sup>일시적인</sup> _____ state of complete happiness, calmness — and inactivity.

11. 11)힌트를 참고하여 각 빈칸에 알맞은 단어를 쓰시오.

12. 12)밑줄 친 ⓐ에서, 어법 혹은 문맥상 어색한 부분을 찾아 올바르게 고쳐 쓰시오.

| ⓐ 잘못된 표현 | 바른 표현 |
|---|---|
| ( ) ⇨ ( ) | |
| ( ) ⇨ ( ) | |
| ( ) ⇨ ( ) | |
| ( ) ⇨ ( ) | |
| ( ) ⇨ ( ) | |

## ☑ 다음 글을 읽고 물음에 답하시오. (2023_고2_09_23번)

If cooking is as central to human <sup>정체성</sup> _____, biology, and culture as the biological <sup>인류학자</sup> _____ Richard Wrangham suggests, it stands to reason that the decline of cooking in our time would have serious consequences for modern life, and so it has. Are they all bad? Not at all. The outsourcing of much of the work of cooking to corporations has relieved women of what has traditionally been their exclusive <sup>책임</sup> _____ for <sup>먹여살리다</sup> _____ the family, making it easier for them to work outside the home and have careers. It has headed off many of the domestic conflicts that such a large shift in gender roles and family dynamics was bound to spark. It has relieved other pressures in the household, including longer workdays and <sup>분주한</sup> _____ children, and saved us time that we can now invest in other <sup>활동,일</sup> _____. ⓐ <u>It has also allowing us to diversified our diets substantially, to make it possible even for people with no cooking skills and little money to enjoy a whole different cuisine.</u> All that's required is a microwave.

13. 13)힌트를 참고하여 각 빈칸에 알맞은 단어를 쓰시오.

14. 14)밑줄 친 ⓐ에서, 어법 혹은 문맥상 어색한 부분을 찾아 올바르게 고쳐 쓰시오.

| ⓐ 잘못된 표현 | 바른 표현 |
|---|---|
| ( ) ⇨ ( ) | |
| ( ) ⇨ ( ) | |
| ( ) ⇨ ( ) | |

☑ **다음 글을 읽고 물음에 답하시오.** (2023_고2_09_24번)

(가) <u>이미 알고 있겠지만, 여러분이 무엇을 어떻게 구매하는지는 정치적일 수 있다.</u> To whom do you want to give your money? Which companies and corporations do you value and respect? Be <sup>주의를 기울이다</sup> _____ about every purchase by carefully researching the corporations that are taking our money to decide if they deserve our support. Do they have a record of <sup>오염시키다</sup> _____ the environment, or do they have fair-trade practices and an end-of-life plan for the products they make? Are they <sup>헌신하다</sup> _____ to bringing about good in the world? For instance, my family has found a company producing recycled, plastic-packaging-free toilet paper with a social <sup>양심</sup> _____. They contribute 50 percent of their profits to the construction of toilets around the world, and we're <sup>진심으로</sup> _____ happy to spend our money on this special toilet paper each month. ⓐ <u>Remember that the corporate world build on consumers, so as a consumer you have the power to vote with your wallet and encourage companies embraced healthier and more sustainable practices with every purchase you choose make.</u>

15. <sup>15)</sup>힌트를 참고하여 각 <u>빈칸</u>에 알맞은 단어를 쓰시오.

16. <sup>16)</sup>밑줄 친 ⓐ에서, 어법 혹은 문맥상 어색한 부분을 찾아 올바르게 고쳐 쓰시오.

| ⓐ | 잘못된 표현 | | 바른 표현 |
|---|---|---|---|
| ( | ) | ⇨ ( | ) |
| ( | ) | ⇨ ( | ) |
| ( | ) | ⇨ ( | ) |

17. <sup>17)</sup>위 글에 주어진 (가)의 한글과 같은 의미를 가지도록, 각각의 주어진 단어들을 알맞게 배열하시오.

(가) how / you / and / be / you / As / can / already / political / buy / may / know, / what

☑ **다음 글을 읽고 물음에 답하시오.** (2023_고2_09_26번)

Camille Flammarion was born at Montigny-le-Roi, France. He became interested in <sup>천문학</sup> _____ at an early age, and when he was only sixteen he wrote a book on the origin of the world. The <sup>원고</sup> _____ was not published at the time, but it came to the <sup>관심</sup> _____ of Urbain Le Verrier, the director of the Paris Observatory. He became an assistant to Le Verrier in 1858 and worked as a <sup>계산원</sup> _____. ⓐ <u>At nineteen, he wrote another book called The Plurality of Inhabited Worlds, which he passionately claimed that life exists outside the planet Earth.</u> His most successful work, Popular Astronomy, was published in 1880, and eventually sold 130,000 copies. With his own funds, he built an observatory at Juvisy and spent May to November of each year there. (가) <u>1887년에 그는 French Astronomical Society를 설립했고 그것의 월간 간행물의 편집자로 일했다.</u>

18. <sup>18)</sup>힌트를 참고하여 각 <u>빈칸</u>에 알맞은 단어를 쓰시오.

(.hwp) (.pdf) → www.englishjmygod.com

**19.** 19)밑줄 친 ⓐ에서, 어법 혹은 문맥상 어색한 부분을 찾아 올바르게 고쳐 쓰시오.

ⓐ      잘못된 표현          바른 표현

(               ) ⇨ (            )

**20.** 20)위 글에 주어진 (가)의 한글과 같은 의미를 가지도록, 각각의 주어진 단어들을 알맞게 배열하시오.

(가) the / editor / of / founded / its / French / publication. / and / In 1887, / he / monthly / Astronomical / served as / Society

---

## ☑ 다음 글을 읽고 물음에 답하시오. (2023_고2_09_29번)

There is little <sup>의심</sup> _____ that we are driven by the sell-by date. Once an item is past that date it goes into the waste <sup>흐름</sup> _____, further increasing its carbon <sup>발자국</sup> _____. ⓐ Remember those items have already travelling hundreds of miles reached the shelves and once they go into waste they started a new carbon mile journey. But we all make our own <sup>판단</sup> _____ about sell-by dates; those brought up during the Second World War are often <sup>경멸하는</sup> _____ of the terrible waste they believe such caution encourages. ⓑ The manufacturer of the food have a view when making or grow something that by the time the product reach the shelves it has already been travel for so many days and possibly many miles. The manufacturer then decides that a product can <sup>합리적으로</sup> _____ be consumed within say 90 days and 90 days minus so many days for travelling gives the sell-by date. (가) 그러나 그것이 유독해지는지는 각 개인이 결정할 수 있는 것이다. It would seem to make sense not to buy large packs of perishable goods but non-perishable items may become cost-effective.

**21.** 21)힌트를 참고하여 각 빈칸에 알맞은 단어를 쓰시오.

**22.** 22)밑줄 친 ⓐ~ⓑ에서, 어법 혹은 문맥상 어색한 부분을 찾아 올바르게 고쳐 쓰시오.

ⓐ      잘못된 표현          바른 표현

(               ) ⇨ (            )

(               ) ⇨ (            )

(               ) ⇨ (            )

ⓑ      잘못된 표현          바른 표현

(               ) ⇨ (            )

(               ) ⇨ (            )

(               ) ⇨ (            )

(               ) ⇨ (            )

**23.** 23)위 글에 주어진 (가)의 한글과 같은 의미를 가지도록, 각각의 주어진 단어들을 알맞게 배열하시오.

(가) becomes / each / But / whether / can / something / is / it / toxic / decide. / individual

☑ **다음 글을 읽고 물음에 답하시오.** (2023_고2_09_30번)

The "jolt" of caffeine does wear off. Caffeine is removed from your system by an <sup>효소</sup> _____ within your <sup>간</sup> _____, which gradually degrades it over time. Based in large part on <sup>유전학</sup> _____, some people have a more efficient version of the enzyme that degrades caffeine, allowing the liver to rapidly clear it from the <sup>혈류</sup> _____. (가) <u>이 몇 안 되는 사람들은 저녁과 함께 에스프레소를 마시고도 아무 문제 없이 한밤중에 깊이 잠들 수 있다.</u> Others, however, have a slower-acting version of the enzyme. It takes far longer for their system to eliminate the same amount of caffeine. As a result, they are very sensitive to caffeine's effects. ⓐ <u>One cup of tea or coffee in the morning will last much of the day, and should they have had a second cup, even early in the afternoon, they will find it difficult fall asleep in the evening.</u> <sup>노화</sup> _____ also alters the speed of caffeine <sup>제거</sup> _____: the older we are, the longer it takes our brain and body to remove caffeine, and thus the more sensitive we become in later life to caffeine's <sup>수면방해</sup> _____ influence.

24. 24)힌트를 참고하여 각 <u>빈칸에 알맞은</u> 단어를 쓰시오.

25. 25)밑줄 친 ⓐ에서, 어법 혹은 문맥상 어색한 부분을 찾아 올바르게 고쳐 쓰시오.

   ⓐ      잘못된 표현         바른 표현

   (            ) ⇨ (         )

   (            ) ⇨ (         )

26. 26)위 글에 주어진 (가)의 한글과 같은 의미를 가지도록, 각각의 주어진 단어들을 알맞게 배열하시오.

(가) problem. / without / midnight / rare / individuals / These / an / fall / and / can / espresso / a / asleep / with / dinner / drink / fast / at

☑ **다음 글을 읽고 물음에 답하시오.** (2023_고2_09_31번)

(가) <u>반항자들은 자신들이 반항자라고 생각할지도 모르지만, 영리한 마케터들은 나머지 우리에게 그러듯이 그들에게 영향을 준다.</u> Saying, "Everyone is doing it" may turn some people off from an idea. These people will look for <sup>대안</sup> _____, which (if cleverly planned) can be exactly what a marketer or <sup>설득자</sup> _____ wants you to believe. If I want you to consider an idea, and know you strongly <sup>거부하다</sup> _____ popular opinion in favor of maintaining your independence and uniqueness, I would present the <sup>대중적인</sup> _____ option first, which you would reject in favor of my actual <sup>선호</sup> _____. ⓐ <u>We are often tricking when we try to maintain a position of defiance. People use this reversal make us "independently" choose an option of which suits their purposes.</u> Some brands have taken full effect of our <sup>반항</sup> _____ towards the mainstream and positioned themselves as rebels; which has created even stronger brand loyalty.

27. 27)힌트를 참고하여 각 <u>빈칸에 알맞은</u> 단어를 쓰시오.

(.hwp) (.pdf) → www.englishjmygod.com

28. 28)밑줄 친 ⓐ에서, 어법 혹은 문맥상 어색한 부분을 찾아 올바르게 고쳐 쓰시오.

| ⓐ 잘못된 표현 | 바른 표현 |
| --- | --- |
| ( ) ⇨ ( | ) |
| ( ) ⇨ ( | ) |
| ( ) ⇨ ( | ) |

29. 29)위 글에 주어진 (가)의 한글과 같은 의미를 가지도록, 각각의 주어진 단어들을 알맞게 배열하시오.

(가) of / marketers / just / but / them / rebels, / Rebels / think / influence / may / they're / us. / like / clever / the rest

---

☑ **다음 글을 읽고 물음에 답하시오.** (2023_고2_09_32번)

A typical soap opera creates an <sup>추상적인</sup> _____ world, in which a highly complex web of relationships connects <sup>허구적인</sup> _____ characters that exist first only in the minds of the program's creators and are then <sup>재현하다</sup> _____ in the minds of the viewer. If you were to think about how much human <sup>심리</sup> _____, law, and even everyday <sup>물리학</sup> _____ the viewer must know in order to follow and <sup>추측하다</sup> _____ about the plot, you would discover it is considerable — at least as much as the knowledge required to follow and speculate about a piece of modern mathematics, and in most cases, much more. Yet viewers follow soap operas with ease. How are they able to cope with such <sup>추상</sup> _____? Because, of course, the abstraction is built on an extremely familiar <sup>틀</sup> _____. ⓐ The characters in a soap opera and the relationships between them is very much like the real people and relationships we experienced every day. (가) 드라마의 추상은 현실 세계에서 불과 한 걸음 떨어져 있다. The mental "training" required to follow a soap opera is provided by our everyday lives.

30. 30)힌트를 참고하여 각 빈칸에 알맞은 단어를 쓰시오.

31. 31)밑줄 친 ⓐ에서, 어법 혹은 문맥상 어색한 부분을 찾아 올바르게 고쳐 쓰시오.

| ⓐ 잘못된 표현 | 바른 표현 |
| --- | --- |
| ( ) ⇨ ( | ) |
| ( ) ⇨ ( | ) |

32. 32)위 글에 주어진 (가)의 한글과 같은 의미를 가지도록, 각각의 주어진 단어들을 알맞게 배열하시오.

(가) the / a / world. / only / opera / is / removed / soap / of / real / from / a / abstraction / The / step

☑ **다음 글을 읽고 물음에 답하시오.** (2023_고2_09_33번)

As always happens with natural selection, bats and their <sup>먹잇감</sup> _____ have been engaged in a life-or-death sensory arms race for millions of years. ⓐ <u>It's believe that hearing in moths arise specifically in response to the threat of eating by bats.</u> (Not all insects can hear.) Over millions of years, moths have <sup>진화하다</sup> _____ the ability to <sup>감지하다</sup> _____ sounds at ever higher frequencies, and, as they have, the <sup>주파수</sup> _____ of bats' vocalizations have risen, too. Some moth species have also evolved <sup>비늘</sup> _____ on their wings and a fur-like coat on their bodies; both act as "acoustic camouflage", by <sup>흡수하다</sup> _____ sound waves in the frequencies emitted by bats, (가) <u>그것으로 음파가 되돌아가는 것을 방지한다.</u> The B-2 bomber and other "stealth" aircraft have <sup>기체</sup> _____ made of materials that do something similar with radar beams.

33. 33)힌트를 참고하여 각 <u>빈칸에 알맞은</u> 단어를 쓰시오.

34. 34)밑줄 친 ⓐ에서, 어법 혹은 문맥상 어색한 부분을 찾아 올바르게 고쳐 쓰시오.

| ⓐ | 잘못된 표현 | | 바른 표현 |
|---|---|---|---|
| ( | ) | ⇨ ( | ) |
| ( | ) | ⇨ ( | ) |
| ( | ) | ⇨ ( | ) |

35. 35)위 글에 주어진 (가)의 한글과 같은 의미를 가지도록, 각각의 주어진 단어들을 알맞게 배열하시오.

(가) waves / from / those / sound / back. / thereby / bouncing / preventing

☑ **다음 글을 읽고 물음에 답하시오.** (2023_고2_09_34번)

ⓐ <u>Much of human thought is designed screen out information and to sort the rest into a manageable condition. The inflow of data from our senses to create an overwhelming chaos, especially give the enormous amount of information available in culture and society.</u> Out of all the sensory impressions and possible information, it is <sup>중요하다</sup> _____ to find a small amount that is most relevant to our individual needs and to organize that into a usable stock of knowledge. <sup>예상들</sup> _____ accomplish some of this work, helping to screen out information that is irrelevant to what is expected, and focusing our attention on clear <sup>모순들</sup> _____. The processes of learning and memory are marked by a steady elimination of information. People notice only a part of the world around them. Then, (가) <u>그들이 알아차린 것의 일부만 처리되어 기억에 저장된다.</u> And only part of what gets committed to memory can be <sup>회수하다</sup> _____.

36. 36)힌트를 참고하여 각 <u>빈칸에 알맞은</u> 단어를 쓰시오.

37. 37)밑줄 친 ⓐ에서, 어법 혹은 문맥상 어색한 부분을 찾아 올바르게 고쳐 쓰시오.

| ⓐ | 잘못된 표현 | | 바른 표현 |
|---|---|---|---|
| ( | ) | ⇨ ( | ) |
| ( | ) | ⇨ ( | ) |
| ( | ) | ⇨ ( | ) |

(.hwp) (.pdf) → www.englishjmygod.com

38. 38)위 글에 주어진 (가)의 한글과 같은 의미를 가지도록, 각각의 주어진 단어들을 알맞게 배열하시오.

(가) of / memory. / stored / what / only / they / gets / a fraction / processed / into / notice / and

☑ **다음 글을 읽고 물음에 답하시오.** (2023_고2_09_35번)

The irony of early <sup>민주주의</sup> _____ in Europe is that it <sup>번성하다</sup> _____ and prospered <sup>정확하게</sup> _____ because European rulers for a very long time were <sup>현저하게</sup> _____ weak. For more than a millennium after the fall of Rome, European rulers lacked the ability to <sup>평가하다</sup> _____ what their people were producing and to <sup>부과하다</sup> ____ substantial taxes based on this. (가) <u>유럽의 약함을 설명하는 가장 눈에 띄는 방법은 그들이 거둔 세입이 얼마나 적은지를 보여주는 것이다.</u> Europeans would eventually develop strong systems of revenue collection, but it took them an awfully long time to do so. In <sup>중세기</sup> _____, and for part of the early modern era, Chinese emperors and Muslim caliphs were able to <sup>얻어내다</sup> _____ much more of economic production than any European ruler with the exception of small city-states.

39. 39)힌트를 참고하여 각 <u>빈칸에 알맞은</u> 단어를 쓰시오.

40. 40)위 글에 주어진 (가)의 한글과 같은 의미를 가지도록, 각각의 주어진 단어들을 알맞게 배열하시오.

(가) weakness / striking / how / to / most / The / way / is / illustrate / collected. / European / show / to / they / revenue / little

☑ **다음 글을 읽고 물음에 답하시오.** (2023_고2_09_36번)

If you drive down a busy street, you will find many <sup>경쟁하는</sup> _____ businesses, often right next to one another. For example, in most places a consumer in search of a quick meal has many choices, and more fast-food restaurants appear all the time. These competing firms <sup>광고하다</sup> _____ heavily. The <sup>유혹</sup> _____ is to see advertising as driving up the price of a product without any benefit to the consumer. However, this <sup>오해</sup> _____ doesn't account for why firms advertise. In markets where competitors sell slightly <sup>차별화된</sup> _____ products, advertising enables firms to inform their customers about new products and services. Yes, costs rise, (가) <u>소비자들은 구매 결정을 내리는 데 도움이 되는 정보도 얻는다.</u> Consumers also benefit from added variety, and we all get a product that's pretty close to our <sup>상상</sup> _____ of a perfect good — and no other <sup>시장구조</sup> _____ delivers that outcome.

41. 41)힌트를 참고하여 각 <u>빈칸에 알맞은</u> 단어를 쓰시오.

42. 42)위 글에 주어진 (가)의 한글과 같은 의미를 가지도록, 각각의 주어진 단어들을 알맞게 배열하시오.

(가) but / make / purchasing / gain / information / decisions. / consumers / also / help / to

☑ **다음 글을 읽고 물음에 답하시오.** (2023_고2_09_37번)

Architects might say a machine can never design an innovative or impressive building because a computer cannot be "creative". Yet consider the Elbphilharmonie, a new concert hall in Hamburg, which contains a remarkably beautiful <sup>강당</sup> _____ composed of ten thousand <sup>맞물리는</sup> _____ acoustic panels. It is the sort of space that makes one <sup>본능적으로</sup> _____ think that only a human being — and a human with a remarkably refined creative sensibility, at that — could design something so <sup>미적으로</sup> _____ impressive. Yet the auditorium was, in fact, designed algorithmically, using a technique known as "parametric design". The architects gave the system a set of <sup>기준</sup> _____, and it generated a set of possible designs for the architects to choose from. (가) <u>유사한 소프트웨어가 다른 많은 것들 중에서도 경량 자전거 프레임과 더 튼튼한 의자를 디자인하는 데 사용되어 왔다.</u> Are these systems behaving "creatively"? No, they are using lots of processing power to blindly generate <sup>다양한</sup> _____ possible designs, working in a very different way from a human being.

43. 43)힌트를 참고하여 각 <u>빈칸에 알맞은</u> 단어를 쓰시오.

44. 44)위 글에 주어진 (가)의 한글과 같은 의미를 가지도록, 각각의 주어진 단어들을 알맞게 배열하시오.

(가) sturdier / chairs, / design / used / else. / and / has / Similar / to / frames / been / lightweight / software / much / among / bicycle

☑ **다음 글을 읽고 물음에 답하시오.** (2023_고2_09_38번)

The brain is a high-energy consumer of <sup>포도당</sup> _____, which is its fuel. (가) <u>그러나 여러분의 뇌는 연료를 저장할 수 없고, 따라서 '활동하는 대로 대가를 지불'해야 한다.</u> Your brain can't store fuel, however, so it has to "pay as it goes". Since your brain is incredibly <sup>적응력이 뛰어난</sup> _____, it economizes its fuel resources. Thus, during a period of high stress, it shifts away from the analysis of the <sup>미묘한 차이</sup> _____ of a situation to a singular and fixed focus on the stressful situation at hand. You don't sit back and speculate about the meaning of life when you are stressed. Instead, you <sup>헌신하다</sup> _____ all your energy to trying to figure out what action to take. Sometimes, however, this <sup>이동</sup> _____ from the higher-thinking parts of the brain to the automatic and <sup>반사적인</sup> _____ parts of the brain can lead you to do something too quickly, without thinking.

45. 45)힌트를 참고하여 각 <u>빈칸에 알맞은</u> 단어를 쓰시오.

46. 46)위 글에 주어진 (가)의 한글과 같은 의미를 가지도록, 각각의 주어진 단어들을 알맞게 배열하시오.

(가) 3 / of / person's / available / the / accounts / a / consumes / 20 / the / body / of / brain / weight, / it / percent / percent / fuel. / merely / Although / for

(.hwp) (.pdf) → www.englishjmygod.com

☑ **다음 글을 읽고 물음에 답하시오.** (2023_고2_09_39번)

Much research has been carried out on the causes of <sup>몰입</sup> _____, an issue that is important from both a theoretical and practical standpoint: identifying the drivers of work engagement may enable us to <sup>조작하다</sup> _____ or influence it. The causes of engagement fall into two major camps: situational and personal. The most influential situational causes are job resources, feedback and leadership, the latter, of course, being responsible for job <sup>자원</sup> _____ and feedback. Indeed, leaders influence engagement by giving their employees honest and constructive feedback on their performance, and by providing them with the necessary resources that enable them to perform their job well. It is, however, noteworthy that although engagement drives job performance, job performance also drives engagement. ⓐ <u>In other words, when employees are able to do their jobs well — to the point that they match or exceeded their own expectations and ambitions — they will engage more, be proud of their achievements, and found work more meaningful.</u> (가) 이것은 사람들이 그들의 가치와 일치하는 직무에 종사했을 때 특히 분명하다.

47. 47)힌트를 참고하여 각 <u>빈칸에</u> 알맞은 단어를 쓰시오.

48. 48)밑줄 친 ⓐ에서, 어법 혹은 문맥상 어색한 부분을 찾아 올바르게 고쳐 쓰시오.

| ⓐ | 잘못된 표현 | | 바른 표현 |
|---|---|---|---|
| ( | ) | ⇨ ( | ) |
| ( | ) | ⇨ ( | ) |

49. 49)위 글에 주어진 (가)의 한글과 같은 의미를 가지도록, 각각의 주어진 단어들을 알맞게 배열하시오.

(가) evident / is / jobs / in / align / This / their values. / that / people / when / especially / are / employed / with

☑ **다음 글을 읽고 물음에 답하시오.** (2023_고2_09_40번)

In 2006, researchers <sup>수행하다</sup> _____ a study on the motivations for helping after the September 11th terrorist attacks against the United States. In the study, they found that individuals who gave money, blood, goods, or other forms of <sup>도움</sup> _____ because of other-focused motives (giving to reduce another's discomfort) were almost four times more likely to still be giving support one year later than those whose original motivation was to reduce personal <sup>고통</sup> _____. This effect likely stems from differences in emotional <sup>자극</sup> _____. The events of September 11th emotionally affected people throughout the United States. Those who gave to reduce their own distress reduced their emotional arousal with their initial gift, <sup>해소</sup> _____ that emotional distress. (가) 하지만, 다른 사람들의 고통을 줄이기 위해 베푼 사람들은 공격 이후 오랫동안 계속해서 고군분투하는 피해자들에게 공감하기를 멈추지 않았다.

50. 50)힌트를 참고하여 각 <u>빈칸에</u> 알맞은 단어를 쓰시오.

51. 51)위 글에 주어진 (가)의 한글과 같은 의미를 가지도록, 각각의 주어진 단어들을 알맞게 배열하시오.

(가) to / empathizing / with / stop / struggle / not / distress / the / did / reduce / victims / gave / who / However, / who / long / those / to / others' / after / continued / attacks.

☑ **다음 글을 읽고 물음에 답하시오.** (2023_고2_09_41, 42번)

In England in the 1680s, it was unusual to live to the age of fifty. This was a period when knowledge was not spread widely, there were few books and most people could not read. As a consequence, knowledge passed down through the <sup>구전</sup> _____ traditions of stories and shared experiences. And since older people had <sup>누적된</sup> _____ more knowledge, the social <sup>규범</sup> _____ was that to be over fifty was to be wise. This social perception of age began to shift with the <sup>출현</sup> _____ of new technologies such as the printing press. Over time, as more books were printed, literacy increased, and the oral traditions of knowledge transfer began to <sup>사라지다</sup> _____. With the fading of oral traditions, the wisdom of the old became less important and as a consequence being over fifty was no longer seen as <sup>의미하다</sup> _____ wisdom.   (가) <u>우리는 생활 연령과 생물학적 연령 사이의 격차가 빠르게 변하고 사회적 규범이 적응하기 위해 분투하는 시기에 살고 있다.</u> ⓐ<u>In a video produced by the AARP (formerly the American Association of Retired Persons), young people were asked to do various activities 'just like an old person'. When older people joined them in the video, the gap between the stereotype and the older people's actual behaviour were striking. It is clear which in today's world our social norms needs to be updated quickly.</u>

52. <sup>52)</sup>힌트를 참고하여 각 <u>빈칸에 알맞은</u> 단어를 쓰시오.

53. <sup>53)</sup>밑줄 친 ⓐ에서, 어법 혹은 문맥상 어색한 부분을 찾아 올바르게 고쳐 쓰시오.

　　ⓐ 　　　 잘못된 표현 　　　　　 바른 표현
　　( 　　　　　　 ) ⇨ ( 　　　　　 )
　　( 　　　　　　 ) ⇨ ( 　　　　　 )
　　( 　　　　　　 ) ⇨ ( 　　　　　 )

54. <sup>54)</sup>위 글에 주어진 (가)의 한글과 같은 의미를 가지도록, 각각의 주어진 단어들을 알맞게 배열하시오.

(가) struggling / between / and / a  period / living / in / are / the  gap / We / chronological / adapt. / age / social / fast / when / is / norms / biological / where / are / and / to / changing

☑ **다음 글을 읽고 물음에 답하시오.** (2023_고2_09_43, 43, 45번)

When Jack was a young man in his early twenties during the 1960s, he had tried to work in his father's <sup>보험</sup> _____ business, as was expected of him. His two older brothers fit in easily and seemed to enjoy their work. But Jack was bored with the insurance industry. "It was worse than being bored", he said. "I felt like I was dying inside". Jack felt drawn to hair styling and dreamed of owning a hair shop with a <sup>활기찬</sup> _____ environment. (가) <u>그는 자신이 그것의 창의적이고 사교적인 측면을 즐길 것이고 성공할 것이라고 확신했다.</u> When he was twenty-six, Jack approached his father and expressed his intentions of leaving the business to become a hairstylist. As Jack anticipated, his father raged and <sup>비난하다</sup> _____ Jack of being selfish, ungrateful, and unmanly. In the face of his father's fury, Jack felt confusion and fear. His <sup>결심</sup> _____ became weak. But then a force filled his chest and he stood <sup>확고하다</sup> ____ in his decision. In following his path, Jack not only ran three flourishing hair shops, but also helped his clients experience their <sup>내면의</sup> _____ beauty by listening and encouraging them when they faced dark times. His love for his work led to donating time and talent at nursing homes, which in turn led to becoming a hospice volunteer, and eventually to starting fundraising efforts for the hospice program in his community. (나) <u>그리고 이 모든 것은 그의 삶에서 또 다른 용기 있는 움직임을 위한 견고한 디딤돌을 놓았다.</u> When, after having two healthy children of their own, Jack and his wife, Michele, decided to bring an orphaned child into their family, his father threatened to disown them. ⓐ <u>Jack understood which his father feared adoption, in this case especially because the child be of a different racial background than their family. Jack and Michele risked rejection and go ahead with the adoption. It took years but eventually Jack's father loved the little girl and accepting his son's independent choices.</u> Jack realized that, although he often felt fear and still does, he has always had courage. In fact, courage was the <sup>발판</sup> _____ around which he had built richness into his life.

55. <sup>55)</sup>힌트를 참고하여 각 빈칸에 알맞은 단어를 쓰시오.


56. <sup>56)</sup>밑줄 친 ⓐ에서, 어법 혹은 문맥상 어색한 부분을 찾아 올바르게 고쳐 쓰시오.

| ⓐ | 잘못된 표현 | | 바른 표현 |
|---|---|---|---|
| ( | ) | ⇨ ( | ) |
| ( | ) | ⇨ ( | ) |
| ( | ) | ⇨ ( | ) |
| ( | ) | ⇨ ( | ) |

57. <sup>57)</sup>위 글에 주어진 (가) ~ (나)의 한글과 같은 의미를 가지도록, 각각의 주어진 단어들을 알맞게 배열하시오.

(가) the / creative / he'd / social / and / He / that / successful. / enjoy / sure / it / he / that / be / of / would / aspects / was / and


(나) this / a strong / another / courageous / move / his / for / And / stone / laid / life. / stepping / in / all

# 정답

## WORK BOOK

2023년 고2 9월 모의고사 내신대비용 WorkBook & 변형문제

# Answer Keys

CHAPTER

Prac 1 **Answers**

1) at which
2) that
3) either
4) grateful
5) remind
6) exists
7) that
8) seeing
9) desperate
10) bordered
11) bothered
12) trivial
13) statue
14) hugging
15) Inscribed
16) were
17) race
18) Empathizing
19) dealing
20) that
21) exhibited
22) making
23) traits
24) performing
25) late
26) are
27) much
28) how
29) little
30) than
31) fights
32) emerge
33) infected
34) were
35) needed
36) Diversity
37) dependent on
38) collapse
39) dominate
40) positive
41) relax
42) that
43) unwind
44) outcome
45) objective
46) *last*
47) relaxed
48) motivated
49) inevitable
50) arise
51) true
52) undercut
53) inactivity
54) identity
55) reason
56) decline
57) relieved
58) exclusive
59) feeding
60) it
61) them
62) shift
63) including
64) to diversify
65) little
66) political
67) corporations
68) purchase
69) deserve
70) committed
71) producing
72) construction
73) encourage
74) to
75) sustainable
76) interested
77) astronomy
78) Observatory
79) assistant
80) in which
81) successful
82) year
83) served
84) little
85) that
86) that
87) further
88) increasing
89) reach
90) judgement
91) brought
92) during
93) scornful
94) caution
95) that
96) by
97) travelling
98) consumed
99) gives
100) individual
101) make
102) perishable
103) non-perishable
104) which
105) degrades
106) degrades
107) allowing
108) clear
109) asleep
110) slower-acting
111) far
112) eliminate
113) sensitive
114) should they
115) will
116) alters
117) longer
118) remove
119) sensitive
120) influence
121) turn
122) alternatives
123) which
124) what
125) reject
126) favor
127) independence
128) majority
129) preference
130) defiance
131) reversal
132) defiance
133) rebels
134) loyalty
135) abstract
136) connects
137) exist
138) were
139) speculate
140) considerable
141) much
142) ease
143) abstraction
144) familiar
145) are
146) removed
147) been engaged
148) sensory
149) arose
150) being eaten by

148

(.hwp) (.pdf) → www.englishjmygod.com

151) detect
152) risen
153) emitted
154) from
155) made
156) overwhelming
157) relevant
158) irrelevant
159) contradictions
160) elimination
161) retrieved
162) that
163) weak
164) lacked
165) assess
166) substantial
167) weakness
168) little
169) revenue
170) extract
171) competing
172) firms
173) up
174) why
175) where
176) inform
177) gain
178) added
179) outcome
180) Yet
181) composed
182) think
183) refined
184) as
185) choose from
186) design
187) blindly
188) varied
189) different
190) which
191) accounts for
192) however
193) adaptive
194) singular
195) fixed
196) Instead
197) trying
198) automatic
199) without
200) causes
201) identifying
202) enable
203) influence
204) with
205) enable
206) although
207) engage
208) meaningful
209) conducted
210) because of
211) other-focused
212) more
213) than
214) reduced
215) discharging
216) empathizing
217) unusual
218) few
219) accumulated
220) shift
221) literacy
222) less
223) signifying
224) where
225) adapt
226) joined
227) striking

228) was
229) approached
230) of
231) unmanly
232) laid
233) adoption
234) does
235) around which

# Answer Keys

## Prac 1 Answers

1) at which
2) that
3) either
4) grateful
5) remind
6) exists
7) that
8) seeing
9) desperate
10) bordered
11) bothered
12) trivial
13) statue
14) hugging
15) Inscribed
16) were
17) race
18) Empathizing
19) dealing
20) that
21) exhibited
22) making
23) traits
24) performing
25) late
26) are
27) much
28) how
29) little
30) than
31) fights
32) emerge
33) infected
34) were
35) needed
36) Diversity
37) dependent on
38) collapse
39) dominate
40) positive
41) relax
42) that
43) unwind
44) outcome
45) objective
46) *last*
47) relaxed
48) motivated
49) inevitable
50) arise
51) true
52) undercut
53) inactivity
54) identity
55) reason
56) decline
57) relieved
58) exclusive
59) feeding
60) it
61) them
62) shift
63) including
64) to diversify
65) little
66) political
67) corporations
68) purchase
69) deserve
70) committed
71) producing
72) construction
73) encourage
74) to
75) sustainable
76) interested
77) astronomy
78) Observatory
79) assistant
80) in which
81) successful
82) year
83) served
84) little
85) that
86) that
87) further
88) increasing
89) reach
90) judgement
91) brought
92) during
93) scornful
94) caution
95) that
96) by
97) travelling
98) consumed
99) gives
100) individual
101) make
102) perishable
103) non-perishable
104) which
105) degrades
106) degrades
107) allowing
108) clear
109) asleep
110) slower-acting
111) far
112) eliminate
113) sensitive
114) should they
115) will
116) alters
117) longer
118) remove
119) sensitive
120) influence
121) turn
122) alternatives
123) which
124) what
125) reject
126) favor
127) independence
128) majority
129) preference
130) defiance
131) reversal
132) defiance
133) rebels
134) loyalty
135) abstract
136) connects
137) exist
138) were
139) speculate
140) considerable
141) much
142) ease
143) abstraction
144) familiar
145) are
146) removed
147) been engaged
148) sensory
149) arose
150) being eaten by

(.hwp) (.pdf) → www.englishjmygod.com

151) detect
152) risen
153) emitted
154) from
155) made
156) overwhelming
157) relevant
158) irrelevant
159) contradictions
160) elimination
161) retrieved
162) that
163) weak
164) lacked
165) assess
166) substantial
167) weakness
168) little
169) revenue
170) extract
171) competing
172) firms
173) up
174) why
175) where
176) inform
177) gain
178) added
179) outcome
180) Yet
181) composed
182) think
183) refined
184) as
185) choose from
186) design
187) blindly
188) varied
189) different
190) which
191) accounts for
192) however
193) adaptive
194) singular
195) fixed
196) Instead
197) trying
198) automatic
199) without
200) causes
201) identifying
202) enable
203) influence
204) with
205) enable
206) although
207) engage
208) meaningful
209) conducted
210) because of
211) other-focused
212) more
213) than
214) reduced
215) discharging
216) empathizing
217) unusual
218) few
219) accumulated
220) shift
221) literacy
222) less
223) signifying
224) where
225) adapt
226) joined
227) striking
228) was
229) approached
230) of
231) unmanly
232) laid
233) adoption
234) does
235) around which

## Prac 2 Answers

1) draw
2) attention
3) frequently
4) halfway
5) unaware
6) ignore
7) past
8) grateful
9) remind
10) prepared
11) improvement
12) faithfully,
13) desperate
14) quarter.
15) irritation.
16) trivial
17) garage
18) placed
19) glanced
20) statue
21) Inscribed
22) race
23) purchase
24) frequently
25) employee
26) Empathizing
27) helpful.
28) dealing
29) particular,
30) exhibited
31) Avoid
32) suggestions
33) traits
34) acceptable
35) unreliability
36) how
37) fungi
38) forward
39) species
40) assume
41) victorious
42) pathogen
43) infected
44) advantageous
45) sprout
46) Diversity
47) security
48) fungi
49) dependent
50) collapse
51) ensure
52) dominate
53) positive
54) fantasies
55) relax
56) physiological
57) unwind,
58) fantasizing
59) outcome
60) objective
61) *last*
62) relaxed
63) energized
64) motivated
65) engaged
66) inevitable
67) challenges
68) undercut
69) temporary
70) inactivity
71) central
72) identity,
73) anthropologist

74) reason
75) decline
76) outsourcing
77) corporations
78) exclusive
79) feeding
80) headed
81) domestic
82) conflicts
83) gender
84) spark
85) elieved
86) overscheduled
87) invest
88) substantially,
89) cuisine.
90) political.
91) value
92) mindful
93) deserve
94) support.
95) polluting
96) committed
97) producing
98) conscience.
99) contribute
100) genuinely
101) corporate
102) wallet
103) embrace
104) sustainable
105) purchase
106) astronomy
107) manuscript
108) attention
109) assistant
110) calculator.
111) called
112) passionately
113) successful
114) eventually
115) observatory
116) founded
117) served
118) editor
119) publication
120) doubt
121) sell-by
122) waste
123) increasing
124) carbon
125) footprint
126) shelves
127) judgement
128) brought
129) scornful
130) caution
131) encourages
132) manufacturer
133) travelling
134) reasonably
135) gives
136) toxic
137) perishable
138) cost-effective
139) removed
140) liver,
141) degrades
142) genetics,
143) efficient
144) degrades
145) rapidly
146) fast
147) midnight
148) eliminate
149) sensitive
150) should

151) asleep
152) Aging
153) clearance
154) longer
155) remove
156) sensitive
157) sleep-disrupting
158) influence.
159) clever
160) turn
161) alternatives,
162) persuader
163) reject
164) opinion
165) maintaining
166) independence
167) majority
168) reject
169) preference.
170) maintain
171) defiance.
172) reversal
173) suits
174) purposes
175) defiance
176) rebels
177) loyalty.
178) abstract
179) fictional
180) psychology,
181) speculate
182) considerable
183) required
184) speculate
185) mathematics,
186) ease.
187) abstraction
188) abstraction
189) framework.
190) abstraction
191) removed
192) mental
193) selection,
194) prey
195) arose
196) threat
197) detect
198) frequencies,
199) frequencies
200) vocalizations
201) scales
202) acoustic
203) camouflage
204) emitted
205) aircraft
206) made
207) screen
208) manageable
209) inflow
210) overwhelming
211) chaos
212) available
213) vital
214) usable
215) Expectancies
216) accomplish
217) screen
218) irrelevant
219) contradictions.
220) elimination
221) fraction
222) processed
223) committed
224) retrieved.
225) democracy
226) thrived
227) rulers

228) weak
229) millennium
230) lacked
231) assess
232) levy
233) illustrate
234) revenue
235) awfully
236) medieval
237) emperors
238) extract
239) exception
240) competing
241) advertise
242) temptation
243) benefit
244) misconception
245) account
246) why
247) differentiated
248) inform
249) gain
250) purchasing
251) variety
252) vision
253) delivers
254) innovative
255) remarkably
256) auditorium
257) composed
258) instinctively
259) sensibility,
260) aesthetically
261) criteria,
262) lightweight
263) behaving
264) blindly
265) glucose,
266) merely
267) available
268) store
269) adaptive,
270) shifts
271) singular
272) devote
273) automatic
274) reflexive
275) engagement,
276) practical
277) drivers
278) manipulate
279) causes
280) influential
281) situational
282) constructive
283) noteworthy
284) engagement
285) exceed
286) ambitions
287) achievements,
288) meaningful.
289) evident
290) align
291) conducted
292) goods,
293) assistance
294) discomfort)
295) original
296) arousal
297) emotionally
298) arousal
299) initial
300) discharging
301) distress
302) victims
303) struggle
304) unusual

305) spread
306) oral
307) accumulated
308) norm
309) perception
310) advent
311) literacy
312) fade.
313) signifying
314) period
315) chronological
316) Retired
317) asked
318) various
319) joined
320) stereotype
321) behaviour
322) striking.
323) updated
324) insurance
325) aspects
326) intentions
327) raged
328) confusion
329) flourishing
330) donating
331) courageous
332) orphaned
333) racial
334) scaffolding
335) richness

Prac 2  Answers

1) draw
2) attention
3) frequently
4) halfway
5) unaware
6) ignore
7) past
8) grateful
9) remind
10) prepared
11) improvement
12) faithfully,
13) desperate
14) quarter.
15) irritation.
16) trivial
17) garage
18) placed
19) glanced
20) statue
21) Inscribed
22) race
23) purchase
24) frequently
25) employee
26) Empathizing
27) helpful.
28) dealing
29) particular,
30) exhibited
31) Avoid
32) suggestions
33) traits
34) acceptable
35) unreliability
36) how
37) fungi
38) forward
39) species
40) assume
41) victorious
42) pathogen
43) infected
44) advantageous
45) sprout
46) Diversity
47) security
48) fungi
49) dependent
50) collapse
51) ensure
52) dominate
53) positive
54) fantasies
55) relax
56) physiological
57) unwind,
58) fantasizing
59) outcome
60) objective
61) *last*
62) relaxed
63) energized
64) motivated
65) engaged
66) inevitable
67) challenges
68) undercut
69) temporary
70) inactivity
71) central
72) identity,
73) anthropologist

(.hwp) (.pdf) → www.englishjmygod.com

74) reason
75) decline
76) outsourcing
77) corporations
78) exclusive
79) feeding
80) headed
81) domestic
82) conflicts
83) gender
84) spark
85) elieved
86) overscheduled
87) invest
88) substantially,
89) cuisine.
90) political.
91) value
92) mindful
93) deserve
94) support.
95) polluting
96) committed
97) producing
98) conscience.
99) contribute
100) genuinely
101) corporate
102) wallet
103) embrace
104) sustainable
105) purchase
106) astronomy
107) manuscript
108) attention
109) assistant
110) calculator.
111) called
112) passionately
113) successful
114) eventually
115) observatory
116) founded
117) served
118) editor
119) publication
120) doubt
121) sell-by
122) waste
123) increasing
124) carbon
125) footprint
126) shelves
127) judgement
128) brought
129) scornful
130) caution
131) encourages
132) manufacturer
133) travelling
134) reasonably
135) gives
136) toxic
137) perishable
138) cost-effective
139) removed
140) liver,
141) degrades
142) genetics,
143) efficient
144) degrades
145) rapidly
146) fast
147) midnight
148) eliminate
149) sensitive
150) should

151) asleep
152) Aging
153) clearance
154) longer
155) remove
156) sensitive
157) sleep-disrupting
158) influence.
159) clever
160) turn
161) alternatives,
162) persuader
163) reject
164) opinion
165) maintaining
166) independence
167) majority
168) reject
169) preference.
170) maintain
171) defiance.
172) reversal
173) suits
174) purposes
175) defiance
176) rebels
177) loyalty.
178) abstract
179) fictional
180) psychology,
181) speculate
182) considerable
183) required
184) speculate
185) mathematics,
186) ease.
187) abstraction
188) abstraction
189) framework.
190) abstraction
191) removed
192) mental
193) selection,
194) prey
195) arose
196) threat
197) detect
198) frequencies,
199) frequencies
200) vocalizations
201) scales
202) acoustic
203) camouflage
204) emitted
205) aircraft
206) made
207) screen
208) manageable
209) inflow
210) overwhelming
211) chaos
212) available
213) vital
214) usable
215) Expectancies
216) accomplish
217) screen
218) irrelevant
219) contradictions.
220) elimination
221) fraction
222) processed
223) committed
224) retrieved.
225) democracy
226) thrived
227) rulers

228) weak
229) millennium
230) lacked
231) assess
232) levy
233) illustrate
234) revenue
235) awfully
236) medieval
237) emperors
238) extract
239) exception
240) competing
241) advertise
242) temptation
243) benefit
244) misconception
245) account
246) why
247) differentiated
248) inform
249) gain
250) purchasing
251) variety
252) vision
253) delivers
254) innovative
255) remarkably
256) auditorium
257) composed
258) instinctively
259) sensibility,
260) aesthetically
261) criteria,
262) lightweight
263) behaving
264) blindly
265) glucose,
266) merely
267) available
268) store
269) adaptive,
270) shifts
271) singular
272) devote
273) automatic
274) reflexive
275) engagement,
276) practical
277) drivers
278) manipulate
279) causes
280) influential
281) situational
282) constructive
283) noteworthy
284) engagement
285) exceed
286) ambitions
287) achievements,
288) meaningful.
289) evident
290) align
291) conducted
292) goods,
293) assistance
294) discomfort)
295) original
296) arousal
297) emotionally
298) arousal
299) initial
300) discharging
301) distress
302) victims
303) struggle
304) unusual

305) spread
306) oral
307) accumulated
308) norm
309) perception
310) advent
311) literacy
312) fade.
313) signifying
314) period
315) chronological
316) Retired
317) asked
318) various
319) joined
320) stereotype
321) behaviour
322) striking.
323) updated
324) insurance
325) aspects
326) intentions
327) raged
328) confusion
329) flourishing
330) donating
331) courageous
332) orphaned
333) racial
334) scaffolding
335) richness

(.hwp) (.pdf) → www.englishjmygod.com

## Quiz 1 Answers

1) ②
2) ③
3) ②
4) ④
5) ⑤
6) ②
7) ④
8) ④
9) ⑤
10) ③
11) ②
12) ②
13) ③
14) ④
15) ②
16) ③
17) ③
18) ⑤
19) ④
20) ②
21) ②
22) ②
23) ②
24) ③
25) (D)-(C)-(E)-(B)-(A)
26) (A)-(C)-(B)
27) (A)-(C)-(B)-(E)-(D)
28) (B)-(D)-(A)-(C)
29) (B)-(A)-(C)-(D)
30) (E)-(B)-(D)-(A)-(C)
31) (C)-(B)-(D)-(A)
32) (B)-(A)-(C)
33) (B)-(C)-(A)-(D)
34) (B)-(E)-(A)-(C)-(D)
35) (B)-(E)-(A)-(D)-(C)
36) (B)-(E)-(A)-(D)-(C)
37) (B)-(D)-(C)-(A)
38) (A)-(C)-(B)
39) (B)-(A)-(C)-(D)
40) (D)-(E)-(C)-(B)-(A)
41) (B)-(A)-(C)
42) (A)-(C)-(D)-(B)
43) (C)-(B)-(A)
44) (D)-(A)-(B)-(C)
45) (C)-(B)-(A)
46) (B)-(C)-(D)-(A)

## Quiz 2 Answers

1)
[정답] ② ⓓ, ⓔ
[해설]
ⓓ be appeared ⇨ appear
ⓔ which ⇨ that

2)
[정답] ④ ⓐ, ⓑ, ⓔ, ⓖ
[해설]
ⓐ was appeared ⇨ appeared
ⓑ x ⇨ for
ⓔ Described ⇨ Inscribed
ⓖ to race ⇨ race

3)
[정답] ③ ⓐ, ①

[해설]
ⓐ been acted ⇨ acted
① which ⇨ that

4)
[정답] ② ⓐ, ⓕ, ①
[해설]
ⓐ is ⇨ are
ⓕ which ⇨ that
① it ⇨ them

5)
[정답] ④ ⓐ, ⓔ, ⓗ, ①
[해설]
ⓐ relaxing ⇨ relax
ⓔ subjective ⇨ objective
ⓗ engaging ⇨ engaged
① principal ⇨ principle

6)
[정답] ② ⓑ, ⓒ, ⓖ
[해설]
ⓑ is ⇨ has
ⓒ cooperations ⇨ corporations
ⓖ that ⇨ it

7)
[정답] ① ⓑ, ⓕ
[해설]
ⓑ cooperations ⇨ corporations
ⓕ bring ⇨ bringing

8)
[정답] ④ ⓐ, ⓓ, ⓔ, ⓕ
[해설]
ⓐ astrology ⇨ astronomy
ⓓ what ⇨ which
ⓔ which ⇨ that
ⓕ observant ⇨ observatory

9)
[정답] ③ ⓐ, ⓒ, ⓗ
[해설]
ⓐ a little ⇨ little
ⓒ Remembering ⇨ Remember
ⓗ grow ⇨ growing

10)
[정답] ⑤ ⓕ, ①
[해설]
ⓕ illuminate ⇨ eliminate
① that ⇨ it

11)
[정답] ① ⓐ, ⓑ
[해설]
ⓐ influence on ⇨ influence
ⓑ after ⇨ for

12)
[정답] ⑤ ⓑ, ⓓ, ⓕ, ⓗ
[해설]
ⓑ are existed ⇨ exist
ⓓ considerate ⇨ considerable
ⓕ themselves ⇨ them
ⓗ is required ⇨ required

13)
[정답] ① ⓐ, ⓒ
[해설]
ⓐ engaged ⇨ been engaged
ⓒ eating ⇨ being eaten

14)
[정답] ③ ⓑ, ⓒ, ⓗ
[해설]
ⓑ giving ⇨ given
ⓒ which ⇨ it
ⓗ processing ⇨ processed

15)
[정답] ⑤ ⓓ, ⓖ, ⓘ, ⓙ
[해설]
ⓓ access ⇨ assess
ⓖ illuminate ⇨ illustrate
ⓘ contract ⇨ extract
ⓙ expectations ⇨ exception

16)
[정답] ④ ⓑ, ⓔ, ⓖ
[해설]
ⓑ competitive ⇨ competing
ⓔ informing ⇨ to inform
ⓖ income ⇨ outcome

17)
[정답] ⑤ ⓒ, ⓓ, ⓕ, ⓘ
[해설]
ⓒ consisted ⇨ composed
ⓓ confined ⇨ refined
ⓕ which ⇨ it
ⓘ worked ⇨ working

18)
[정답] ④ ⓒ, ⓕ, ⓗ
[해설]
ⓒ therefore ⇨ however
ⓕ try ⇨ trying
ⓗ reflective ⇨ reflexive

19)
[정답] ② ⓓ, ⓗ
[해설]
ⓓ influenced ⇨ influential
ⓗ proceed ⇨ exceed

20)
[정답] ② ⓐ, ⓔ, ⓕ
[해설]
ⓐ conducting ⇨ conducted
ⓔ discharged ⇨ discharging
ⓕ to empathize ⇨ empathizing

21)
[정답] ③ ⓐ, ⓒ, ⓖ
[해설]
ⓐ a few ⇨ few
ⓒ advertent ⇨ advent
ⓖ changed ⇨ changing

22)
[정답] ④ ⓖ, ⓗ

[해설]
ⓖ experiencing ⇨ experience
ⓗ it ⇨ them

---

Quiz 3 Answers

1)
[정답] ①②③⑤
[해설]
① x ⇨ to
② is occurred ⇨ occurs
③ be appeared ⇨ appear
⑤ drive ⇨ driving

2)
[정답] ③
[해설]
③ Described ⇨ Inscribed

3)
[정답] ③④
[해설]
③ remembering ⇨ remember
④ which ⇨ that

4)
[정답] ①④⑤
[해설]
① is ⇨ their
④ which ⇨ that
⑤ independent ⇨ dependent

5)
[정답] ①②③④
[해설]
① getting ⇨ get
② subjective ⇨ objective
③ enough energized ⇨ energized enough
④ engaging ⇨ engaged

6)
[정답] ①③⑤
[해설]
① is ⇨ has
③ makes ⇨ making
⑤ been allowed ⇨ allowed

7)
[정답] ①③
[해설]
① taken ⇨ taking
③ been found ⇨ found

8)
[정답] ③④⑤
[해설]
③ what ⇨ which
④ observant ⇨ observatory
⑤ found ⇨ founded

9)
[정답] ②③
[해설]
② reach at ⇨ reach

(.hwp) (.pdf) → www.englishjmygod.com

③ while ⇨ during

10)
[정답] ①②③④⑤
[해설]
① removes ⇨ is removed
② allowed ⇨ allowing
③ illuminate ⇨ eliminate
④ be lasted ⇨ last
⑤ disrupted ⇨ disrupting

11)
[정답] ①②④⑤
[해설]
① after ⇨ for
② containing ⇨ maintaining
④ definition ⇨ defiance
⑤ them ⇨ themselves

12)
[정답] ①④
[해설]
① what ⇨ which
④ contraction ⇨ abstraction

13)
[정답] ④
[해설]
④ making ⇨ made

14)
[정답] ②③
[해설]
② which ⇨ it
③ help ⇨ helping

15)
[정답] ①③④⑤
[해설]
① what ⇨ that
③ that ⇨ what
④ a little ⇨ little
⑤ contract ⇨ extract

16)
[정답] ①④
[해설]
① are appeared ⇨ appear
④ raise ⇨ rise

17)
[정답] 없음

18)
[정답] ②③
[해설]
② therefore ⇨ however
③ adoptive ⇨ adaptive

19)
[정답] ①②③④⑤

[해석]


[해설]

① identified ⇨ identifying
② it ⇨ them
③ proceed ⇨ exceed
④ meaningfully ⇨ meaningful
⑤ alien ⇨ align

20)
[정답] ①②⑤
[해설]
① what ⇨ that
② who ⇨ whose
⑤ to empathize ⇨ empathizing

21)
[정답] ①②④
[해설]
① a few ⇨ few
② been accumulated ⇨ accumulated
④ more ⇨ less

22)
[정답] ①⑤
[해설]
① boring ⇨ bored
⑤ is ⇨ does

Quiz 4 Answers

1)
[정답]
③ that ⇨ which
⑤ which ⇨ that

2)
[정답]
① was appeared ⇨ appeared
② x ⇨ for
③ bother ⇨ be bothered
④ to hug ⇨ hugging
⑥ was ⇨ were
⑦ to race ⇨ race

3)
[정답]
① been acted ⇨ acted
② Empathized ⇨ Empathizing
④ to deal ⇨ dealing
⑥ what ⇨ that
⑦ to make ⇨ making

4)
[정답]
① is ⇨ are
② is ⇨ their
③ fight ⇨ fights
⑤ the ⇨ a

5)
[정답]
① relaxing ⇨ relax
② when ⇨ that
③ getting ⇨ get
④ to fantasize ⇨ fantasizing
⑤ subjective ⇨ objective

⑥ relaxing ⇨ relaxed
⑦ enough energized ⇨ energized enough
⑧ engaging ⇨ engaged
⑨ arouse ⇨ arise
⑩ principal ⇨ principle
⑪ temporal ⇨ temporary

6)
[정답]
① they ⇨ it
③ cooperations ⇨ corporations
⑤ inclusive ⇨ exclusive
⑥ makes ⇨ making
⑩ makes ⇨ making
⑪ requiring ⇨ required

7)
[정답]
① who ⇨ whom
② cooperations ⇨ corporations
④ that ⇨ if
⑤ committing ⇨ committed
⑥ bring ⇨ bringing
⑧ constitute ⇨ contribute
⑩ what ⇨ that
⑪ embracing ⇨ to embrace

8)
[정답]
③ was called ⇨ called
④ what ⇨ which
⑤ which ⇨ that

9)
[정답]
① a little ⇨ little
② farther ⇨ further
③ Remembering ⇨ Remember
④ reach at ⇨ reach
⑤ while ⇨ during
⑥ discourages ⇨ encourages
⑦ to make ⇨ making
⑧ grow ⇨ growing
⑨ reaches out ⇨ reaches
⑩ giving ⇨ gives
⑪ that ⇨ whether

10)
[정답]
③ affectionate ⇨ efficient
④ allowed ⇨ allowing
⑤ therefore ⇨ however
⑦ sensible ⇨ sensitive
⑧ be lasted ⇨ last
⑩ disrupted ⇨ disrupting

11)
[정답]
① influence on ⇨ influence
③ that ⇨ which
⑤ what ⇨ which
⑥ been taken ⇨ taken
⑦ definition ⇨ defiance

12)
[정답]
① what ⇨ which
④ considerate ⇨ considerable
⑤ contraction ⇨ abstraction
⑧ is required ⇨ required

13)
[정답]
① engaged ⇨ been engaged
② arouse ⇨ arose
③ eating ⇨ being eaten
④ been risen ⇨ risen
⑤ omitted ⇨ emitted
⑥ making ⇨ made
⑦ similar something ⇨ something similar

14)
[정답]
① overwhelmed ⇨ overwhelming
⑥ focus ⇨ focusing

15)
[정답]
① what ⇨ that
② processed ⇨ prospered
④ access ⇨ assess
⑤ that ⇨ what
⑥ leving ⇨ to levy
⑦ illuminate ⇨ illustrate
⑨ contract ⇨ extract

16)
[정답]
① are appeared ⇨ appear
② competitive ⇨ competing
③ Therefore ⇨ However
④ identical ⇨ differentiated
⑥ raise ⇨ rise
⑦ income ⇨ outcome

17)
[정답]
① considering ⇨ consider
② that ⇨ which
③ consisted ⇨ composed
④ confined ⇨ refined
⑤ desinging ⇨ designed
⑥ which ⇨ it
⑦ Dissimilar ⇨ Similar
⑧ designing ⇨ design
⑨ worked ⇨ working

18)
[정답]
① is accounted ⇨ accounts
② presumes ⇨ consumes
③ therefore ⇨ however
⑥ try ⇨ trying
⑦ anatomic ⇨ automatic
⑧ reflective ⇨ reflexive

19)
[정답]

① carried ⇨ been carried
⑤ later ⇨ latter

20)
[정답]
① conducting ⇨ conducted
② what ⇨ that
④ affected on ⇨ affected
⑥ to empathize ⇨ empathizing

21)
[정답]
⑤ more ⇨ less

22)
[정답]
① for ⇨ during
② boring ⇨ bored
⑬ when ⇨ which

## Quiz 5 Answers

1) 나타나다,보이다 - appear // 무시하다 - ignore // 감사하다 - grateful // 상기시키다 - remind // 개선점 - improvement
2) ⓐ
who ⇨ whom
drawing ⇨ to draw
occur ⇨ occurs
where ⇨ which
3) 절실하다 - desperate // 짜증 - irritation // 사소한 - trivial // 쥐어주다 - placed // 구매 - purchase
4)
(가) As I watched him race back to the garage sale, I smiled with a heart full of happiness.
5) 심리학자 - psychologist // 공감하다 - Empathizing // 특성 - traits // 수행 - performing
6) ⓐ
which ⇨ when
remembering ⇨ remember
which ⇨ who
exhibit ⇨ exhibited
7)
(가) It is difficult for employees to change who they are
8) 균류 - fungi // 우세하다 - victorious // 이점 - advantage // 안전 - security // 무너지다,붕괴하다 - collapse // 확실히 하다 - ensure // 우세하다 - dominate
9) ⓐ
sprout ⇨ 싹을 틔우다
10)
(가) Among trees, each species fights other species.
11) 주목할 만 한 - remarkable // 범위 - extent // 생리학적 - physiological // 목적 - objective // 활력을 얻다 - energized // 피할수 없는 - inevitable // 장애물 - obstacles // 일시적인 - temporary
12) ⓐ
getting ⇨ get

going ⇨ go
close ⇨ closing
fantasize ⇨ fantasizing
enjoying ⇨ enjoy
13) 정체성 - identity // 인류학자 - anthropologist // 책임 - responsibility // 먹여살리다 - feeding // 분주한 - overscheduled // 활동,일 - pursuits
14)
ⓐ
allowing ⇨ allowed
diversified ⇨ diversify
to make ⇨ making
15) 주의를 기울이다 - mindful // 오염시키다 - polluting // 헌신하다 - committed // 양심 - conscience // 진심으로 - genuinely
16) ⓐ
build ⇨ is built
embraced ⇨ to embrace
make ⇨ to make
17)
(가) As you may already know, what and how you buy can be political
18) 천문학 - astronomy // 원고 - manuscript // 관심 - attention // 계산원 - calculator
19)
ⓐ
which ⇨ in which
20)
(가) In 1887, he founded the French Astronomical Society and served as editor of its monthly publication.
21) 의심 - doubt // 흐름 - stream // 발자국 - footprint // 판단 - judgement // 경멸하는 - scornful // 합리적으로 - reasonably
22) ⓐ
travelling ⇨ travelled
reached ⇨ to reach
started ⇨ start
ⓑ
have ⇨ has
grow ⇨ growing
reach ⇨ reaches
travel ⇨ travelling
23)
(가) But whether it becomes toxic is something each individual can decide.
24) 효소 - enzyme // 간 - liver // 유전학 - genetics // 혈류 - bloodstream // 노화 - Aging // 제거 - clearance // 수면방해 - sleep-disrupting
25) ⓐ
have had ⇨ have
fall ⇨ to fall
26)
(가) These rare individuals can drink an espresso with dinner and fall fast asleep at midnight without a problem.
27) 대안 - alternatives // 설득자 - persuader // 거부하다 - reject // 대중적인 - majority // 선호 - preference //

반항 - defiance

28) ⓐ

tricking ⇨ tricked

make ⇨ to make

of which ⇨ which

29)

(가) Rebels may think they're rebels, but clever marketers influence them just like the rest of us.

30) 추상적인 - abstract // 허구적인 - fictional // 재현하다 - recreated // 심리 - psychology // 물리학 - physics // 추측하다 - speculate // 추상 - abstraction // 틀 - framework

31) ⓐ

is ⇨ are

experienced ⇨ experience

32)

(가) The abstraction of a soap opera is only a step removed from the real world.

33) 먹잇감 - prey // 진화하다 - evolved // 감지하다 - detect // 주파수 - frequencies // 비늘 - scales // 흡수하다 - absorbing // 기체 - fuselages

34) ⓐ

believe ⇨ believed

arise ⇨ arose

eating ⇨ being eaten

35)

(가) thereby preventing those sound waves from bouncing back.

36) 중요하다 - vital // 예상들 - Expectancies // 모순들 - contradictions // 회수하다 - retrieved

37) ⓐ

screen out ⇨ to screen out

to create ⇨ could create

give ⇨ given

38)

(가) only a fraction of what they notice gets processed and stored into memory.

39) 민주주의 - democracy // 번성하다 - thrived // 정확하게 - precisely // 현저하게 - remarkably // 평가하다 - assess // 부과하다 - levy // 중세기 - medieval times // 얻어내다 - extract

40)

(가) The most striking way to illustrate European weakness is to show how little revenue they collected.

41) 경쟁하는 - competing // 광고하다 - advertise // 유혹 - temptation // 오해 - misconception // 차별화된 - differentiated // 상상 - vision // 시장구조 - market structure

42)

(가) but consumers also gain information to help make purchasing decisions.

43) 강당 - auditorium // 맞물리는 - interlocking // 본능적으로 - instinctively // 미적으로 - aesthetically // 기준 - criteria // 다양한 - varied

44)

(가) Similar software has been used to design lightweight bicycle frames and sturdier chairs, among much else.

45) 포도당 - glucose // 적응력이 뛰어난 - adaptive // 미묘한 차이 - nuances // 헌신하다 - devote // 이동 - shift // 반사적인 - reflexive

46)

(가) Although the brain accounts for merely 3 percent of a person's body weight, it consumes 20 percent of the available fuel.

47) 몰입 - engagement // 조작하다 - manipulate // 자원 - resources

48) ⓐ

exceeded ⇨ exceed

found ⇨ find

49)

(가) This is especially evident when people are employed in jobs that align with their values.

50) 수행하다 - conducted // 도움 - assistance // 고통 - distress // 자극 - arousal // 해소 - discharging

51)

(가) However, those who gave to reduce others' distress did not stop empathizing with victims who continued to struggle long after the attacks.

52) 구전 - oral // 누적된 - accumulated // 규범 - norm // 출현 - advent // 사라지다 - fade // 의미하다 - signifying

53) ⓐ

were ⇨ was

which ⇨ that

needs ⇨ need

54)

(가) We are living in a period when the gap between chronological and biological age is changing fast and where social norms are struggling to adapt.

55) 보험 - insurance // 활기찬 - lively // 비난하다 - accused // 결심 - resolve // 확고하다 - firm // 내면의 - inner // 발판 - scaffolding

56) ⓐ

which ⇨ that

be ⇨ was

go ⇨ went

accepting ⇨ accepted

57)

(가) He was sure that he would enjoy the creative and social aspects of it and that he'd be successful.

(나) And all this laid a strong stepping stone for another courageous move in his life.

23년 고2
9월 모의고사

마
이
갓

어법&어휘 문제
약 200문제 이상
빈칸 연습문제
약 200문제 이상
적중예상&서술형 대비
약 100문제 수록

마이갓
2023년 고2 9월 모의고사

값 15,000원

보듬책방

53740
9 791190 959759
ISBN 979-11-90959-75-9

21년 고2
3월 모의고사

마
이
갓

연습과 실전 모두 잡는 내신대비 완벽
| workbook |

1 등급을 위한
**5단계 노하우**

2 **21년
고2 3월**

3 **내신변형**
완전정복

어법&어휘 문제
약 200문제 이상
빈칸 연습문제
약 200문제 이상
적중예상&서술형 대비
약 100문제 수록

21년 3월 모의

**2학년**

보듬책방